Taking Japan Seriously

Taking
Japan
Seriously

*A Confucian perspective
on leading economic issues*

RONALD DORE

STANFORD UNIVERSITY PRESS
STANFORD, CALIFORNIA

Stanford University Press
Stanford, California
© 1987 Ronald P. Dore
Originating publisher:
The Athlone Press, London
First published in the United States by
Stanford University Press, 1987
Printed in the United States of America
Cloth ISBN 0-8047-1350-2
Paper ISBN 0-8047-1401-0
Last figure below indicates year of this printing:
98 97 96 95 94 93 92 91 90 89

Contents

Preface   vii

Acknowledgements   x

I The enterprise and income determination

1 Introduction   3

2 Training in industry   20

3 Dual economy or spectrum economy?   48

4 Building an incomes policy to last   68

5 Authority, hierarchy and community   85

6 Long-term thinking and the shareholders' role   108

7 Innovation, entrepreneurship and the Community model   125

8 The firm as community: The road to industrial democracy   145

II The linking institutions

9 Goodwill and the spirit of market capitalism   169

10 Industrial policy   193

11 Meritocracy, employment and citizenship   204

12 Home thoughts from America   226

References   247

Index   255

Preface

Perhaps the 'Confucian perspective' of my sub-title needs some explanation.

After nearly a decade of privatization, monetarist economic policies, and deregulation of markets, the phrase 'the mixed economy' has all but disappeared from serious political discourse. It used to stand for a recognition of the possibility of a halfway house between a free enterprise and a planned economy. It used to stand, also, for a recognition that people work for a variety of motives, that the pursuit of self-interest can, and in a decent society is, mixed with other desires – to do a good job, to serve society, to share in effort and reward, to evoke smiles and not frowns from other people.

Motives are what this book is primarily about. There is nothing like spending one's life studying Japan and thinking about the differences between Japan and Britain and America for making one reflect: why do people work? Why do they do what their foremen and managers tell or ask them to do? Why do people sometimes cooperate, sometimes compete? What makes them sometimes obstinate, sometimes ready to compromise? What makes things seem fair to some people and not to others, and what makes some people care more than others whether something is fair or not?

Start from the assumptions of original sin, as did some of the Confucianists' opponents in ancient China, and as did the Christian divines of the eighteenth century societies in which our western economic doctrines evolved, and you get one set of answers. It is the set of answers which Mrs Thatcher and Mr Reagan have recently reasserted with force and clarity. People work for self-interest. If you want a peaceful and prosperous society, just set up institutions in such a way that people's self-interest is mobilized and let the invisible hand of the market do the rest. Reduce everything to the bottom line.

If, by contrast, you start, as at least the followers of Mencius among the Confucianists did, from the assumption of original virtue, then something else follows. You assume that bonds of friendship and fellow-feeling are also important, and a sense of loyalty and belonging – to one's community, one's firm, one's nation – and the sense of responsibility which goes with it. And you would be likely to assume that economic institutions which bring out the best in people, rather than the worst, make for a more pleasant and peaceful, and probably in the end more generally prosperous, society.

But it seems pretty clear that the sort of institutions which will bring out the best in the Japanese people, are not necessarily those which will bring out the best in people in Britain or America. It is precisely the much greater egalitarianism and individualism, and almost instinctual anti-authoritarianism of European, and especially Anglo-Saxon, cultural traditions which make the link between 'fairness' and 'bringing out the best in people' so much more important in Britain than in Japan.

That is a dominant theme of this book, both of Part 1 which concerns relations within the enterprise, and of Part 2 which looks at certain aspects of the national structure – business relations between firms, industrial policy, meritocracy and the distribution of income. Fairness is a recurring theme in the chapters on industrial training and the wage spectrum, as in those on industrial democracy, on authority in industry, and on incomes policy.

The other dominant theme of the book is the way the accumulation of technological knowledge – the steady and, I would say, accelerating onward march of science – affects the quest for social and economic efficiency. (As that quest itself is intensified by the way new technologies cheapen transport and communication and so sharpen international trade competition. 'Competitiveness' is the buzz-word of the decade.)

New technologies call forth new forms of work. New forms of work require new skills, new motivations, new forms of organization. Increasing government intervention in industry, within-enterprise training, the development of wage spectrums within occupations, moves towards industrial democracy or profit-sharing, growing meritocratic hierarchy in education, are all, in a sense, 'on the cards', trends rooted in the growing complexity of technology which we ignore at our peril. Japan helps here not as Confucian country so much as *qua* late-developer. Having laid the basis for its industrialization with big technology in big organizations, (largely because it started so much later than we did), Japan is in many respects further along, down a road which we are also travelling. Japan helps by clarifying our options, by helping us to decide what to take as a horrible warning (Japanese levels of meritocracy, I suggest), and what as a trend we might approve of and seek to accelerate – like, I suggest, organization-oriented employment patterns.

The book contains a number of concrete institutional suggestions – for a loan/insurance fund for employee training, for a synchropay-based incomes policy, for a new kind of board/council structure for enterprise democracy, for new rules on takeovers, for a citizens' trust and a citizen dividend. Megalomaniac social engineering illusions, some will say. Maybe. But at least I *try* to present them as modest suggestions.

'Stale 1970s stuff'. 'The discredited corporatist recipe' will be the other kind of charge. Certainly our 1970s corporatism fumbled and stumbled. But we should just learn to do our corporatism better, because it *was* a response to underlying long-term trends for which the leave-it-all-to-the-market recipes of our present rulers have no answers. They have no answers even in America, as I suggest in the last chapter; much less in Britain where residual concerns for fairness and community preclude some of the more ruthless forms of marketism practised across the Atlantic.

Acknowledgements

Many of the paragraphs, and chunks of whole pages, have appeared before in various other places, and I am grateful for permission to quote earlier writings to the ESRC Newsletter (Chapter 1), the Tawney Society (Chapter 4), and the editors and publishers of *Government and Opposition* (Chapter 5), *Policy Studies* (Chapter 6), the Imperial College-SPRU-TCC Lecture series (Chapter 7), the *British Journal of Sociology* (Chapter 9), *Catalyst* (Chapter 10). I am grateful to Maria Spoors for the editorial and bibliographical work, as well as the typing, which turned a collection of bits and pieces into something more like a whole. I must also gratefully acknowledge, with the usual absolutions, the help of many friends who have commented on various parts of the book at various stages in their evolution: Chris Beauman, Charles Carter, Rodney Clark, Sally Dore, Tony Flower, Prosser Gifford, Mark Goyder, Howell Harris, Chris Huhne, Arthur Knight, Zoe Mars, Susan Pharr, John Pinder, Takashi Suzuki, Robert Wade, Bruce Williams, Michael Young. Zoe Mars was, indeed, much more than commentator on Chapter 3; provider of many of the ideas and much of the information. To Nancy Dore go thanks for a great deal more than her help with the index.

I
The enterprise and income determination

1
Introduction

One of the more interesting aspects of the way the 'state of Britain' debate has evolved over the last ten years is the increasing frequency with which Japan is referred to with respect as a country from which we have much to learn. To be sure there is still plenty of dismissive complacency around. The cultural and racial stereotypes which being top nation for a century gives a people, do not disappear overnight. To the complacent ones on the Left, Japan is a harsh and oppressive society whose competitive success rests on exploitation of low-paid workers. For the complacent ones on the Right . . . well, they're a lot of little swots, aren't they? Good imitators. No humour, no originality. It's hard to take them seriously.

Gradually, these are becoming fringe views. As regional development authorities compete with each other to attract Japanese investment, and as more and more British firms enter into agreements to license Japanese technology, there is no longer much doubt as to who is teacher and who is taught as far as the hardware and software of production technology are concerned. But what about the underpinning social technology? What *are* the institutions of Japan's society and economy, what *are* the policies of Japanese governments which account for Japan's industrial success? Can we copy them? Should we want to?

Here there is no unanimity. Send a British parliamentary delegation to Japan and the result is like the Rashōmon film: versions of the story so unlike that they appear to be set in different countries. Right-wing MPs come back full of praise for a system whole-heartedly devoted to free enterprise competition, for unions which cooperate with management, for a society which accepts the discipline of the market, which devotes only a small proportion of its Gross National Product to public spending, which holds down inflation by tight monetary control. Those on the Left return with stories of effective state planning, of wise industrial policy initiatives, of corporations which accept trade union participation, of judicious demand management as a means of stimulating low-inflation growth, of financial controls which keep Japan sheltered from the gale-force blasts of hot money which make monetary management so difficult in other countries.

Nor is there agreement as to whether there is much to admire in Japan *besides* its economic performance. Probably more people know about political corruption and the exclusion of women from any important role in public or business life than about the low crime rate or the fact that the Japanese have just overtaken the Icelanders to become the people with (for both sexes) the longest life-expectancy in the world. And interpretations differ about what people do know. Is long life-expectancy a reflection of the quality and efficiency of their health service? Or is it just because the Japanese are health fanatics? Low crime rates? Well, with all that indoctrination, that is what you would expect, wouldn't you? Trains that run on time? Well, Mussolini exposed the true value of *that* as a national virtue. Public telephones – actually working – in every corner tobacconist's, and breakdowns on domestic phones running at once-in-twenty-years instead of once-every-two-years as in Britain? Well, perhaps they are more efficient in some ways, but at what price?

This book is not an attempt to answer any general question as to whether Japan is a society worthy of general approbation and imitation or not. Nor is it a catalogue of the institutional bits and pieces which we might think of borrowing, in the way that an interior decorator might come back from a tour of the grand houses full of ideas about brightening up living-rooms. It is, rather, an attempt to spell out some of the things that observing and thinking about Japan have taught me about my own society and the ways it might be improved.

Comparison: instructive even when invidious

All learning – all science – proceeds by comparison. There is no better way of learning how societies in general work than by studying, and living in, a country very different from one's own, observing the differences, asking why, watching one's own reactions, learning to look a little wide-eyed at things one has always taken for granted.

When I first went to Japan I was not surprised that Japanese politics seemed to make a great thing of the budget. So did ours, with all those newspaper photographs of chancellors holding up despatch boxes and great national excitement as to whether there would be a penny, or twopence, on a pint of beer. A budget, I imagined, was all about revenue plans, how and how much the Government was going to squeeze the public. But I soon found out that that was not what the Japanese annual budget ritual was about at all. Taxation structures are something which can be altered at any time of the year by administrative order or *ad hoc* legislation. 'The budget' that everyone was talking about was the detailed overall expenditure plan – which in Britain is dealt with only in grossest outline in the budget announcement and filled in by debates on departmental estimates at various times through the year. And, far from the Japanese budget being prepared in desperate secrecy until the moment of dramatic unveiling, it goes through three public drafts. The Ministry of Finance publishes the first in December. Then follows a month of intense public debate and private lobbying by, and on behalf of, all those government departments and their client groups whose pet projects have failed to get financed. Then the second draft is published. More weeks of lobbying, most intensely by those whose projects were in the first draft but got squeezed out of the second. The third draft, sometimes delayed a day or two by the, now quite frantic, last-minute negotiations, is final.

What are the differences symptomatic of? A long period of fast growth plus enough moderate inflation to yield a good 'natural increase' in revenue which kept it growing faster than GNP and so made taxation plans relatively unproblematic? Partly, no doubt (and in itself instructive of the different *political* problems and possibilities of growing and stagnant economies), but they are symptomatic also, surely, of different popular conceptions of the state, and of its role in the economy. On the one hand is a view of the state as a barely necessary evil: the night-watchman got above himself, now giving orders as to who should have keys, who can go where and do what; the state as the home of unthinking, oppressive, faceless bureaucrats, always thrusting forms under the noses of wealth-creating businessmen. On the other, in contrast, is the idea of the state as coordinator of a development drive towards objectives shared by the whole nation: prosperity and national strength, 'catching up with more advanced countries'; the state as animator, providing funds and valued imprimaturs to organizations with plausible plans to contribute to those objectives; the state also as pork barrel from which politicians provide hand-outs to buy or consolidate votes; the state as an arena of conflict between generally animator-minded civil servants and pork-barrel-keeper-minded politicians.

These differences between basic conceptions of the state – the regulatory state and the developmental state – are crucial to an understanding of the limits of industrial policy, and how those limits differ between Britain and Japan. When I did a survey of Japanese efforts at energy conservation in industry during the high-energy-price period of the late 1970s, I was most impressed by two things. The first was the ease with which the Japanese passed a law requiring all large firms to have a qualified energy manager (and mobilized for token rewards the efforts of large numbers of industrial engineers to devise the syllabus and run the very tough national certificate examinations). The second was the detail and complexity of the form on which the government required firms to report the most intimate details of all their major energy-using equipment (partly, in fact, for didactic purposes – to prompt them to measure performance indicators they had never measured before). I have reflected on this form frequently when I have heard of the recent swingeing cut-backs in the British Production Census – a crucial source of the information on which any industrial policy, and even macroeconomic policy, must be based – or when I hear of the difficulty civil servants experience in getting ministerial permission to 'bother businessmen' with survey inquiries which are fundamental to the assessment of costly government initiatives.

These differences in basic assumptions, in political culture, mean that there would seem little to be gained from suggesting that the Department of Trade and Industry (DTI) should suddenly start behaving like the Ministry of International Trade and Industry (MITI) and offer 'administrative guidance' to British firms. And yet. . . . There is danger, too, in learning from comparisons. One can easily end up with over-emphasized contrasts, with all-or-nothing national stereotypes. In fact, of course, both Britain and Japan are diverse heterogeneous societies – Britain considerably more so than Japan. Japan, too, has its minority of 'my factory is my castle' businessmen, who loudly decry government interference. Britain, likewise, has a good many loyal businessmen involved in the committees of the National Economic Development Office (NEDO) who believe that only a lot of cooperative effort between businessmen and civil servants can bring the British economy round. I recently made a study of the working of the Product and Process

Development Scheme – a government scheme to aid new product development – in the British pump industry. I found, admittedly, a number of instances of generalized animosity towards government and government officials – 'not worth the money to put up with all their forms and fussing' – but also a large number of cases of friendly and frank collaboration, of businessmen acknowledging not only the helpfulness but the expertise of the DTI officials, acknowledging that they had learned a thing or two from the contact. 'Administrative guidance' may not work in Britain as a means of getting a TV company to cancel a film about a Saudi princess, but the British are not so uniformly individualistic that it can never work in more modest and tentative forms.

So, to sum up on the use and abuse of comparison, it gives one, primarily, a framework for judgement. It gives one a sense of *the dimensions of variation* in the ways human beings have devised for making social and political and economic arrangements. One starts off taking the role of the state and views of its limitations current in Britain today for granted. The next step is a sense of the polarized dichotomy: Japan/developmental state–Britain/regulatory state. The third step is the realization that this is not in fact a dichotomy but a spectrum, that in getting a sense of the contrast between the two polar states at the opposite ends of the spectrum, one has got hold of a new tool of analysis, a new dimension, a new means of measuring changes as a shift along that dimension, a new means, say, of analysing the compatibility of different institutions which may belong to different parts of that dimension. Comparisons, if they are done properly, take you from the black and white world of either/or to the greyer ambiguities of more or less.

Culture and its homogeneity

And so it is with most of those dichotomous broad-brush contrasts commonly drawn between British and Japanese cultures (and so often invoked by those who say that there is nothing much we can learn from Japan): our individualism versus their groupishness; their acceptance of hierarchy versus our manly refusal to knuckle under to non-accountable authority. No use thinking, many would say, that one can adopt Japanese management practices in British factories: you will never get British workers singing the company song and touching their forelocks to their managers.

That there is, indeed, a difference in the proportion of Britons and

Japanese who would take kindly to an intensely loyalty-demanding work organization is true. But it *is* a matter of proportions. Britain has no great difficulty in finding enough people to sign up for lifetime careers in the Army or the Civil Service. And what more loyalty-demanding, hierarchical organizations can one imagine than those? In that very individualistic country America, that very Japanese company IBM even has a company song, which is more than the vast majority of Japanese companies do. Workers in none of the Japanese companies operating in Britain sing songs, as far as I know, but a good many of them take kindly to factory uniforms (which the managers also wear) and morning meetings. With total manufacturing employment down to less than a quarter of total employment, and only a minority in the high-investment, high-scale-economy areas which need large corporations or public monopolies, an individualistic society does not need too many de-viant 'organization men' to staff the kind of organizations that re-quire them. Modern societies provide wide scope for diversity and specialization. The outlook and values of the few thousand people who staff Britain's administrative Civil Service could hardly be said to represent the central tendencies of British contemporary culture as effectively as Terry Wogan or Geoffrey Boycott, but that does not prevent them playing a crucial role in our society.

The late-development effect

Many of the differences between Japan and Britain are in any case not primarily cultural in origin, but a product of Japan's history as a latecomer to industrialization. The 'developmental state' syndrome, for instance, owes a lot of its strength to the fact that for the whole of the last century Japan has had one compelling shared objective around which the nation could rally: 'catching up with the West'. In the industrial sphere, too, a lot of the differences derived – as I concluded after making a detailed study of technically similar British and Japanese factories fifteen years ago – from the different trajectories of industrialization of the two countries.

Britain was the pioneer. Industrialization based on the increasing mobilization of inanimate energy started in the eighteenth century. It was a long slow process. The accumulation of capital, the incor-poration of new techniques, the modest annual growth in output, were the work not of large corporations but predominantly of small enterprises, producing for highly competitive product markets, drawing their workers from competitive labour markets in which every occupational skill had its market price, its going rate. Our institutions, particularly the employment and industrial relations practices which grew out of attempts to regulate those labour markets, were constrained by those circumstances and the assumptions which went with them – easy mobility for the worker from firm to firm; freedom for the employer to hire and fire; the 'equal pay for equal work' notion of a going rate for occupational skills; the craft/occupational organization of trade unions as combinations of those with a common interest in keeping up the going rate for a particular skill – and bargaining fragmented into 'rate for the job' arguments for different groups rather than about the share of enterprise revenue due to whole workforces.

Japan, by contrast, came to industrialization late. It started with more advanced technology in bigger capital lumps. The 'catch-up effect' provided faster growth rates in leading sector firms. Also, the importance of state involvement, the availability of new corporate models of business organization as they were beginning to emerge in the West (Krupp and National Cash Register were admired and studied), together with the lumpishness of the capital requirements for entry into the newer fields, all conspired to make large corporations the pace-setters of industrialization in crucial sectors of the economy. Using novel technologies, they needed novel skills, and only the corporations themselves could teach them. A well-developed school system provided plenty of able and willing learners and the criteria with which to select the most able. Having trained these young workers, the firms had a strong interest in keeping them. Their stable oligopoly position in their product markets made it easy enough to afford to do so, to offer seniority increments and welfare benefits, to formalize internal promotion chains. And the contrast between these privileged conditions of work (in what were in any case high-prestige firms) and conditions in the small enterprises of the more traditional industries meant little difficulty in stabilizing their workforces. Thus was the lifetime-employment, seniority-wage – and later enterprise-union – syndrome ('internal labour market' as economists like to call it, though it is not a market at all) created and established as the 'modern sector' norm, and eventually, as the medium and small enterprises began to emulate the large, it became also the norm (though less often, in the smaller firms, the practice) for the whole economy.

Thus, largely out of the circumstances of late development, Japan got a set of employment and industrial relations institutions which were very different from ours. And institutions for regulating product as well as labour markets, too. Japan could jump straight into the large-corporation era of product-market oligopoly and segmented internalized labour markets and create from the very beginning institutions which made them efficient – all the apparatus of recession cartels and investment cartels and watchdog commissions to regulate oligopolies on the one hand, and on the other the whole structure of enterprise unions, enterprise training, and enterprise bargaining within the framework of a national 'Spring Offensive' wage-norm system which serves as a powerful brake on inflationary leap-frogging.

Japan: the model of our future?

But *we* have moved into the era of large-corporation oligopoly, too. Many of our markets are also dominated by oligopolies, and a vast *ad hoc* regulatory system has sprung up to deal with them. As Chapter 3 analyses at some length, within the framework of our occupation-based fragmented union structure, and our 'rate for the job' wage assumptions, there seems to be a different, much more Japanese kind of system struggling to get out – one based on plant or enterprise bargaining, long service in the same firm, rewards in promotion prospects as well as cash, bargaining by appeal to the level of the firm's performance rather than ruling wage rates in the external market. Labour market competition, in Thurow's (1975) useful classification, becomes less and less 'wage competition' with wage levels being signals that prompt people to move, or get pushed, in and out of jobs; instead it becomes more and more 'job competition' with relatively secure tenures, wages and conditions set internally without too much concern for the external market, and all the competition concentrated at limited 'entry ports' – which is where, in the younger age groups, unemployment is concentrated when the system is doing badly.

Now – and here we come to the main point, and, I believe, the timeliness of this book – there are two views of these trends in the British economy (pretty much paralleled throughout Europe and in the US). The dominant mood ten years ago was one of puzzlement, a certain acceptance that something irreversible was happening, a search for ways of accommodating the trends by *ad hoc* adjustments to promote efficiency and fairness, a sort of corporatism by default which included largely unimplemented planning agreements between government and private firms, national enterprise boards under constant pressure to rescue lame ducks, and patchwork incomes policies lacking in conviction – and, as it turned out, lacking in effect.

The new Right, which controls the ideological airspace today, is very different. Puzzlement is banished. We now *know* that these fudging compromising trends are our downfall. They introduce rigidities into our economies which prevent market forces from operating freely to promote efficiency. They lead to feather-bedding and unjustified privilege. The intrusion of government can only stifle enterprise. The bureaucratized large corporation is less efficient, less vigorous than the small business. Employment rigidities produce inefficient over-manning and wage levels unresponsive to market conditions, thereby perpetuating inflation and unemployment. Get government off the backs of the people, stop market regulation by corporate oligopolies, and labour-market regulation by trade-union monopolies, and soon we shall once again have an economy characterized by entrepreneurial vigour, full employment and general growth and satisfaction all round.

One can understand why economists should believe that; why, indeed, perhaps by now a majority of the economics profession has a doctrinaire attachment to views such as that. Markets, and the adjustment of price and quantity through the operation of impersonal forces, are what the most clever and intellectually exciting equilibrum economics is about. And one can see how many other people besides economists should be driven to such views by the failure of ineffective 1970s-style corporatism to stem Britain's decline.

But the solution is too simple. And anyone who takes Japan seriously, anyone who is used to thinking in terms of developmental state–regulatory state, or wage competition–job competition dimensions, and who knows a bit of history, must realize that it is. All those rigidities that we complain of – large segments of product markets under oligopoly, high labour immobility, a high level of government intervention in private industry's planning decisions – are well-established characteristics of Japan's economy. And yet they seem there to have a benign effect. How can this be?

Eleven ingredients of the Japanese recipe

This book does not set out to provide a detailed account of the working of the Japanese economy. For that the reader is referred to the companion volume to this one: *Flexible Rigidities: Industrial policy and structural adjustment in the Japanese economy 1970–80* (Dore, 1986). But it may be useful here to summarize briefly what seem to me the main distinctive characteristics of the Japanese economy. All such lists are bound to be a bit tendentious; I find that this one, though, satisfies a fairly wide range of observers.

1   *The Japanese work hard*   A sociologist blushes, of course, to say anything so unsubtle and so easily mistaken for a quotation from the *Daily Mail* discussing British workers' tea breaks, but the unsubtle is often very important. It is not so much a matter of manual workers' steady input of effort throughout the day, nor of the 2,100 hours a year (compared with our 1,900) of the workers covered by the Organization for Economic Co-operation and De- velopment (OECD) statistics. (That still leaves Japan with higher hourly wage costs than us in most industries.) What is more important in all those industries in which innovation and product quality are crucial is that *managers and technologists* work hard – the research team nearing a breakthrough who stay in their labs until midnight for days on end, the engineer who never lets up until he has seen the last detail of a retooling off the drawing- board. All sorts of both institutional and cultural characteristics lie behind this – what the Japanese have learned to call work- aholism.

2   *The Japanese are well educated*   Over 90 per cent of each age group stays at school until the age of 18. The typical school year contains 240 teaching days. Approaching 40 per cent of the age group proceed to college or university and a fifth of all under- graduates' degrees and a half of masters' degrees are in en- gineering.

3   *Japanese work cooperatively in large corporations*   This co- operativeness is manifest in such features as the Quality Circles through which manual workers contribute ideas for improvement of the production system, or the decision-making processes in management – widespread and slow consultation, a diffusion or blurring of responsibility, but swift execution of agreed decisions. The civil-service-like nature of the employment system, for all

grades, may be thought to foster this characteristic: the assumption of lifetime employment as the norm, and strenuous efforts to avoid redundancies; representation of employee interest by enterprise unions which bargain under the constraint of their members' interest in the long-run health of the firm; promotion by merit along relatively predictable tracks with minimum-seniority thresholds (so that juniors can rarely threaten to replace their immediate superiors); frequent rotation of generalist managers and technologists in the early part of their careers between production, sales, finance, design, personnel, etc.

4 *There is extensive use of subcontracting in manufacturing* This gives some advantages of specialization. The creation of hierarchies by bargaining power and status, legitimating lower wages in small subcontractors than in large corporations, also lowers costs to the latter. The extent to which they reap these advantages, however, is limited by the somewhat 'moralized' pattern of relational subcontracting (*à la* Marks and Spencer) which limits freedom to squeeze subcontractors, but this drawback is seen to be largely compensated for by the guarantees of quality, prompt delivery and rapid response to novel requirements which relational contracting can gain.

5 *Japan has a managerial, production-oriented capitalism, not a shareholder-dominated form of capitalism* Corporations until recently got a very high proportion of their capital in the form of bank loans rather than equity, and a high proportion of their equity, in the case of quoted companies, is held by the banks which finance their loans, the insurance companies which insure their businesses, their suppliers, their distributors and their customers, in other words, other corporations with a stake in the long-term health of the company. At the same time, the stock exchange is, and is believed to be, rife with shady speculation, and movements of share prices are not thought to carry the moral pressure of 'an authoritative judgement of one's peers'. These circumstances give corporate managements elbow room to look to the long term, to foster developments which might only after several years compensate for a short-to-medium-term drain on resources.

6 *Japan has the most effective form of incomes policy outside Austria and Sweden* The whole private sector settles (by individual enterprise bargaining) at the same season with a simultaneous pay-

rise start date of 1 April, the public sector following a few months
later. The Spring Offensive system, as it is called, comprises an
elaborate set of institutionalized rituals between November and
March: negotiations by megaphone between national federations
of enterprise unions and of employers; publication of economic
projections under alternative pay assumptions; newspaper
polemic and commentary by 'disinterested' academics; and much
private feasting and negotiation. By the time enterprise
bargaining begins the range of expected settlement levels has
greatly narrowed, and a few big settlements by pay leaders establishes a norm which is then rapidly followed, with local discounts
and premia for special circumstances.

7 *Japan has a high savings rate and low rates of interest and her
corporations invest 15 per cent of GNP, as do government and
households combined.* Cultural ingredients in this involve prudence
and the willingness to defer gratification. Other factors include:
in the corporate sector, low shareholder pressure for dividend
distribution and high business confidence; in the household
sector, the still meagre provision of state old-age pensions and the
payment of about a third of cash wages in the form of twice-yearly
bonuses, as well as the many (25 per cent of the labour force) self-
employed whose reserves count as household savings in the
statistics.

8 *Japan is still a relatively 'small government' country* The tax
take has recently been around 24 per cent of national income
compared with a British figure of around 40 per cent. This,
however, is more a function of the low level of defence expenditure, the relatively recent arrival of affluence and the consequently low level of accumulation of social security demands,
and of the scale advantages of a large population with centralized
administration, than of hostility to public sector expansion as
such, though the accumulation of large public debts in the 1970s
has prompted strenuous efforts to hold back public expenditure
in recent years – attended by no greater success than in Britain.

9 *Japanese corporations are very good at forming cartels* In consumer goods markets, particularly expanding ones, and even
markets dominated by three or four producers, competition is
extremely keen. But even in those industries Japan has an im-
pressive array of strong industry associations; there being no
conglomerates of any significance in Japan (the takeover also

being unknown), every firm has what it regards as its 'home industry'. These industry associations, as well as sometimes providing the framework for illegal price-fixing conspiracies in fields where markets are stagnant, are also the vehicle for a wide range of concerted activities, frequently conducted under the guidance, surveillance, covert condoning, or subsidization of their sponsoring ministry – in most cases MITI. These activities include research reports of the kind produced by the best of the British NEDO's Sector Working Parties, and recession cartels (shared production cut-backs to deal with a cyclical fall in demand). They also organize research clubs to tackle research problems of remote rather than immediate commercial significance. Japanese managers show a keenly calculative sense of where rationally to put the boundary between competition and cooperation.

10 *The Japanese value and honour the public service, and an intelligent industrial policy is one consequence of this* As used to be the case in Britain until a few years ago, competition to enter government service is keen. Ministries – especially high-prestige ministries like the Ministry of Finance and MITI – recruit some of the most gifted members of their generation. A large proportion of them in the case of MITI are from science and engineering faculties. This helps to give MITI the respect of business managers which permits close and continuous consultation. The ability to build up a consensus about the direction of needed change in the industrial structure (periodically enshrined in publication of a forecasting document or 'Vision') provides a framework in which industrial policy initiatives can be intelligently planned and cooperatively carried out. This has been most important for the smooth running down of depressed industries and for technological development. MITI's role in the latter has diminished since the ending of exchange control removed its regulation of technology imports, but it has played a major part in organizing long-range club research projects, of which the current fifth-generation computer project is the most famous. Direct subsidy of these programmes has been relatively limited – a good deal smaller than British government expenditure under the Industry Act. (Also, the effective rate of taxation on corporation profits in Japan is over 50 per cent, compared with under 20 per cent in Britain.)

11   *By contrast, the Japanese do not much honour politicians, whose role in running the economy is small*   Given the electoral strength of the dominant Liberal Democratic Party, in power for thirty continuous years, the only effective electoral competition is between the factions of rival candidates for the prime ministership, and policy is rarely an issue in these contests. Politicians are more-or-less corrupt brokers for interest groups who have limited powers of veto over bureaucratic initiatives, but rarely take initiatives of their own. As ministers they need not, for example, master legislation they sponsor since bureaucrats come to the Diet to answer questions of detail at the committee stage. The consequent absence of any electoral-cycle swings of economic policy has been an important precondition for business confidence and has given time for the institutionalization of such important parts of the economic structure as the wage and price negotiation mechanisms.

So what does it all amount to? First, what it does *not* amount to is free-for-all market capitalism, whether one is talking about the employer–employee relation in labour markets, about the large-firm-producer–subcontractor relation in intermediate goods markets, about investor–banker–entrepreneur relations in financial markets, about competitor–competitor relations in final product markets, or about interventions of governments in *all* those markets. It is harder to imagine an economy more sharply different from the free enterprise ideals which currently find their expression in the speeches of English-speaking political leaders on both sides of the Atlantic, and find their theoretical endorsement (as the high road to efficiency) in the writings of the majority of the economics profession.

What is so often overlooked is that there are two kinds of efficiency. There is the efficiency with which economists are most concerned, namely allocative efficiency or accounting efficiency. This is the sort of efficiency which comes from getting all the economy's resources put to the use in which they will yield most value – as free-market prices currently measure value. It involves making sure that when you buy a machine the capital cost is not greater than the cost of the labour it replaces (and, for the macroeconomic manager, it means creating the conditions in which the costs of capital and labour that the machine-buyer takes account of are undistorted true costs as they would be set, impersonally, by the balance of supply and demand in a free market). It involves not making an investment in a dying industry, if the same amount of money will yield a higher return in a new one. It involves keeping billions of pounds in cash mountains like GEC's when, discounting suitably for risks, the yields from lending it to other people are greater than any plausible projects for investing it in the making of electrical or electronic goods.

And then there is the other kind of efficiency, the efficiency which comes from paying attention to the work you are doing and not boring holes in the wrong place and having to scrap an expensive work-piece, from calculating just how many machining blanks you need to have in the stockpile to avoid having the machinists run out of work to do, from the conscientiousness that sees to it that deliveries to keep up that stockpile arrive on time. It is the efficiency which ensures that a small-businessman's application for a loan is processed by the bank in three days not three weeks, that hospitals do not get patients' papers mixed up and amputate the leg of an appendicitis case. It comes from making the right decisions because you have done your homework, got hold of all the market forecasts, collected as much information on your competitors' development plans as possible. It comes from caring about the quality of the work you produce and the service you give your customers, and from giving thought to how you can improve them. With some exceptions – notably the Harvard economist, deemed something of a maverick by his fellows, who calls this 'x-efficiency' to distinguish it from allocative efficiency and writes about it all the time (Leibenstein, 1966) – most members of the economics profession simply do not like analysing this sort of efficiency. It is hard to put numbers on it. It does not lead to very exciting algebra. It involves getting inside people's heads. A man's wages, the total labour costs he incurs, you can measure; his marginal revenue you have to calculate, and you simply can't *do* calculations if you assume that it varies from individual to individual or from day to day, depending on how intelligent or careful a man is, or which side he got out of bed, or how well he gets on with the foreman, or how interesting or meaningful his work. You simply have to take an average figure from past statistics, treat that as normal, and not enquire about the variations.

But what Japan tells us is that one *should* enquire, and that what the statistics show to be 'normal' in one society is not necessarily normal in another. Japan's competitive edge is not a matter of efficiency in the allocative sense. Doubtless the wage structure set by lifetime employment systems, the prices of sub-assemblies set in the subcontractors' 'customer markets', the results of oligopoly collusion aided and abetted by government in depressed industry markets, *involve allocative inefficiences on a grand scale*. But this is made up for, and apparently quite amply made up for, by the fact that all these social arrangements – the compromises made in favour of people who would lose out from the free working of market forces, the mobilizing of a sense of obligation and personal commitment in employment relations and 'customer market' relations – generate a sense of fairness which enables people to work cooperatively, conscientiously and with a will.

The message

This chapter has outlined the dominant themes of the essays on various aspects of contemporary economic structures and policy-making contained in this book, namely:

1   'x-efficiency' or 'production efficiency' is as important as, and probably for explaining differences in national economic performance *more* important than, allocative efficiency.

2   A sense of the *fairness* of social and economic arrangements is a crucial precondition for that kind of efficiency.

3   That sense of fairness cannot be achieved in the rough and tumble which results when each actor in the market is encouraged to maximize his own short-term benefits, unconstrained by anything except the hard reality of market forces – not, at any rate, in modern societies, with modern concepts of citizenship and the acompanying rights to be respected and consulted and to receive a minimum level of income and security. It requires, instead, a good deal of personal compromise and often corporatist compromise – compromise between the leaders of groups able to make promises for, as well as demanding benefits for, their members. It requires restraint in the use of market power out of consideration for the interests of bargaining partners/adversaries, or for the interests of a whole to which both belong. And that process of compromise will often require a good deal of umpiring, conciliating, cajoling, coordinating, incentive-providing, adjudicating – in short, intervention – by government.

'Taking Japan seriously' is meant in contrast to 'looking at Japan superficially'. It means not just being impressed by bits of social technology like Quality Circles and seeking to borrow them. It means asking what lies behind Quality Circles, what characteristics of the enterprise they are symptomatic of, what there is that is different about British and Japanese enterprises which explains why they developed in Japan rather than in Britain, and what this might suggest about how the structure of British enterprises or assumptions about industrial relations would have to change for Quality Circles to be effective.

This is not to scorn the borrowing of discrete bits of social technology – all the specific lore of how to organize Quality Circles, what sort of analytical techniques people should be taught, what sort of motivations can be appealed to, and so on. The world is full of institutional devices we would do well to consider borrowing, and Japan, simply *because* it is so different, is fuller of them than most countries. One of them, for instance, – which the Japanese got to by accident rather than by design – figures largely in Chapter 4: the synchronization of the pay round.

But not all Japanese institutions will 'fit' in Britain. What Japan offers us is the opportunity to show our ingenuity as well as to demonstrate the proper humility of those willing to learn. Japan shows the efficiency gains to be made through the working of institutions designed to produce a general sense of the fairness of social arrangements. What institutions do *we* need to produce the same sense of fairness in a society which is more heterogeneous, more individualistic, less groupish than Japan?

It is around that question – around the manifold interrelationships of fairness and efficiency – that the following chapters revolve, beginning with the enterprise, its structure, its ideologies, and its market context, and moving on to certain crucial areas of the macroeconomy: incomes policy for those in work, and the welfare system for those who are not.

2
Training in industry

A good example to start with, of opportunities to try to achieve by British means the same ends as the Japanese achieve by different, distinctively Japanese means, is to be found in the murky field of vocational training.

One can hardly pick up the *Financial Times* these days without finding a report of some new ministerial speech berating British employers for their miserly unwillingness to invest in the training of their employees. Levels of occupational competence in Britain, it is suggested, never very high in comparison with other countries, are in danger of falling further.

The sharp decline in traditional apprenticeships in manufacturing is one piece of frequently cited evidence. A yearly intake of about 25,000 in the mid 1970s was 9,000 a decade later. Not everyone sees that as catastrophic, of course. New technologies made many traditional skills obsolete. And the dead hand of corporate conservatism weighs on nothing more heavily than the tripartite training organizations. Changes in content have been difficult. Even more tenacious has been the union opposition (often aided and abetted by personnel managers) to efforts to introduce a system of objective testing of standards of achievement to replace the nineteenth-century (or rather sixteenth-century) system of 'time-serving'. Not until April 1986 did the engineering union finally agree in principle that Britain could no longer afford the sloppy standards inherent in a system which admitted men to the overall lifelong status of 'skilled craftsmen' simply by the passage of a prescribed number of years in apprenticeship.

There are obvious advantages in bypassing traditional systems and introducing new sorts of traineeships – new in substantive content and in the rigour with which performance is tested. They could be free of one oppressive constraint under which British training systems have hitherto laboured – the need to fit into simple union ideas of what does or does not qualify one for the status of craftsman. The appointment by the Manpower Services Commission (MSC) of a Working Group to review Britain's whole system of vocational qualifications offered an opportunity to get away from the notion that in any industry there are three, and only three, status levels into which all manual workers can be fitted – the skilled, the semi-skilled and the unskilled – a notion which has been the source of endless dispute as to whether, for instance, a tool-room fitter should be able to claim a higher wage than, or separate representation from, other kinds of fitters who share the same 'craftsman' classification. Recognition of the variety of skills and of the variety of ways of acquiring them to acceptable standards other than having the once-for-all chance of being selected for an apprenticeship at the age of 17, could help in creating more flexible, realistic and fair job-grading and wage systems – in British engineering especially. Unfortunately the Working Group simply worked to entrenched tradition. It saw its main task as providing a 'clear classification and hallmarking system for vocational qualifications', which means in practice confirming the four-status-level system. The British training industry is condemned to a future of endless dispute as to whether any particular piece of learning fits into Level III or Level IV of the National Vocational Qualification (MSC, 1986).

Inadequate response

But the defects of the qualification system are only one reason, and probably not the most important one, why the forms of vocational training made necessary by new technology and the intensification of world competition have been slow to develop. Employers ('what do we pay taxes for, after all?') expect the technical colleges, polytechnics and universities to develop the courses, and prefer to hire people who have taken the courses at the state's or their own expense rather than to take on trainee-employees and share the expense of day-release or block-release training. At higher levels, they show a reluctance to sponsor students on university and polytechnic courses, or to accept for their practical training students going through sandwich courses. Select committees and government-sponsored reports alternately deplore employers' lack of interest in training, and wonder, sadly, why individuals in Britain seem less willing than in the United States to invest their own money in the upgrading of their own skills. These, for instance, were the conclusions of a joint MSC–NEDO survey:

British companies do not act on the US model and themselves set up or support whatever facilities they need (e.g., engineering education and training) but usually expect somebody else to do it (e.g., the Government). Nor do they come to a long term institutional arrangement, like their German or Japanese counterparts. UK employers, individually or collectively, rarely assess what they ought to spend on education and training in human and financial terms and they are not sure whether it would be worth while making an effort (MSC–NEDO, 1984, p. 90).

And, again, a Coopers and Lybrand report to MSC and NEDO suggested that:

In contrast with Germany and with the USA, there is little pressure for training coming from individual employees. Much of the difference can be explained in cultural/historical terms but there is also little doubt that the incentives for individuals to press for training are noticeably less in Britain than Germany and the USA . . . Furthermore, differentials in pay and status are rarely linked to the attainment of qualifications or to attendance at training courses, so they provide little incentive to British employees to seek further training (Coopers and Lybrand Associates, 1985, p. 14).

Much of the discussion of training concerns initial training of new entrants to industry and business. But there is also an increasing need for retraining. The pace of technological change is accelerating, and the acceleration seems inbuilt as international competition supplements inter-firm competition to cause the percentage of national incomes spent on research and development to rise steadily. An accelerating pace of technological change means an increasing obsolescence of old skills, increasing requirements for new skills. It means an increasing need for individuals to add new skills to their repertoires, or sometimes to make fresh starts, accept the lack of demand for their steelmaking skills, their skills in judging the temperature of a baker's oven, or their skills at mental arithmetic or at teaching Russian, and learn something new. Retraining of those made redundant from declining industries is very commonly agreed to be properly left to the state or individual initiative. It is topping-up additions to skill-repertoires – nowadays so often a matter of teaching people how to use computers, but by no means confined to that – which is more obviously seen to be the responsibility of employers, and again a responsibility which they are in general loath to discharge, with sorry consequences for levels of competence, if we are to believe, say, recent, detailed comparison of work practices in British and German factories (Daly *et al.*, 1985; Bessant and Grant, 1985).

Facts about training expenditure are notoriously hard to come by. Coopers and Lybrand's researchers were told by some training managers that they kept full details of training costs from their boards, because, if full costs were known, they would probably try to reduce them (Coopers and Lybrand Associates, 1985, p. 6). The most widely quoted survey – 500 telephone interviews conducted by Industrial Facts and Forecasting (1985) – concludes that the average British company spends 0.15 per cent of turnover on training, vastly less than the 3 to 4 per cent spent elsewhere, say scolding ministers in their speeches and press interviews ('futile government finger-wagging', a Labour MP said in a House of Commons debate) – elsewhere being, of course, the US, West Germany and Japan, where employers' attitudes to training are said to be very different.

And of course, in Japan they *are* different. In the big-firm sector of the Japanese economy the whole notion of skills, occupational identity, training and who gets what out of it, is different from ours. We share with other European and the American economies what may be called the basic market paradigm. They do not. To make the point clear, let me explain what I mean by 'the market paradigm'. Economists will recognize the model classically elaborated by Becker (1975) as 'human capital theory'.

The market paradigm

The essential idea is that skills are a kind of capital owned by, and embodied in, individuals, and that labour services, utilizing those skills, are bought and sold by those individuals in the market in much the same way as any other commodity: that is to say that forces of demand and supply determine the price (wage, salary) which different kinds of service will fetch. Individuals have an incentive to acquire skills so long as there is a market for the labour services those skills render possible, and so long as the cost of acquiring those skills does not exceed the likely gains in higher wages, bearing in mind that the costs are likely to bear fairly immediately on the individual at the time at which he decides to take training, whereas the gains are spread out over a longer future period and have to be discounted for their remoteness and uncertainty. If people show reluctance to undertake training, then (eventually) there will be a scarcity of the labour services embodying their skills and a rise in wages which will attract extra recruits to correct the balance. The 'invisible hand' may take a bit longer to do its balancing act than in the market for bread, or even for pigs, but work it eventually does.

As for the role of employers in all this, no single employer can hope by his own subsidy of training to increase the supply of skilled labour sufficiently to bring the price down (everybody is a price-taker in these labour markets) so employers have no more interest in paying directly for training than the buyer of cherries has for subsidizing the fruit-grower's fertilizer (he's already going to pay for it once in the wage/price of cherries). At least this applies to *general* skills which might be sold to a wide range of employers, like welding or typing or hairdressing. What the employer *does* have an incentive to subsidize is training in 'specific skills' – blast-furnaceman's skills in a region which has only one steelworks, railwayman's skills where there is only one railway – because he is probably the only one who can give the training efficiently and cheaply, and as the monopsonist buyer of the skill he can hold down the wages to recoup the training costs.

National and local political authorities have reasons to subsidize training also, because there are certain external benefits not reflected in the wages the trained person receives: the fact that fitters can only work if there is also an adequate supply of forgers and founders, for instance. So a rational world is a world in which general training is paid for by the individual being trained, and by the state, while an employer pays only for training in some sense specific to his enterprise.

And the real world?

It is all rather remote from the world we know. The world we know is one in which most people are *not* constantly looking around the labour market for somebody to buy their services, but instead are employed on a fairly long-term basis. It is a world where employers talk of 'turnover costs' and try to avoid them, a world in which many organizations have promotion chains, so that a machinist promoted to supervisor, or an accounts clerk appointed to be investment manager, or a draughtsman appointed to be designer, are faced with the need to know and to be able to do things which they never knew nor did before. It is a world in which a firm which scraps an electromechanical machine and gets one with electronic controls does not immediately sack its maintenance electricians and replace them by others with electronic skills – it may well, indeed, be precluded by a union agreement from doing so – but tries to adapt them to the demands of the new machine. It is a world, in other words, in which the motive for getting the skill frequently arises out of the job – the employment relation – itself; a situation as far from the 'get skills: go into market: find buyer' model as it is possible to get.

Certainly, there *are* a lot of jobs to which the market paradigm applies. A heavy-goods-vehicle (HGV) licence, for example, costs a fairly clearly defined amount to acquire, and usually leads to a job at a wage just that much higher than an ordinary lorry driver's. A course in shorthand or word-processing costs an equally calculable amount and adds, similarly, to the salary a secretary can expect. These are for various reasons 'mobile occupations'. Here is a real market for skills because they are used by a wide variety of enterprises in any one district, because the amount of 'enterprise-specific knowledge' – knowing the who's who and the what's where in a firm – which the job requires is relatively small, and because there are enough people in the market at any one time in large centres for a 'going rate', a market wage, to be established. These are also the sort of skills in which – along with wholly unskilled work – market forces actually bring down wages because the forces of supply and demand really are at work on the wage, and although employers rarely actually cut the wages of employees, they may take the opportunity of staff turnover to lower the wage they offer to replacements.

But are these the typical occupations of our society? Are the majority of British employees in such 'market jobs', or in the sort of 'organization jobs' of the first kind described, in which employment is relatively stable and training needs arise out of organizational contingencies? The fact that the creation of a pool of 3½ million unemployed has done very little to reduce – and certainly totally failed to halt – the rise in real wages of those already in employment, should be a clue to the extent to which market forces do, or rather do not, work on wage rates in the classical way, and a clue, therefore, to the extent to which the 'market paradigm of training' can safely be taken as representing reality. Secretaries and HGV drivers may conform to that paradigm, and so perhaps do a lot of construction workers and hotel staff and in some districts other people with distinct transferable skills, like welders; but probably not the majority of people in today's labour markets, and certainly not the people in the banks, insurance companies, hospitals, the hi-tech robotics, electronics, instrumentation industries, and so on. Those sectors of the economy where techniques change most rapidly, where there is the greatest need for continuous revision and development of initial training courses, and the greatest need for mid-career topping up of skills – it is precisely in those areas that employment tends to be most stable, internal promotion chains and job security guarantees tend to be most institutionalized, and consequently the need for training most likely to arise out of organizational contingencies. These are, in other words, the fields *par excellence* where the market paradigm is least likely to be applicable, though even here there are exceptions to which the paradigm *does* apply, skills like computer programming, for instance – a discrete and self-contained body of techniques required in a wide variety of enterprises and in short supply. They are likely to be the subject of active poaching, leading to a perceptible rise in wages, and a clear perception by possessors of the skill that they face a seller's market and would be counted fools not to exploit their advantage.

Persistence of the market paradigm: the crucial role of mobility

It is perhaps because of these conspicuous examples that, in spite of the fact that the market paradigm does not provide an adequate modelling of the motives to get and give training over most of the economy, it is nevertheless the paradigm that governs a lot of our thinking about the matter. It is the basis, for example, for the laments about the low level of enthusiasm the British, as compared with the American, population shows for buying their own training and marketable skills. It is the basis for the only training loan scheme so far started in Britain – the MSC's 1985 initiative designed to give incentives to individuals who might be contemplating getting training, to re-weight a little their calculations of costs and benefits. But at the same time we *also* think in terms of the 'organizational exigencies' paradigm, which lies behind all those attacks on British employers for not spending enough on training.

What gives a particular plausibility to the market paradigm is that one central feature of it – the notion that skills are the property of the individual – remains true. People *are* mobile in our society and when they move they take their skills with them. They are not necessarily mobile for the reasons postulated by the 'market paradigm' because, having acquired a new skill (through their work experience in their existing job, say) they need to re-enter the market in order to exploit it. They *do* move for that reason, but they also move because promotion blockages at their place of work make 'spiral mobility' a faster means of career progression than staying where they are. They move because of personal incompatabilities with their colleagues, or because a husband or wife wants to move. Or – a factor not to be despised – they move because moving is a *norm*, because careers officers at school and university tell them that when they choose their first job they should think of where they hope their second job will be in three or four years' time and what sort of work experience would best conduce to getting it. Staying too long with the same employer, especially at a young age, is likely to be condemned as a sign of want of initiative.

So employers have to face the possibility – in the case of young employees, probability – that the people they train will leave soon after training is completed. And this constitutes a perfectly understandable reason for hesitating to invest in training. Once, before the accountants' rigorous and myopic analyses of *internal* rates of return held such sway in managerial decision-making, there was a sense that there was something wrong about being a free-rider on the training efforts of others, doing no training oneself and relying on picking up trained people in the market. There was enough of a community sense among employers in certain traditional manufacturing areas for them to feel that every firm should take its share in the cost of providing a pool of skilled labour available to them all. As this sense began to break down, the training boards were created in the 1960s to formalize the give-and-take. Every employer had to pay a payroll tax to the board and the board offered in return to use the money to pay the cost of any (approved) training courses the employers put on. The idea was a good one. Unfortunately top managers often care so little about real skills and productive competence, are so driven by purely financial criteria, that far too many training managers were given, and their performances were judged by, one single objective: 'get the levy back' – get enough training courses approved to recoup the levy in subsidies. This often led to such a proliferation of phoney and quasi-phoney courses that the whole system was corrupted and lost its credibility.

For initial training there remains some incentive for employers in that young trainees could be persuaded to pay for their training to some extent in lower salaries and by doing useful work while they are training at lower wages than would otherwise have to be paid. But this does not apply to mid-career retraining. Wages cannot be lowered for the 30-year-old electrician whom the firm wants to get electronic maintenance skills. And the newer and scarcer the skill, and the greater the importance (for the economy as a whole) of investing in it, so the greater the likelihood that poachers will be after anyone an actively training employer decides to train.

Hence, an impasse. Hence, much less vocational training in Britain than we need if one accepts that there *is* a national need to maintain the competitiveness of the British economy in internationally traded goods, in comparison with the training investments of some of our competitors. The Good and the Great may invoke the genuine-reality roots of the 'organizational exigencies' paradigm when they exhort employers to do more training, but in fact the incentives of the market paradigm are the only ones which the actual structure of our economy allows to be invoked – and they fail us.

Training in a lifetime employment world

So how does thinking about Japan help to resolve the issue? It sharpens up the choices because it shows us what the 'organizational exigencies' model which is struggling to get out of our basically market-model system could look like when it is fully developed. It *is* fully developed in the large-firm sector in Japan, because in that sector there is very little mobility between firms, and (just as in Britain, bank employees used to get poached by insurance companies, but not by other banks) almost no mobility at all between direct competitors.

The 'lifetime employment' pattern of employment for all employees in the typical large Japanese business firm is well known. It is paralleled in the West only in public sector organizations such as the civil service, police and army, and in the managerial ranks of a few leading firms: BP, ICI, IBM, major banks, etc. Lifetime employment is the central feature of Japan's 'organization-oriented' system of employment. Let me briefly list the other, interrelated, features of that system in contrast to the 'market-oriented' system of employment once dominant in the practice, and still dominant in the thinking about practice, of the typical British firm.

Market-oriented	*Organization-oriented*
1 Frequent mobility from firm to firm. Workers frequently in, always watching, the market.	Low mobility. Recruits leave the educational system for 'lifetime careers' in firms which accept 'no redundancy' as a dominant imperative of personnel policy, and expect to fill all except junior jobs (including board directorships) by internal promotion. Only bankruptcies and 'dire emergency' redundancies send workers back into the market.
2 Terms of worker contract (period of notice) vary only with status (blue, white collar, etc.).	Sharp distinction between permanent workers to whom above applies and temporary, part-time workers to whom it does not.
3 Wages = 'the rate for the job', the 'going rate' in the market. Fairness = 'equal pay for equal work' = 'work of equal value to employer'.	Pay on incremental scales differentiated by qualification level. Incremental progression depends on seniority and assessed 'merit'. 'Fairness' = 'equal pay for equal levels of qualification, service, willingness, cooperativeness,' etc.
4 *Trade* unions, combining all those with the same skill to sell in the market in a cooperative effort to raise the going rate for their skills.	*Enterprise* unions, combining all the lower ranks of those who have thrown in their lot with the same employer, in a cooperative effort to ensure that they get a fair share of the proceeds of the firm's collective endeavour, are not abused by, and are taken as seriously as the shareholders by, the enterprise managers.

5 Welfare/social security is looked after by the state or the individual's own savings and insurance effort rather than by the firm.

The firm assumes more, and the state less, of the responsibility for social security.

And, to extend the comparison to the field of training in more detail:

6 (a) Skills, once acquired, are individual property. Individuals can take them into the market, looking for a new employment contract, at any time it seems to their advantage.

In practice, difficult to leave a major firm and expect to get a job with a competitor firm of equal standing.

   (b) The possibility of mobility is a fairly salient thought in the minds of both employers and employees.

The likely market value of a skill they might acquire is of little concern to employees who do not foresee any great likelihood of their being in the market.

   (c) Employee who acquires a new skill and remains in the same employ can expect a new job at a new rate – a factor mutually reinforcing and reinforced by the salience of the consciousness of the 'market price' of skill.

Employee's wage not immediately dependent on job-function. Hence, not necessarily altered by his acquiring a new skill. A factor mutually reinforcing, and reinforced by, the lack of consciousness of the 'market price' of a skill.

   (d) Employers see training as an alternative to buying-in skills.

Employers see training as a means of getting their employees to do better the job they are pretty well committed to doing anyway; purchase of necessary skills in the market is not normally considered a possible substitute.

(e) Calculation of the costs of internal training must include subsequent payment of wages equal to the cost of buying the skills from the outside.

The costs of training are the direct costs only. No on-costs in raised wages.

(f) Gains uncertain because of the likelihood of trained employees leaving.

Gains may not be easily calculable, but at least the firm appropriates them all.

(g) Employers deterred from training.

Employers encouraged to train.

The contrast is clear enough. The whole logic of the situation is different in the two countries. Admittedly, in many sectors of the British economy, as noted earlier, mobility is declining: long-service employees *are* becoming more numerous. (Only 12 per cent of British employees had less than one year of service in their present job, according to a recent OECD (1984) survey.) Recessions always have that effect, but the tendency for turnover to decline can be traced back in the statistics to much earlier dates, to the late 1960s in fact.

So Britain, too, may be shifting *towards* the organization-exigencies paradigm, but not yet far enough to alter the perceptions and (quite reasonable) expectations of most employers. Ministers who issue exhortations to British employers to be like the Japanese are missing the point that they live in a different world from the Japanese, and are subject to different constraints. British firms, despite their domination by accountants who want properly calculated rates of return, still do invest in new machines even though they can only roughly calculate what might be the rate of return on the investment. They might be willing to make the same sort of bread-on-the-waters investment in their employees, if the employees were as unlikely as the machines to walk out of the door.

Matching Japanese training levels: less mobility?

One possible response to this contrast is to suggest that Britain, too, should move further from a market-oriented system towards a Japanese-type organization-oriented system, far enough for lifetime employment to become the new norm, thereby sharply altering employers' calculations of the costs and benefits of training investments. There is a lot of room for legitimate doubt both about the feasibility and the desirability of this solution.

First, feasibility. From the employee's point of view a generalized lifetime employment system implies a considerable restriction of freedom of choice. In an individualistic society like Britain, where people are less prone to identify fully with, or to develop intense loyalties towards, the organizations they join, such long-term commitments are more likely to be seen as a surrender of a desirable freedom than as a gain in security and sense of belonging. Moreover, even if it *were* culturally feasible (and we do not, after all, have too much difficulty in finding recruits to lifetime employment organizations like the Civil Service and the police and armed services), there is the problem of how to get from here to there. Suppose that a single employer did try, by giving guarantees of employment security, by paying attention to the structuring of career progressions, and by building wage structures around seniority-incremental scales, to retain his employees. He still could not hope, single-handed, to change the mobility *norm* of the society: the common idea that not moving shows a lack of initiative, the idea which is sustained by what people say, by the everyday judgements of others' behaviour, by the advice careers advisers give. An employer can *offer* the attractions of long-service employment, but cannot force his employees to accept them and stay with him after he has given them expensive training. To be sure, elite firms in monopoly positions in their product markets can afford to make employment conditions so attractive that few people can actually better themselves by moving elsewhere, thereby having a better chance of getting a low mobility response from their employees and recouping their training costs. And it was the practice of elite firms which established the system in Japan. But there were *also*, in Japan after 1919, very deliberate attempts to propagate the new norms by business and government organizations. In the same way, in Britain too, to effect a really substantial change in norms, it will be necessary for employers *collectively* to engage in propaganda efforts, to try to change the advice that careers officers give, for instance.

And that collective effort is unlikely to be forthcoming as long as there are doubts about the *desirability* as well as the feasibility of the reduction in mobility. Mobility is thought to be very good for an economy in various ways. First it is thought to diffuse knowledge of techniques and good industrial practice around the economy, and so contribute to the general raising of standards. (This asssumes that people prefer the highest when they see it. Otherwise it might just as well diffuse sloppy practice.) Secondly, it is seen as an essential means of adjustment: firms in expanding industries expand and need extra people, firms in contracting industries need to lose people; well-managed efficient firms expand, their less efficient competitors contract. These are not definitive arguments because Japanese large-firm industry manifestly achieves a high level of efficiency without these advantages. They compensate for the first by intensive and systematic efforts at information-gathering through trade and professional journals, trade fairs, trade associations, and so on, and by their success in generally maintaining a 'learning environment' in the firm, something which, as we shall see in Chapters 5 and 7, is promoted by the lack of occupational specialization and occupational identification: generalist managers and generalist craftsmen expect constantly to be having to learn new skills in mid-career. Japanese firms compensate for the second, adjustment, effect of mobility by efforts of large firms in declining industries to diversify, to find new products and markets to occupy the people whom they are more or less committed to employing anyway; that is one reason why they are more innovative firms than ours are: necessity is the mother of innovation. The idea of a GEC, sitting on liquid resources of £1½ billion, simultaneously making people redundant by closing factories, is incomprehensible to a Japanese manager. Some British firms do diversify too, of course, but in a different way. Courtaulds' expansion of its paint manufacture to compensate for the decline of its traditional textiles provided very little employment for the redundant workers who lost jobs in the textile factories they closed, and finding such jobs was not a dominant motive for diversification. And the favourite British means of diversification is through acquisition – acquiring new employees with the new business – whereas in Japan it involves, usually, setting up task forces which train themselves for a new product line.

Obviously, the degree to which British business culture is likely to be Japanized to compensate for the loss of mobility and its advantages is limited. Is there not, then, some way in which British employers can be given an incentive to train in spite of mobility?

Matching Japanese training levels: other incentives

One commonly mooted idea is that of the remissible training tax such as the French have. The major problem with that solution is the same as with the levy grant system: the danger of a proliferation of spurious courses and the need for an inspection bureaucracy to prevent it. (Levels of gobbledy-gookism in the advertising literature of the training industry exceed that of most other industries by a considerable margin. For choice examples of the even greater excesses of the American industry see Ivar Berg's classic *Education and Jobs: The Great Training Robbery*, 1971.) A better idea might be a loan scheme to provide a kind of insurance cover for the employer who invests in the training. Quite simply, the loan covers the costs of training, including salary while training, and the responsibility for repayment is shared between the employer and the person trained. However, the employer actually pays only for as long as the person trained stays in his employ. If he leaves he takes the debt with him, but presumably persuades his new employer to take over the repayments. If the employer does not actually need the loan, the whole transaction can be nominal up to the point at which the person trained changes jobs. For those interested in how the scheme might work out in detail, the following description explores some of its implications, including the safeguards needed to protect employees.

Employee Training Loan Insurance Scheme (ETLIS)

1 *The purpose*

(a)   There is a widespread assumption that the current demand by employers for the training of their employees (both employees of long-standing and those newly hired) is lower than the 'need' for such training. The difference between demand and need can be framed in terms of:
— the difference between private cost-benefit analyses which do not, and a social cost-benefit anlaysis which does, take account of externalities;
— the difference between rational and irrational employers, accepting their objective functions as given;
— the difference between 'good' (long time-horizon) objective functions and 'bad' (short-term bottom-line) objective functions (on the assumption that the correct balance between short- and long- term maximization is *not* to be determined solely by the rate of interest);
— more intuitively, and more germane to the discussion of political practicabilities than any of the above, the difference between what British employers do and what foreign employers do.

(*b*) A variety of factors is invoked to explain differences between the enthusiasm for employee training of British and foreign firms: a lesser willingness of British employees individually to share the cost of training than American employees; a more generally philistine managerial culture in Britain, placing less value on trained expertise than on the exercise of authority, as compared, say, with a Germany or a Sweden; a greater danger of having the people one trains leave to work for other employers in the mobile British labour market than in a Japan where the 'lifetime employment' norm prevails.

(*c*) Doubtless there are many factors involved, but almost everyone has some anecdotal evidence to indicate that the last – the fear of losing trained employees soon after their training – is *one* of those factors, and probably an important one. From the firm which refuses to take raw electronic engineering graduates and prefers to pick up already experienced employees in the market, to the small employer who has stopped spending the £600 to £700 needed to train his drivers for an HGV licence because half of those he has trained have gone off to drive cross-Channel trucks at twice the wage he offers, there is plenty of evidence that many employers' perfectly rational profit-maximizing decisions lead them to prefer to be free-riding poachers rather than providers of training.

(*d*) ETLIS is designed to alter that particular incentive pattern, by providing employers who do invest in training their employees with some insurance cover – cover designed to compensate them if the employees they train should leave them before they have derived such profit from their training investment.

2 The scheme

(*a*) The idea is simple in outline. An ETLIS Bank is established. It advances loans to cover the cost of training (fees, equipment, wages during training less any contributions to production made during training) of people already in employment. The loans are taken out jointly by the employer and the employee receiving the training, but repayment of the loan is the responsibility of the employer for as long as the employee does not voluntarily leave his employment. If he does leave before the end of the term set for repayment he, the employee, assumes responsibility for the remaining payments. The assumption is that he would negotiate with his new employer to compensate him for this, or – and tax arrangements would presumably make this preferable – to take over direct responsibility for those repayments.

(*b*)   A firm which did not need the loan and wished to finance the training itself could do so, and still register the loan with the Bank. No actual transactions would take place unless the trained employee left before the notional loan was paid off. In that case the Bank would undertake the collection of the remaining payments and pay the employer a lump sum representing the present value of the expected payments, less the collection charge.

(*c*)   Dismissal of the employee would leave the repayments as the responsibility of the employer.

(*d*)   If the interest rate on the loan approximated market rates, there would be no need to exercise any but the broadest monitoring control over the genuineness or the usefulness of the training for which the loan is contracted. (This is the great advantage of the scheme as compared with, say, remissable training taxes. One important reason for the general loss of confidence in the training boards' levy-grant system – an earlier attempt to share training costs between conscientious training firms and would-be free-riders – was the cost, the bureaucratic elaborateness, the tendency to 'old-boy' corruption, and ultimately the ineffectiveness of the vetting system, made necessary to prevent phoney courses from being botched up 'to get the levy back'.) One can work on the assumption that, as freely bargaining agents, neither employer nor employee would embark on a training arrangement under this scheme if they were not both convinced that it would be worth while.

(*e*)   However, employer and employee are usually not freely bargaining agents with equal clout. There would need to be several safeguards to prevent employers from taking advantage of vulnerable employees as a result of the scheme.

First, there is a genuine information problem. The employee is expected to buy a training the quality of which he may not be able to judge very accurately, probably less accurately than the employer. Suppose, having signed a loan document, he discovers the training to fall far below expectation. Should he not have some way of repudiating the agreement? Perhaps the best solution would be to make a provisional agreement on the loan at the beginning, and then to confirm it at the midpoint of the training period.

Second, employees should not be under pressure to accept loan obligations if they see them as reducing their options and conferring no great corresponding advantage. To deal with this problem one might, first, make it the Bank's task to make sure that the employee understands the terms of the agreement and is not coerced, and secondly, one might make 'unfair pressure to accept a training loan' an unfair labour practice which, like 'unfair dismissal' may be taken to an industrial tribunal.

A third problem is that an employee who has a loan obligation is at a disadvantage in subsequent negotiations with his employer if he does not, for family reasons perhaps, have the option of moving to another firm which will accept his loan obligations. He might be put at a disadvantage in asking for wage increases or in resisting unreasonable demands from his employer. To deal with this the original agreement should specify whether or not promotion or wage increase would be expected to follow after the training is completed, 'unfair coercion of employees bearing a training debt obligation' should be added to the list of unfair labour practices which can be taken to an industrial tribunal and, in view of the interest an employer might have in avoiding overt dismissal and engineering a voluntary resignation instead, the safeguards against 'constructive dismissal' developed by the tribunals in unfair dismissal cases may need strengthening where outstanding loan repayments are involved.

To iron out any problems of the above kind before they get to industrial tribunals, firms over a certain size should be required to set up a Training Council made up of management and union or employees' representatives. This could operate both as a first court of appeal for disputes about the treatment of individuals, and also as a forum for discussion of the firm's training strategies.

One alternative to much of the above, one which would offer greater protection for employees, but possibly at the expense of unduly restricting the scheme, is to confine the scope of the scheme to firms which formally *join* it. Member firms would receive the advantages of the scheme only if they accepted to pay the loan repayments of any poachees who had been trained by other member firms. Employees would not be personally liable to repay the loans if they left their original employment to join a non-member firm or to live in a rural commune on a legacy or supplementary benefit. The scheme would, however, be viable on this basis only if membership in fact became near-universal.

(*f*) The scheme could cover both the initial training of newly appointed staff (who might be paying partly for the training anyway by accepting low wages, thereby lowering the value of the loan required) and for in-service training, retooling, or upgrading of long-established employees receiving their full wage during training. It is for the latter type of training that the cost, and arguably also the demand–need gap, is greater.

(*g*) Repayment terms would have to be relatively short not to seem too burdensome, perhaps not more than five years for a two-year course of training.

(*h*) In order to keep the loans at market rates there would probably have to be state subsidy to cover administration and bad debts. Bad debts would arise from bankruptcy (the Bank would become one of the bankrupt firm's creditors, collecting what it can) and from the emigration or evaporation of individuals who cannot be traced. If the demand–need gap were seen to be serious enough, subsidy could well be used to lower interest rates below market levels. Any attempts to use this loan finance for other purposes should be relatively easy to frustrate.

(*i*) Interest rates have a two-edged effect, however. A high interest rate deters a firm which is actually taking a loan from the bank and also deters an employee from accepting a training offer. But a high interest rate provides an incentive to a firm which is using its own money because it increases the compensation payment it might subsequently collect if the employee leaves.

(*j*) Likewise the scheduling of the loan repayments has variable implications. A high degree of front-loading is a deterrent to the firm to offer training, but an incentive to the employee to accept it. Given the plausibility of the view of training as an 'investment' analogous to investment in equipment, the analogy of depreciation allowances would seem to justify a fair degree of front- loading.

3 *The advantages*

(a) The scheme can be expected to stimulate employers' propensity to offer training by providing:

— insurance against losing part of the gains from training their employees through employee mobility;

— the automatic availability of loan finance with low transaction costs and, possibly, with low interest costs if subsidy incentives are applied;

— possibly, also, an actual reduction in the mobility of the people they have trained.

(b) The disincentive to employees to accept training should not be great enough to offset employers' increased willingness to offer it, particularly if the safeguards suggested in 2(e) are adopted, given the employee's enhancement of his employability and the likelihood – which experience should soon establish – that other employers would pick up his loan repayment obligations if he moved to another job.

(c) It leads to greater equity in the distribution of the costs of training if 'poachers' have to assume repayment costs for those whom they poach soon after training.

Training in a mobile sector

All the argument so far has been about training in the large corporation sector (where, admittedly, needs for the more sophisticated and novel forms of training are concentrated). There, clearly, some 'Japanese-effects-by-British-means' recipe is important. But neither the British nor the Japanese economy is entirely composed of large firms. There are, for instance, the 25 per cent of the Japanese workforce who are self-employed, or family members working with the self-employed, and the even larger numbers of people working as employees in smaller firms where, however much the lifetime employment pattern may be the ideal, employers cannot in practice offer job security. Here, employee loyalties are personal and more limited, and mobility between firms, and between wage employment and self-employment, approaches British levels. As a consequence, here the 'market paradigm' is a much closer approximation to what happens in Japan too. As far as this sector is concerned, a comparison between Japanese and British practice is instructive in a more direct way, in showing the sort of direction in which a 'strong developmental state' can effectively use its resources, a matter of some interest for our own transition from the regime of a weak regulatory state system to that of a stronger developmental one.

British governments have never fully accepted the principle that the public interest in standards of work competence requires state action. The market ought to sort out the competent from the incompetent, as the latter eventually find no buyers for their services. Skill standards of boilermakers and carpenters can be left to trade unions and employers to arrange among themselves. When the skill is of a higher order and serving a public which cannot easily tell the quacks from the competent practitioners, the usual device to which the weak regulatory state resorts is the licensed monopoly. The Bar Association, the British Medical Association, the engineering institutions, the opticians, the accountants, are able wholly to exclude non-members from the market – or at least put them under severe disadvantages – on the promise that in exchange for these often lucrative monopoly powers they, the corporate bodies, will see to it that the public interest is properly served by maintaining high standards of competence: running professional examinations, striking the incompetent or the immoral from the register, and so on.

Corporatist self-regulation of this kind is seen as sufficient in the weak regulatory state only where personal safety is involved. Where incompetence does not merely lead to, say, a steady fall in the balance of trade in manufactures, but actually endangers human lives, then even the British state with its weak regulatory traditions has stepped in and assumed direct state responsibility for maintaining standards. The driving licence is the obvious example. Others are the licensing of air pilots, pharmacists and those who handle explosives.

Skill-testing in Japan

But in a society with a strong and developmental state like Japan, the public interest in the society's international competitiveness is seen as justifying far more extensive and thorough-going intervention in the maintenance of standards of competence. (And in a late-developing state, as opposed to one that grew slowly through market forces, the coporate bodies of practitioners may not yet exist at the time the need to import professional standards is recognized. There may not *be* any entity to delegate self-regulation powers to.

British colonial administrators, for example, set up skill-test centres for manual skills in Africa, run directly by the colonial state, in the absence of any craft bodies capable of regulating apprenticeship.)

It is not surprising, therefore, to find that Japan licenses its doctors and lawyers directly with state examinations and has, moreover, at quite low craft levels, developed a comprehensive state-organized and state-sponsored skill-testing system. At the national level are central committees to revise and maintain test syllabuses and to ensure national uniformity of standards. Then there is a second tier of committees manned by volunteers at prefectural level to oversee the complex administration of skill-test centres with funds provided ultimately on the Ministry of Labour's budget. The tests range from a diversity of manufacturing skills – three modules for bamboo and basket work, sixteen for metal-shaping, three for founding, three for forging, three for textile dyeing, and so on – to construction, commercial and service trades, including traditional gardening, stonemasonry, photography, watchmaking, etc. The failure rates (passes in 1981 averaged 45 per cent for the lower grade and 43 per cent for the upper grade examinations) suggest that the standards set are quite rigorous. Larger lifetime-employing firms, which have no particular interest in giving their employees qualifications which certify their skills on the labour market, do not encourage them to take these tests, though they do often take part in the 'skill Olympics', the competitive tournaments, primarily in engineering skills, which are a secondary feature of the competence-raising system. They may also encourage their subcontractors to put their employees through the tests as a means of improving quality standards. And a good many of them run their own internal tests which may be imposed on the subcontractors too. But, for the most part, the skill-test system serves the mobile-labour-market sector of the economy where workers do have the incentive to obtain a qualification which will enhance their claim to a job or, if they are self-employed, provide quality-of-service guarantees to their customers. The most popular tests in 1981 were for carpentry, plastering, steel-frame construction, technical drawing, building painting, portrait photography, bath installation (of the large, jacuzzi-fitted, hotel variety), construction machine repair, agricultural machine repair, gardening and some of the more common trades of the small engineering firms.

There is one other use of the skill-test in Japan, however, which does apply to large firms. When standards of competence in a particular field are such that an especially strong public interest is served by maintaining them, the state may legally require firms to train some of their employees to test standards. Thus, having a certain number of employees who have acquired the state architect qualification is a precondition for construction firms receiving certain public works contracts. Another recent example followed from the perception that there was a strong national interest in promoting energy conservation. Two new test syllabuses were devised by committees of practising engineers under MITI auspices, one in heat management, one in electricity management. A law was passed requiring any plant which used a certain quantity of kilowatt hours of electricity to have one electricity manager per x kWh, and plants which used a certain number of calories of industrial heat to have heat managers. The tests, held twice a year, and at first with high failure rates, were run by MITI. A newly established quango, the Energy Conservation Agency, (also a nice new source of post-retirement jobs for a few MITI officials and private-sector managers) wrote textbooks and organized distance learning packages, supplemented by day-release and week-release refresher courses to help people to attain the required standards.

British practice: compromise and flexible standards

In the absence of direct state involvement in skill-testing, something of the same function is performed in Britain for the lower level and intermediate skills for which there are no corporate professional bodies to assume responsibility for standards, by voluntary bodies such as the City and Guilds Institute, the Royal Society of Arts (RSA) and the Business and Technical Education Council (BTEC). Latterly they too have come to receive some assistance from the state. But, generally, the British response to demands for action to raise competence standards has been to put public money into *training* rather than testing, by subsidization of courses run in technical colleges, polytechnics, colleges of further education and universities. The definition of standards and their certification are delegated to the pre-existing corporate bodies which all have their own vested interests: firstly, the corporate professional bodies, which have a primary interest in maintaining their monopoly over certification (not to mention resisting any radical syllabus reform which might imply that existing practitioners are incompetent!); secondly, the training institutions, which have a primary interest on the one hand in maintaining their autonomy and on the other in securing recognition for their courses by the professional bodies; and thirdly, the testing bodies, which have a primary interest in getting their tests and qualifications accepted by training institutions (which are heavily dominant in their councils) and by the professional bodies. The hugger-mugger which often results from this process of nudge and fudge is often plain enough. Of course, all concerned recognize the *public* interest in competence and social efficiency, but the state which is the primary guardian of that public interest is largely reduced to the role of provider of training subsidies, without any control over the definition of standards. It is a typical result of this system that the Finniston Committee's recommendations for a state Engineering Agency which would set national qualification standards for engineering competence finally resulted in a Council, heavily under the influence of professional bodies, whose major standards-raising activity turns out to be 'accrediting' training courses, giving them a stamp of approval on the basis of the apparent 'quality' of their teaching provisions, but leaving them the autonomy to set their own standards of tested competence. The result: pass mark standards differing widely between training institutions, depending primarily on the quality of their student intake (no polytechnic can afford to run courses which a large proportion of their students will fail). In consequence there are no certificates which effectively guarantee standards of known and certain currency in the national market except those still awarded and tested by the professional bodies. One of the major abuses of this system, of course, is that professional bodies which for quite good reasons are given certification monopolies are also given training monopolies; they are allowed to say: 'the only way to reach acceptable standards of competence is to take a course run by our friends, one on which *we* have put our stamp of approval'.

The driving test principle: a model to copy?

The Japanese state has likewise been heavily involved in the subsidization of technical and vocational training since the nineteenth century. But for a wide range of lower and middle level craft skills it has made far more use of what is best described in British terms as 'the driving test principle': use state resources primarily to define standards to be achieved and to organize tests open to all and leave it to individuals to get the training necessary to meet those standards as best they can in the market. As a consequence there *is*, in Japan, a very flourishing free-enterprise training industry of vocational schools of all descriptions, some of which receive public subsidy, but most of which are as unsubsidized as British driving schools.

The whole field of skills in the mobile-labour-market sector – as distinct from the large-enterprise training sector – is an area where, as the British state moves from a regulatory to a more interventionist and developmental role, we might learn more directly from Japan by copying Japanese practices. We might, that is to say, find more applications for the driving test principle: state subsidy and control primarily for the definition, testing and meaningful certification of standards of competence; more reliance on private initiative for the acquisition of the skills themselves; prevention of professional bodies from turning a certification monopoly (if it *is* desirable that they should have one) into a training monopoly too.

The first step would be the establishment of a national network of skill-testing centres which would provide a framework for all testing activities for skills primarily bought and sold in the *local* labour markets (i.e., lower-than-graduate-level skills), for rationalizing the activities of the existing testing institutions – like City and Guilds, RSA, etc. – to provide economies of scale and, not least, to secure the independence of the testing institutions from the training institutions, as is necessary if skill certificates are to have as widely trusted a validity as the driving licence. Probably it would be essential that the new national skill test service should be created within the Department of Trade and Industry, or jointly between it and the Department of Employment (DE). The Department of Education and the MSC are too deeply involved with the training industry to deal with the vested interests which would be challenged.

The starting point: a tale of two sectors

The complexities of the vocational training field were a good place to start because they show that there is no simple formula for deriving instructive lessons from a detailed comparison of British and Japanese practice. The following five points summarize what I have been suggesting in the broadest terms.

1   Training practices in Japan differ quite sharply between the large-firm, lifetime-employment sector, and the more-mobile-labour-market/self-employment sector.

2 Training *needs* differ similarly in Britain too: it is primarily large firms or high technology firms which have the need to invest in the training of people who are already their employees, or to provide initial training – often in very enterprise-specific skills – which is not available from training institutions in the market.

3 But training practices do not differ sharply between the two sectors in Britain because, as is not the case in Japan, large-firm employees are also highly mobile. The 'market paradigm' which relies on individual self-betterment as the major motive for acquiring training, is the dominant approach to training in *both* sectors.

4 In order to ensure that British large firms invest as heavily in training as their Japanese competitors it is possibly necessary, therefore, for the state to provide supplementary incentives, of which one of the cheapest and most effective might be a training loan scheme to provide insurance cover for firms which train their employees, only to have them poached, shortly thereafter, by other firms.

5 The importance given to skill-testing in the mobile-labour-market sector in Japan suggests that we too might benefit from the wider application of the driving-test principle: invest state resources in the definition and testing of skills; rely more on individual initiative and the market for acquiring those skills. A network of national skill-test centres and a national skill-testing service run by the DTI or the DTI and DE would be the way to start moving in this direction.

The cultural/ideological residual

Adopting reform measures of the kind outlined here might make a lot of difference, but we should not expect that it would automatically transform large British firms into 'learning organizations' in quite the same way as Japanese firms are, nor that we should become a nation of avid test-takers keen to collect certificates as boy scouts collect badges. It would be foolish to claim that there are only institutional, and not also cultural, factors involved in the differences between the two countries. Read about traditional Japanese apprenticeships in sword-making or print-making, or the way in which calligraphy beginners were expected to spend their first three months mastering the intricacies of the simple single horizontal stroke. There seems, particularly where psycho-motor skills were involved, to have been a somewhat greater rigour and insistence on perfection in traditional Japanese than in traditional European forms of apprenticeship.

But the other part of the cultural element is not so much a matter of long-standing tradition as of more recent habits induced by historical circumstances. Once again this is a question of the late-development effect. For more than a century Japanese society as a whole has defined itself as a learning society. From the 1870s, when they hired an Englishman at a salary higher than that of their own prime minister to establish a national Mint with the very latest techniques, to the 1980s when it is still only a minority of Japanese who say that Japan has little more to learn and now a lot to teach foreigners, the Japanese have seen 'catching up with the West' as a dominant objective and have had the humility to 'accept the status of pupil' as the best means of achieving it.

And a learning society naturally needed its business firms to be learning organizations. Britain's leading firms developed largely by slow incremental improvement of their own technology, each new step being absorbed, as it came, into the skill repertory of its designers and workmen: learning on the job. Japan's leading firms, latecomers to the world's industrial revolution, often started, or achieved crucial stages in their growth, by importing a radically new technology from abroad, a technology which often required mastery of new *kinds* of knowledge and skills; hence, often, new kinds of systematic training, new standards of competence. And usually there was no alternative but for the firm itself to do the training: new skills had no established means of transmission in state training colleges. In these circumstances, the development of the 'learning organization' tradition is understandable. And so is the concern of the enterprise with its employees' standards of competence. In Britain in the 1930s a railway fireman whom the seniority promotion system would soon allow to become a driver had to pass a rather perfunctory test of his knowledge of the workings of a steam engine. The training – on the Southern Railway at least – was organized not by the firm but by the trade union: the employees were going to gain from the promotion, so they should bear the cost. When they had become drivers and were to drive over a route new to them, they were allowed a fixed number of hours riding the footplate with another driver, after which they were presumed (without any test) to 'know the road'. In Japan, as one of the social realist novels of the 1930s describes, the national railway showed a great concern with developing its workers' skills. There were competitions for firemen, with careful measures of the degree to which they succeeded in distributing coal evenly over the surface of a long firebox. A leader of the railway workers' union who had been a champion driver of Akita Prefecture, once described to me the tests of driver skill used in the competition. For the 'smooth stop' section of the test, the judges sat solemnly in the restaurant car with a row of metal bars stood on end. They were of identical cross-section but different lengths. The longer the bar the more readily it toppled in a jerky stop. Driver skill was measured by the longest bar to remain upright.

There is no obvious way in which these cultural traditions and ideological prescriptions of the learning society and the learning enterprise can be reproduced in Britian, neither those of long standing, nor those which are part of the late-development syndrome. The humility required in 'accepting the status of pupil' does not come so easily to Britons as it does to those born in Japan's more hierarchical society: witness the contrast between the way Japanese government reports still in 1985 deplore the 'backwardness' of Japan's research and development institutions, the shortage of creative skills, and so on, and the way British politicians reassure us (recently, often, on the basis of a misquotation of a 'Japanese survey' which turns out to be derived from a dubious American study) that we are basically the most creative people in the world, responsible for the major scientific breakthroughs since the war, temporarily experiencing a little local difficulty in putting our ideas into production practice. (See a speech by the Minister of State at the Department of Trade and Industry, Geoffrey Pattie, *The Times*, 2 April 1985.)

To be sure, if the realization of the nature of our plight as a trading nation does grow strong enough to break through this complacency, and the recovery of a lost capacity to compete internationally in goods and services does become defined in the public consciousness as a dominant national objective, then we might finally benefit from a late 're-development effect' ourselves. The title of the recent MSC–NEDO report, *Competence and Competition*, may already be an indication of a shift of consciousness in that direction. If that happens, then perhaps, eventually, even British Rail and its drivers and signalmen and maintenance men will come to care more about perfecting the skills they use at work, and we shall get as high a proportion of our trains running on time as the Japanese.

3
Dual economy or spectrum economy?

The last chapter drew a distinction between the 'organization-oriented' large firm in Japan with its stable lifelong employment, and what was called the mobile-labour-market sector, the world of self-employment and small firms closer to the 'market-oriented system' – mobile employment, rate-for-the-job wages, no enterprise unions, training at the individual's expense – which is seen as the norm in Britain.

It was suggested there that British large firms were in many respects moving towards a Japanese-type 'organization-oriented' system, with important leverage in this direction being supplied by the way in which training needs, arising out of organizational exigencies, cannot be easily met from the market. The two quite different recipes for improving skill-training in Britain are perhaps symptomatic of an emerging British 'dual economy' similar to the familiar Japanese dual economy.

On the one hand is a privileged sector of government and the public sector and large firms which are more price-makers than price-takers in their product markets, a sector in which job tenures are relatively secure and (because they are privileged) the rate of voluntary job resignations also fairly low, a heavily unionized sector where real wages continue to rise even in a recession, a sector characterized by Thurow's (1975) 'job competition' rather than 'wage competition'.

On the other hand is an unprivileged sector where job tenures are less secure, mobility much greater; where wage competition still serves to hold down, and even reduce, real wages when unemployment rises. Most of the jobs undertaken by people who left school at the age of 18 and over, and most of the middle-class incomes, are to be found in the former rather than in the latter sector.

If there is some truth in the idea that this is indeed the direction in which we are tending, it is worth while looking at Japan, the most obvious exemplar of a 'dual structure' among modern industrial economies, to gain an idea as to what might be the implication of an extrapolation of these trends – for industrial relations, wages and incomes policy, for education and social security, for political cohesion and the notion of citizenship in our society. This chapter will look at wage-setting mechanisms.

Ask a Japanese about the dual structure and he's almost certain to define it primarily in terms of wages. The figures which show that, for example, the differential between firms with over 1,000 workers and those with between 10 and 29 is of the order of 100:60 – even within the same industry – are among the most familiar of Japanese economic statistics. Comparable British statistics are hard to come by, but partial surveys of earlier decades have produced figures of 100:85 or 100:80.

A key role in producing this dualism in Japan has been played by technological advantage and control over product markets. The large firms which created the organization-oriented system and which allowed it – largely in the post-war period after enterprise unions entered on the scene – to become also a high-wage system, were firms which were at the forefront in importing high technology and enjoyed, by virtue of their technological lead, some degree of monopoly control over their product markets. They could afford to privilege their workers compared with 'going rates' in the mobile-labour market (but not compared with their small number of hi-tech competitors; oligopoly firms tended to move together) precisely because they had little difficulty in passing on the costs to consumers; and the advantages in stability of the workforce, skill-quality, loyal commitment, seemed worth having.

Could the same thing be happening in Britain? The dominant view is that it is unlikely because we have an active labour market. There may actually be a considerable spectrum of wage rates in different enterprises for what is to all appearances the same skill. But these are just variations around an underlying 'going rate'. They are due to imperfections and rigidities which *slow down* the operation of the principle that workers who are mutually substitutable in skill will tend to be paid the same wage, no matter who hires them. Removal of the rigidities will help the principle to operate faster and remove the anomalies of a broad spectrum of inter-firm differentials. But the imperfections are not so great that we need think in terms of the submergence of the principle, in terms of a wholly new system.

Market forces?

There is an alternative view. It goes as follows:

> The *appearance* of a 'going rate' for skills around which actual
> wage rates cluster has not for a long time, over most of the
> economy, *really* been a consequence of market principles, of the
> principle that within the same market substitutable products will
> tend towards the same price. The 'going rate' was, instead, very
> largely the product of the influence on employment contracts of
> ideas of fairness which *simulated* market effects precisely because
> 'equal pay for equal work' was at the basis of those ideas. But,
> employment contracts in Britain are now changing in such a way
> as to alter basic ideas of fairness. Not only will market forces cease
> to work: it will cease even to look as if they are working. Already
> the tendency of real wage rates over much of the private sector to
> continue to rise in spite of a steady increase in unemployment is
> an indication of the non-functioning of market forces.

The tenacity with which belief in market forces is adhered to in
contemporary economic analysis is remarkable. For example, the
Oxford Economic Forecasting model, a refinement of the Treasury's
small model, which apparently successfully sells its predictive wares
to private business says, of its wage equation, that it:

> is of central importance in the model . . . broadly labour is
> analysed like any other tradeable good. Its price is assumed to be
> determined by the market mechanism with demand and supply
> equilibrating . . . On the supply side, the major determinants are
> assumed to be: the real wage that employees receive; and the level
> of public sector spending (which acts as a proxy for the supply of
> labour to the private sector). An interesting and powerful feature
> here is that if income taxes are cut and thus real take home pay is
> raised the supply of labour is assumed to rise in consequence and
> so wages fall . . .

It would be plausible to assume that the real world works
effectively like that if employment predominantly followed the 'spot
contract' pattern of, for example, traditional daily-hire dock work.
Then changes in labour supply might well be expected to have a
rapid effect on the wage. Employers might actually lower their offer
wages to the point at which there were not enough workers willing to
take them. As suggested in the last chapter, there *is* a sector of the
economy, and certain occupations, where labour is sufficiently

mobile for that effect to be noticeable – though with a considerable. time lapse – as a result of turnover and accumulation of new hirings. But over a large segment of the economy and a wide range of occupations, the reality is different, being characterized by:

1 Quite stable employment;

2 Wage-setting not so much by individual contract as by collective bargaining between the managers of single firms and representatives of employees;

3 Institutionalized practices by which those negotiations of new wage scales are put on a regular annual cycle;

4 The implication, in that collective bargaining, of various principles of fairness.

What is 'fair'?

It is the notion of fairness which this chapter is principally about. Let us begin the discussion of the light which Japanese practice might shed on trends in Britain, by distinguishing between four different principles of fairness which might be invoked in these negotiations.

1 *'Equal pay for equal work'* fairness (hereafter EPEW fairness). This principle is satisfied if each worker in the firm is paid as much as his or her 'comparators', people doing the same work in other firms. It is the principle, as noted above, which simulates the effects of market forces.

2 *'Equal percentage pay increases for all'* fairness (EPPI fairness). People learn to live with existing differentials over time, and any disturbance thereof usually strikes the *relative* loser as unfair, though in some circumstances there can be acceptance of the fairness of each disturbance. Thus, one reason why miners had an easy climb up the differentials scale in the early 1970s – apart from changing fuel prices lowering managers' concession costs – was because their doing so did not offend fairness principles. (As Tylecote (1981) notes, during the UK strike in 1974 it was hard for a miner to pay for his own drink in a pub; hard for an electric power worker to get served.) General standards of work comfort had risen sufficiently in previous decades for people to feel that a revaluation of the 'heat and danger premium' paid to miners was

not unreasonable. So one should fully spell out EPPI as: 'equal percentage pay increases for all, unless for some good reason'.

3 '*Equal shares in the fruits of shared effort*' fairness (ESSE fairness). This is the principle that, the enterprise in some sense being a community, when it does well all its members should do well: higher-than-average profits should be reflected not only in higher-than-average dividends but also in higher-than-average wages. One can also count as part of ESSE fairness the 'no loss' principle that everyone has a right to be compensated for rises in the cost of living, rephrased in ESSE terms that can be spelled out as 'if there has been no diminution in our contribution to the firm there should be no reduction in our real reward'.

4 '*Equal pay for enterprises of equal standing*' (EPEES fairness). This is a principle which can only be applied in an economy, like Japan's, in which a hierarchy of firms has been established. When a truck driver in the British Steel Corporation thinks himself entitled to the same wage as a truck driver in ICI, but sees no reason to compare his wage with that of a truck driver in a small transport firm, EPEES is beginning to operate. In Japan, it is well established. The Hitachi union, seeking bargaining criteria, checks with the Toshiba union the rate for, say, 40-year-old graduate managers or for 35-year-old craftsmen electricians, but it would never think of checking on the wages paid to electricians in the small electrical firm around the corner, nor would the union in the small firm – if there was one – aspire to parity with Hitachi.

The central point already made – that it is the strength of EPEW arguments in wage negotiations, as much as genuine market considerations like the ease or difficulty of recruiting or retaining workers, which sustains the appearance of a 'going rate' for skills – is not new, of course. John Stuart Mill was very clear about the way ideals of justice sometimes override market considerations. More recently Ross (1958) talked of 'the force of equitable comparison' in US bargaining, and Wood (1978) and Tylecote (1981) have spelled out some of the reasons why fairness arguments work: because a sense of *un*fairness involves costs to the employer, from reduced enthusiasm and conscientiousness at work to outright strikes.

It may be true that trade-union negotiators will use any argument to hand: ESSE when profits are high, EPEW when they are low. Fairness, some would way, is a matter of rhetoric; it is power that counts.

But what is power for a trade-union leader? Partly it is a function of the sort of damage the circumstances of the industry allow him to inflict on the employer. Partly it is a matter of his ability to bring his members out on strike. And what determines that? The strength of their feelings, of which the most important is indignation at any deviation from what is thought of as fair.

So fairness does count, but by and large the discussions of institutional economists who have taken such considerations into account have concentrated exclusively on EPEW: people are concerned to know whether they are getting the 'going rate' for their job and look to see what their 'comparators' are getting in other firms.

But it is reasonable to suppose that Britain has changed: EPPI is a product of the changes in economic circumstances and institutions dating only from the last couple of decades. 'If a fireman gets £100 a week so should I', could give way to 'If the firemen are going up ten per cent so should I' only when average percentage increases become the focus of collective bargains and of all newspaper reporting about them, i.e., after endemic inflation raised the percentage figure to sizeable double or high single figures, after incomes policies set norms in those terms, after the notion of an 'annual round' and 'the average settlement figure so far this round' became institutionalized. The Confederation of British Industry (CBI) began its data-bank survey on which such figures are based in July 1977. In the course of the 1981–82 round, more managers responding to the CBI questionnaire ranked 'pay increases nationally' as a 'very important influence' on pay negotiations than put 'comparisons with employees in the same industry' in that category.

EPPI maintains existing relativities. It is ESSE, linking wage rises to the profitability of firms, which can alter them and can be the mechanism for growing differentiation in wage levels between an increasingly – in the terms developed in the last chapter – 'organization-oriented' large-firm oligopoly sector, and a more 'market-oriented' sector of smaller firms facing competitive markets.

There is good circumstantial evidence, at least, to suggest that arguments from ESSE fairness may be of growing importance. The reasoning is best developed by postulating a dimension of 'community' (in the abstract sense of 'communitarian-ness') along which it would be possible to give firms at least an ordinal ranking. The dimension is best defined by describing its polar types, at the one end what we shall call the 'Company Law model' firm and at the other the 'Community model' firm. It will be apparent that the distinction is cognate with several others, Fox's (1974) 'low trust firm' and 'high trust firm' for example. These contrasting types are briefly characterized in the box following.

In the COMPANY LAW MODEL:

1 The firm is primarily defined as the property of the shareholders whose rights are paramount. They have, for instance, an unconstrained right to sell a controlling interest to other parties if they wish.

2 'The management' are the *trusted* agents of the shareholders.

3 The management hires workers. The wage-effort bargain is struck in what is inevitably an adversary relationship in which each side seeks continuously to improve its position. Both sides may behave in scrupulous conformity to market contract rules about conscientiously delivering on promises, etc. But that does not imply a relationship of trust, which could lead, e.g., to exchanging information which the other side might, if you could not trust it not to, use to out-smart you.

In the COMMUNITY MODEL, by contrast:

1 The firm is primarily defined as a social unit made up of all the people who work full-time in it ('in' rather than 'for').

2 The shareholders are, like customers and suppliers and local authorities, one group of outsiders who have to be satisfied if the firm is to prosper. Members of the firm would feel entitled to vociferous protest if they had no say in the transfer of a controlling interest.

3 Every member of the firm can act on the assumption that other members share a desire to make the firm prosper, and this gives enough fellow-feeling for those who have less than a full understanding of the accounts to trust managers not to conceal things from them for manipulative purposes. They are likely to believe that the distribution of rewards is what it appears to be and is fair.

Different national institutions differentially foster the two types. In Japan, as we shall see in Chapter 6, a mixture of the conventions surrounding shareholders' rights and the actual pattern of shareholding decisively fosters the Community model and Japanese firms tend to cluster at that end of the continuum. But even within a British national institutional framework, firms can occupy very different positions between the two poles. My suggestion is that the modal British firm is edging towards the Community end of the spectrum.

Obviously, it is the Community type, encouraging in employees an *organizational* identification with the firm rather than an occupational identification with those others outside the firm who have the same skill to sell on the market, which fosters the ESSE principle of fairness at the expense of the EPEW principle which is naturally consonant with the Company Law model.

What then, is the evidence of an edging along the continuum in the UK private sector?

1   The importance for pay settlements of single employer, plant-level and enterprise-level bargaining is increasing, as documented by Brown (1983), White (1981), and the Department of Employment surveys (Daniel, 1983 and Millward, 1986). This establishes an elementary precondition for developing Community-type conventions. With this has come such 'enterprise union' characteristics as joint factory committees, the check off, and full-time factory convenors. Brown recently estimated that the latter, paid for by the employer, were now twice as numerous as full-time officials employed in the external organization by the unions themselves (Brown, 1983, p. 50).

2   There has been a similar increase in the 1970s in joint consultative committees, as recently documented by Daniel and Millward (1983). Many of these have heavy trade-union representation and blur the line – which unions have traditionally sought to keep sharp – between consultation and collective bargaining. This can be interpreted as conceding, on the union side, that bargaining also has to be constrained by 'responsible' concern for the health of the firm. A recent survey of shop stewards found that a majority recognized that 'involvement in participation committees' would affect 'the stewards' primary role in collective bargaining', but of that majority 'many more felt it would be beneficial rather than detrimental to their bargaining role' (Armstrong and Marchington, 1982, p. 42).

3   A tendency towards small plants is developing, partly as a result of labour-saving process innovation, partly because the difficulties of maintaining peaceable industrial relations in large units are now so generally appreciated. The average size of manufacturing plant, according to the Census of Production estimates, fell from 87 to 60 employees between 1973 and 1980; in metal goods, engineering and vehicles from 100 to 70. Whether the relation is linear or exponential or kinked, 'community' comes more easily in smaller units. Daniel's survey (1976, p. 88) found that union negotiators were more likely to mention the firm's 'ability to pay' as a consideration influencing them in small rather than in large plants: 33 per cent in the 200–500-worker group, 15 per cent in the over 500s.

4   There has been a growth in profit-sharing schemes. They were already found, by the end of 1981 – possibly as a result of the incentive of the 1978 and 1979 tax concessions – in 368 firms covering 1½ million employees (Creigh *et al.*, 1982). The much more significant tax-concessions of the 1987 Budget – inspired by the ideas of the American economist Martin Weitzman – should have a far wider effect.

5   Firms are moving towards 'harmonization', i.e. single status terms of employment (as regards holidays, sick pay entitlements, periods of notice and other conditions of employment), for both manual and non-manual workers. This again, for the lower ranks of the hierarchy, is another precondition for fostering a sense of being a 'full member' of the firm. In some firms there is tenacious opposition from white-collar unions insisting on the preservation of differentials (EPPI fairness), and the extra cost, estimated at between 5 and 12 per cent of labour costs, has doubtless been a deterrent since early 1980 when a management journal celebrated the final 'fading away' of 'the great divide' (Evans, 1980). 'Canteen harmonization', however, has reputedly been accelerated by the cost squeeze of the recession.

6   Labour turnover is declining, with progressively lower rates at the troughs and at the peaks of business cycles over the last 15 years. This may be just the secular trend counterpart of the business cycle tendency for turnover to fall as unemployment rises (unemployment has also been steadily rising at each successive peak of the cycle). At any rate, an OECD survey (1984)

concluded that Britain had one of the highest levels of stability of employment in Europe: only 12 per cent of employees had less than 12 months' service in their present employment. It may be (since a minority of frequent movers have always been responsible for the bulk of turnover) that falling turnover represents a disproportionate loss of jobs in the unskilled 'secondary market': the former frequent movers have now joined the long-term unemployed. It may, alternatively, be the result of firms' deliberate policies to reduce turnover and institutionalize internal labour-market practices. There is no clear evidence to judge, but that some firms *are* making such efforts can be documented (Marsden, 1982), and whatever the causes a lesser frequency of turnover ought to lead to lesser expectations of turnover, longer expectations (on both sides) of a continuance of the employment relationship, and so a stronger sense of organization membership.

7 The tendency for more complex technology to make more industrial skills non-transferable and enterprise-specific – the generally postulated origin of internal labour-market policies on the part of firms (see Doeringer and Piore, 1971, for the classic discussion) – is a tendency which shows little sign of abating. Moreover, as argued in the last chapter, as the pace of technology change increases firms have more frequent occasion (whatever the countervailing disincentives) to invest in the retraining of their employees: hence a greater incentive to keep them within the firm.

8 Even where the specificity of enterprise skills does not require it, job grade schemes are frequently introduced within enterprises partly to recognize that work traditionally done by a 'skilled fitter' is not homogeneous, partly to recognize differences in personal performance, and partly to provide the possibilities of career progressions as a work incentive. This serves to isolate further the internal from the external labour market: 'Fitter Grade III' has meaning only within the single organizational context. 'The loss of job descriptions that are common between firms increases the employee's dependence upon his own employer' (Brown, 1983, p. 50). Formal job evaluation schemes which directly grade all jobs in a plant *only* in relation to other jobs in the plant reinforce this tendency. A 1979 survey found evaluation schemes in 52 out of 82 plants surveyed, and of the 88 schemes (some plants had more than one for different sections) 40 had been started since 1975 (Torrington, 1980).

9   Another development, widespread in the engineering industry for the last decade, is the 'flexibility agreement'. This usually involves not only an easing of union demarcation boundaries, but agreements to pay skilled men their normal wage for turning their hands to unskilled work when there is none of their normal work to be done – an application to manual workers of the principle (hitherto applied only to non-manual workers) of payment according to status within the organization as opposed to the market principle of the rate-for-the-job or the measured value of performance.

10   Finally, there are many signs of the steady incorporation into management ideology of the Community model as an ideal, albeit an ideal shorn of some of its more awkward implications like the right of workers' representatives to question managers' salaries: Company Law ideals can continue to rule in such matters with little clear recognition of the incompatibility. Policies for enhancing 'employee-involvement' – a variety of measures to get workers interested in the success of the company and its objectives, to have a broader understanding of the company's operation than is strictly required for their own job functions, to take part in work planning and process improvement in their own departments, etc. – have been promoted by bodies like the Industrial Society for a long time. (The Community model can, indeed, cover the whole authority-style spectrum from traditional paternalism – both manipulative and altruistic, as far as the two can be distinguished – to the egalitarianism of a small cooperative.) Casual observation – of, for example, the Quality Circle movement, the latest manifestation of involvement policies – suggests that these pressures have intensified in recent years. Likewise the pressure stemming from the European Community for the disclosure of financial information to employees and for the legal enforcement of industrial democracy have already had their effects on the practices of a number of firms, even if they have had only marginal effect on the general climate of managerial opinion and even less on the legal framework. With the abortion of British proposals for industrial democracy legislation in the 1970s, the only substantial embodiment of the Community ideal in national law is the last-minute amendment inserted in the 1982 Employment Act requiring larger companies to report annually on measures they have taken in the previous year to improve their communications with their employees, to consult them on a reg-

ular basis, to encourage their 'involvement in the Company's performance' through share schemes, etc., and to promote a 'common awareness' of the company's financial and economic environment, an agenda which almost exactly follows the urgings of a 'New Year's Resolution' letter to the *Financial Times* from the Director-General of the Institute of Directors (5 January 1982). Earlier, also, there had been a clause in the 1980 Companies Act – found in some form in every draft Companies Bill since 1973 – requiring directors of companies to be concerned about 'the interests of the Company's employees in general as well as the interests of its members'. (The clause goes on to make clear, however, that the directors remain *legally* responsible to the *members* – i.e., shareholders – alone.)

Evidence of rising strength of the ESSE principle

Clearly this 'edging along the continuum' is tentative and hesitant, but the trends set out above do point in the same direction, they do mutually reinforce each other, and most of them do seem to be rooted in what it is reasonable to see as secular, not cyclical, trends: the growing complexity of technology, the erosion of deference towards ascriptive authority and authority based on property rights, and so on. They are promoted in some ways by the weakness of trade unions in the 1980s as they were promoted in other ways by the strengths of the unions in the 1970s. The question whether they have gone far enough for the expected consequence – the strengthening of the ESSE principle against other principles of fairness – to make itself felt and to result in an increase in inter-firm wage differentials, is one which cannot be fully answered on present evidence. There is one suggestive study, however, by Ball and Skoech (1981), who looked at the inter-firm differences in productivity (output per employee) and average earnings in Production Census data for 1973. In almost every one of 15 industries the two were correlated. It is not clear whether the causal chain is (*a*) superior production efficiency → higher real output per employee → higher wages, or (*b*) oligopoly control over markets → readiness to concede higher wages → passing on of wage increase into prices → higher nominal but not real output. The question is of interest for assessing the consequences of the trend for inflation and output, but does not affect the present argument very much; either way the figures show the cumulative effects of some process of differentiation at some time previous to 1973.

Consequences of a stronger ESSE principle

Supposing that there is an increase in inter-firm wage differentials. Should one deplore or welcome the trend? Would it be a good thing or a bad thing if we too, like the Japanese, develop a 'dual economy' with a monopoly/high-technology/high-wage 'primary labour market' sector and a· services/non-tradeables/public-sector/productivity-laggard/low-technology/low-wage sector; or rather, (for Japan, too, is better called a 'spectrum economy' than a 'dual economy') if Britain also saw the growth of a pay gradation (for comparable skills) from the most secure and profitable firms to the least?

First of all, is it feasible? It would certainly represent a considerable departure from the world we know. Blackaby (1980, p. 71) was assuredly reflecting the conventional received wisdom when he wrote: 'the gap between the pay of, say, a computer operator in an oil company and a computer operator in British Rail *cannot* be allowed to widen indefinitely' [my italics].

The fact is that it *can* be allowed to widen as far as the prevailing ideas of justice allow it to, as the example of Japan shows. Market forces would not stop it. All that market forces would cause to happen is that all the good computer operations would go into the oil companies, and British Rail (BR) would have to be content with those who cannot get a job elsewhere (or railway buffs), and both ends of the spectrum would be paying their 'efficiency wage'. (Arguably this is what has been happening anyway, which is the reason why BR reputedly suffers from such poor-quality management. The textile industry is another example where decline/low rewards/poor prospects ensure further decline, thanks to 'last option' recruitment and poor manager and worker quality.) The market does not stop this process because recruitment into computer operating is not adversely affected thereby. When hovering between a computing course and a nursing course, the rational human-capital-investing student, if there is such a creature, calculates his future benefit stream as the sum of the wage in Shell and the wage in BR and all the other jobs in between, each multiplied by the probability of his ending up in each of them. And, it may be said, if such a spectrum of 'organizational standing' develops and the people in top organizations are consciously perceived as having 'made it' in a competition everyone was engaged in, inter-organization differentials within occupations can come to seem no more unjust than traditional inter-occupational differentials.

A lot would depend on the extent to which the national union organizations can maintain national or regional pay-bargaining systems, and there is no reason to suppose that they would be any more successful in resisting the encroachments of enterprise-bargaining in the next decades than they have been in the last. Should the Association of Scientific, Technical and Managerial Staffs (ASTMS) try to stop its computer programmer members in Shell from pushing the wage up as far as it will go? Or insist that a downmarket widget maker has to pay the same wage (for what the union also recognizes to be less qualified people), which it manifestly cannot afford? Would the railway white-collar union, the Transport and Salaried Staffs Association (TSSA), see any mileage in arguing that BR's computer men should have a comparable wage with those in Shell even if getting it required a considerable disturbance of differentials with other occupations TSSA covers, and jeopardized claims for an overall x per cent rise for all its members?

So I conclude that a considerable degree of spectrumization is indeed possible. Inter-firm differentials, not only in average wages, but also in wages within the same occupation, could well grow. If so there would be a number of implications.

Spectrumization and education

First of all, such a change in the labour market would be a reflection of – and would be closely linked in a relation of mutual reinforcement with – the 'spectrumization' of the educational system. One can already see it happening. For example, in the top tertiary segment (13 per cent of the age group) one can detect a gradual formalization, through the mechanisms of entrance competitions based on national General Certificate of Education (GCE) standards, of a national prestige gradient running from Oxbridge (Oxford and Cambridge) through the 'better' redbrick, white-tile and Shakespeare universities to the technological universities, polytechnics and colleges of further education. At every level of the system there may be similar syllabuses in English literature or computer studies or mechanical engineering but the students – selected by their GCE O-level (Ordinary Level) and A-level (Advanced Level) performance – are generally thought to differ between levels in degrees of personal brightness. In terms of their formal possession of a degree, they end up identically 'qualified', but the world discriminates sharply when it comes to hiring them.

Politics

There would be long-run political consequences of this overt transformation of labour markets, too. Market is the basis of class, as Max
Weber recognized when he defined a class as a group which enters
the market with the same commodity – property or skill or brute
labour – to sell. The disappearance even of the assumption of a
uniform market price for a particular skill could well destroy the
basis of a sense of common interest amongst its possessors. Trade
unions might become stronger *within* enterprises with the development of participation schemes. But as the class-consciousness basis
of the Trades Union Congress (TUC)'s authority dwindles, so will
disappear the basis of the traditional British corporatism whose rise
Middlemas (1979) has documented: the recognition (what counted
effectively was recognition by Tory 'wets') of the 'union movement'
as an estate of the realm, as a 'social partner' in tripartite bargaining
relations with government and employers. The Thatcher government is slowly emasculating the formal institutions of that corporatism; spectrumization would undermine its social base in the
consciousness of citizens. The new corporatism would be sectional,
not tripartite. The miners might still use strike muscle to get funds
to keep pits open, but more probably in tacit collusion with British
Coal than with the support of the TUC.

Industrial policy

There is another implication – for industry policy. The traditional
view is that the labour market's enforcement of economy-wide wage
rates has been a prime instrument forcing the structural change
necessary for a progressive economy, as Salter (1966, p. 53) argued:

> Because wages play a major part in inducing such structural
> changes, it is particularly desirable that the market for labour,
> should cut across inter-industry boundaries, thereby ensuring
> that comparable labour has the same price in expanding and
> declining industries. The argument that an industry cannot
> 'afford' higher wages is, in the long run, extremely dangerous. If
> it were accepted and wages were based on the 'capacity to pay',
> employment would be perpetuated (unless labour deserted them)
> in industries which should properly decine *to make way* for more
> vigorous industries [my italics].

The argument may have some force in a full-employment economy where labour shortages in new frontier-breaking industries give some meaning to 'making way for'. When, however, unemployment is 14 per cent, when there are no new jobs available for redundant workers from textile firms which go bankrupt because they cannot both meet the import competition and pay standard wages, and when the fixed assets tied up in those firms have no alternative uses anyway, it is not so clear that lowering the wage as 'capacity to pay' falls – up to the point at which labour does desert – has any disadvantages either for workers, or for capitalists or for the economy's capacity to grow. Certainly, there are former employees of bankrupt textile firms in Blackburn who have taken this option into their own hands. Instead of remaining unemployed they have bought old looms from the former employer and now meet the import competition (as the former employer could not) by working, self-employed, for 55 hours a week to earn about the same income as they formerly received as a wage for 40 hours, a self-imposed 30 per cent cut in hourly wage *rates* which keeps them off the dole and the looms off the scrap-heap.

In short, it is far from obvious that 'spectrumization' would have disastrous effects on the prospects for smooth structural adjustment to the opportunities of new technology. In any case, the general acceptance and expectation of industrial policy intervention in the technology frontier industries has radically altered the significance of market forces in this regard compared with the 1924–50 period which Salter was analysing.

Production efficiency

There will be other economic effects. One should not overlook the intentions of those whose actions are likely to bring spectrumization about or rather bring about the shift' towards the Community model' firm which underlies that process. Managers responsible for those policies clearly believe that they will pay off and improve work efficiency, lead to better patterns of cooperation and the overcoming of adversarial 'us and them' attitudes, and so on. 'Wage increases linked to productivity' is very often an explicit recipe of those who advocate this way forward, an essential ingredient in the project of building efficiently cooperative enterprises.

For any increase in the efficiency of the British economy which results we should all be grateful, but the desirability or otherwise of

the spectrumization trend will depend crucially on the underlying
mechanisms which give some firms higher profits and greater ability
to pay than others. Are they the result of the abuse of a sheltered
monopoly position – the lucrative cost-plus defence contracts which
can mean so much to Britain's electronics industry as well as the
natural monopolies of transport and communications and public
utilities? Or are they the reward for real increases in output and
production efficiency – the just, and temporary, monopoly which
technical innovators can enjoy? An active competition policy, and
strict monitoring of those sectors where corporatist regulation seems
necessary for other reasons, will be a necessary condition for keeping
the spectrumization process benign.

And equality

But what would spectrumization do for the general level of inequality
in our society? Discussions of the difference between the high-wage
large-firm sector and the small-enterprise subcontracting/family-firm
sector in Japan suggest that income inequalities are very great.
Indeed, there are good theoretical reasons for thinking that income
distribution will become more unequal with spectrumization. The
EPEW principle and/or market forces have been the mechanism
whereby the gains from advances in technology, altering the quality
of goods and services and the efficiency of the means of producing
them, have not been monopolized in the industries where a technical
advance occurred, but have been widely distributed through the
society. When new techniques and new bicycle designs raise the
value-added of a maintenance electrician in a bicycle factory, the
need for comparability between his wage and that of a maintenance
electrician in a hospital has helped to ensure that in the long run
everybody shares in the march of science. The bicycle factory electrician's wage is held down by the comparison. The extra efficiency
may lead to higher profits momentarily if the technical advance gives
the firm concerned a sharp competitive edge, but eventually competition should lower bicycle prices to the general benefit. Or,
suppose that the bicycle electricians *do* manage to bump up their
wage when they see the extra profits. The hospital electricians can
and do reasonably claim to follow them to retain comparability:
hospital charges rise if a hospital is in the private sector, or the
general level of taxation if it is in the public sector, and (though in
this case a bit of inflation has gone on in the meantime) the end result

– electricians having the same real wage in both places and bicycles getting cheaper in relation to hospital services – is much the same.

Introduce spectrumization, however, introduce the principle of 'pay increases directly linked to productivity' and weaken the force of 'rate-for-the-job' comparisons, and the way is open for the electricians in the bicycle factory to appropriate a large share of the real income gains from the development of science and technology. The process can still be halted by the EPPI principle ('If they've got ten per cent so should we') where there is a powerful trade union to argue the case, as there is for hospital electricians. It is less easily halted for, say, maintenance electricians in hotels and restaurants, though even there, the employers' calculation 'If I don't give them something close to the ten per cent they know everyone else is getting I shall have trouble: they won't do their work properly' can produce the EPPI effect.

The way it seems to work in Japan is that the spectrum is *created* by emergency situations justifying deviation from the EPPI principle ('We know the one per cent we are offering you is way below everybody else, but we're on the verge of bankruptcy'), and it is thereafter *preserved* by EPPI. There is a ratchet effect, in other words. If one year you get 1 per cent when everyone else got 6, the lost position may never be regained. And differential hiring wages may confirm positions in the spectrum. The figures in Table 1 refer only to inter-industry differentials of major firms (a sample of 288 quoted firms), not to the more interesting differences within industries between the major firms with a large market share and the smaller ones with a less secure position or their subcontractors. They do illustrate the effect of EPPI and the ratchet, however. In a 'normal year' like 1972 or 1981 there is no very wide variation in the percentage rise of nominal wages. (A maximum deviation from the average of 25 per cent in the one year, 10 per cent in the other.) In turbulent moments, however, the spread increases. Coal jumped up the spectrum in 1974 for obvious reasons. Textiles went down in 1975 when the textile industry was in crisis and did not get back to an average wage increase until 1981. (Most firms made losses and paid no dividends in the late 1970s.) Shipbuilding got hit later.

Table 1 Negotiated nominal wage increases: Selected industry averages (Japan)

Industry	1972	1974	1975	1979	1981
Public sector	13.6	29.3	14.1	5.7	7.6
Private industry average	15.3	32.9	13.1	6.0	7.7
Coal	12.7	55.4	14.4	4.5	7.3
Food	17.1	32.6	15.0	4.6	6.9
Textiles	n.a.	31.7	6.1	2.9	7.7
Pulp and paper	13.5	34.1	11.4	5.4	7.1
Cement	13.6	31.3	10.5	6.4	7.7
Steel	11.5	31.3	12.2	5.1	7.0
Metal-machining	16.3	33.3	13.8	6.1	7.6
Cars	16.9	30.2	13.1	6.7	8.0
Shipbuilding	16.9	29.3	15.2	3.3	7.2

Source: Economic Planning Agency, Japan, *Keizai Yōran*, 1982.

It must be said, however, that the degree to which this process contributes to overall inequality in society is rather open to doubt. The following figures for the dispersion of earnings relate the 10th and 90th percentiles to the median for both Britain (April 1983) and Japan (June 1982):

Table 2

	JAPAN		UK	
	1000 yen per month	Index	£ per week	Index
10th percentile	125.7	61.4	96.3	64.1
Median	204.7	100.0	150.3	100.0
90th percentile	339.4	165.8	255.0	169.7

Sources: Japan, Ministry of Labour, *Rodo Tokei Nenkan*, 1982, p. 172; UK, Department of Employment, *Employment Gazette*, 19, x, p. 445, Table 1.

The distributions are not dissimilar. (They would have been more dissimilar if the UK figures had been those for the mid-70s when the dispersion was narrower.) There are, of course, comparability problems. Size cut-off points are similar: Japanese figures are for enterprises with more than nine employees, and the UK ones for those with more than ten, but the Japanese figures include (and the British do not) white-collar as well as manual workers, but on the other hand exclude the public sector. Nevertheless, if there were radical differences in the overall distribution of wages they should show up in figures such as these – and in household income distribution figures – which they do not. One is entitled to conclude that, although we perceive the pattern of differentials differently, being aware of occupational differences between the skilled and the less skilled while the Japanese are aware of differences between high-ranking and low-ranking firms, the actual shape of the distribution is not so very different.

Summary

The trends which are shifting employment patterns in the British large-firm sector towards a more 'organization-oriented' 'Community' model have implicit in them the operation of a principle of fairness – 'equal shares in the fruits of shared effort' – different from the 'equal pay for equal work' principle which so far has operated to reinforce, or to simulate, the market determination of wages. If this be so, wage differences between the privileged sector and the unprivileged sector can be expected to deviate, or rather the spectrum between the more privileged and the less privileged will be stretched. This could have a range of consequences, not least in inhibiting the mechanisms which have served hitherto to diffuse the gains from technical progress and structural change throughout the society, and to prevent their being appropriated disproportionately by those who work in, or own the equity of, the sectors in which the progress occurred.

The extent to which it does so, however, will surely depend on the extent to which incomes policies reinforce the EPPI principle – equal percentage pay increases for all – and it is to the subject of incomes policies that the next chapter is devoted.

4

Building an incomes policy to last

Six years of Thatcher government should be enough to demonstrate that 'free collective bargaining', the one principle on which the Tories and the TUC were united against the Labour establishment in 1979, is a luxury we cannot afford. Their alliance then sprang, of course, from contrasting motives. The TUC was not much worried about inflation, or at least saw it as no responsibility of the TUC to cooperate in stopping it. The Tories did care, but thought they could do the necessary magic solely by monetary and fiscal policy.

Six years of deflationary policies, the creation of a permanent state of surplus supply in the labour market, and still the rise in wages in the large-firm private sector keeps up an inflationary pressure which prevents even mass unemployment from bringing the inflation rate down to target level. Meanwhile, economic policy is hamstrung. Everyone acknowledges that if there *were* to be an attempt to reflate the economy, the inflation rate would start shooting up once again.

In addition, as argued in the last chapter, present movements in wages, and in the mechanisms determining wages, suggest a long-term and not merely short-term tendency for income inequalities to grow, for the spectrum to stretch. The abolition of wage councils in the mobile-market sector will accentuate that trend. Apart from any intrinsic antipathies we might have to inequality, no one can much welcome the growth of social discontent which would follow, nor the increase in social security costs and taxation which would be necessary to treat the symptoms. Better to go for prevention; better to rely on incomes policies to create the conditions for full reflation to full employment, and to prevent the primary distribution of income from shifting too far towards inequality.

Japan is not noted, like Sweden or Norway or Austria, for having an established tradition of incomes policies operated by consensus among 'the social partners'. There is no central council to set the macroeconomic parameters for the following year. There is no government announcement of a wage-increase norm. There is no complex system of calculation of cost-of-living threshold pay, productivity-bargain exemptions, mixtures of flat-rate and percentage increases, inflation taxes, sanctions against infringements, and so on.

And yet, when you go to Tokyo, use the well-tried instant airport research method of asking a taxi driver: 'What was the rate of wage increase in Japan last year?' and do not be surprised if – especially if it is Springtime – he answers: 'Do you mean nominal or real?' and goes on to offer a figure for both to at least one place of decimals. We all know, of course, about the Japanese being *wundermenschen* in matters of numeracy. But that is not the point of the story. The point of the story lies in the kind of numbers the average Japanese worker keeps in his head, in the way the institutions of wage-bargaining work to give him the information and the understanding he has, and in what this means for those who are trying to run the Japanese economy.

The Japanese economy was knocked off course by the oil crisis even more violently than the British. Inflation went up to nearly 25 per cent there as it did in the UK. But the Japanese have long since got inflation under reasonable control. Consumer price inflation has been kept below 6 per cent since 1977. They have won back the right to do a Keynesian reflation and boost employment without the mortal fear that, for inflation or balance-of-payments reasons, every 'go' will have to be followed in twelve months with a 'stop'. And one important reason why they have been able to do so is precisely because of what the taxi drivers and the other wage workers know and understand. It is because, in short, Japan has an incomes policy, or at least a set of wage-bargaining institutions which amount to arriving at a covert consensual incomes policy.

There are three things which make the man on the Shimbashi omnibus different from the man on the Clapham omnibus. First, the former has a clear idea of what the economy-wide wage-increase norm established for the current year is. Secondly, if his own wage increase deviates from the norm (though it usually does not deviate by very much) he will have some views as to the reason why: 'The union put up a good show and squeezed an extra half per cent because we'd been below the norm the year before'; 'The firm did well last year so we got a wee bit extra', 'We were down because we're in a declining industry'; 'Our company's in a bad way because of a bad investment and the union had to agree to less than the average', and so on. The norm, in other words, will be the focal point of all his thinking about his wage, and the central criterion of its fairness. (And this substantially narrows the area of dispute in wage bargains: management and unions are arguing not about the justice of 11 per cent or 3 per cent *in vacuo*, but of being 1 per cent or 2 per cent above or below the reference-point norm.) Thirdly, he knows how to translate his nominal wage increase into real purchasing power. He has been weaned off money illusion by frequent exercises in making such translations – and behind that ability often lie many more elements of understanding about the interrelations of some major macroeconomic variables.

Let us come later to why all of these characteristics seem to me eminently desirable. The first question is: 'How did it get to be that way in Japan?

The Spring Offensive

The answer is: largely by lucky accident. The new industrial bargaining structure with strong enterprise unions started off after the war at a time of high inflation. There was no question that there had to be annual wage adjustments. It became the universal practice to make wage increases from 1 April for two reasons: April is the start of the fiscal year and tax obligations make it a convenient time for firms to close their accounts, too. Secondly, the Japanese lifetime employment and incremental wage-scale system was relevant. March is the end of the school year. Hence 1 April is the normal time for recruiting new workers. Their annual movements up the incremental wage scale (sometimes part-discretionary, sometimes automatic) consequently take place in April, so April becomes the obvious time for renegotiation of the scales themselves.

The simultaneous settlement date provided the unions with the opportunity to strengthen their hands by coordinating their efforts. The so-called Spring Offensive, mounted by the unions' joint Spring Wage Struggle Coordinating Committee, began in the mid-1950s and has since become steadily institutionalized. It is that institutionalization, the containment of the bargaining within a *predictable* procedure, and the heavy involvement of the media in the process, which creates the norm-establishing effect now apparent even in the over-the-shoulder chat of Tokyo's taxi drivers.

The way it works is approximately as follows. The first preparations begin towards the end of the autumn of the previous year. The unions' coordinating committee meets and flies its first kite. With the loss the workers have taken from higher-than-expected inflation last year, they might say, with the extra need to sustain demand at home, given the prospects for exports with the rising yen, and with the increase in productivity still running at a high figure, the unions cannot think of settling for less than *x* per cent, and they will expect a promise of massive tax cuts from the Government too.

The employers' federation replies in kind: There is a need for maintaining restraint; the world recession is bound to reduce the growth of GNP and the Government must get the economy back on a sound footing by reducing the budget deficit, which means taking resources out of private consumption; profits are down; employers cannot possibly contemplate paying more than *y* per cent.

Variations on these arguments appear in the press with increasing frequency as December gives way to January and January to February. Meanwhile every research institute in the business which wishes to be taken seriously organizes a major seminar with full press coverage attended by prominent employers, prominent trade unionists, prominent Government officials, and occasionally even a Minister if he has acquired the reputation of having some influence on the decisions of his Department. The chairman of the seminar, a respected academic, sums up the day's proceedings by suggesting whereabouts, between *x* per cent and *y* per cent, the final settlement probably will, or ought to, find its level. By February, the claims of individual enterprise unions (coordinated closely on an industry basis and more loosely on a national basis by the coordinating committee) will have been put to their managements. The union leaders will go about getting a vote from their members authorizing them to call strikes in support of their claim and a schedule of half-day, 24-hour and 48-hour strikes will be drawn up, industry by industry, putting the unions with the strongest bargaining power at the beginning of the schedule. These are nationally coordinated, too, with the great attention-getting strike of commuter railways, at least in recent years up to 1981, being made the centrepiece with an early strike which it is hoped will make them the pace-setters.

The actual bargaining takes place for the most part at the enterprise level, although there is close coordination between both firms and unions in the oligopoly industries, and in a small number of cases – the private commuter railways being one example – formal bargaining at the industry level. As the first settlements are made, the nightly TV news bulletins report the 'average percentage settlement figures so far', with jumbo-sized digits behind the commentators, calculated to two decimal places, clicking over as new results come in, with ten or fifteen minutes' commentary on where the negotiations have reached, industry by industry differences, and who is waiting for whom to settle. At some point, after a few giants have settled, and a few strikes have been held, the pundits declare that the struggle has 'passed its peak' and that the norm is now pretty finally fixed. There is a certain amount of competition between unions of different complexion to gain the role of pace-setter or peak-passer. In 1982 the engineering federation coordinated the simultaneous announcement of settlements in the major steel, shipbuilding, electrical machinery and car firms (ranging from between 6.36 per cent and 7.5 per cent), thereby stealing the thunder of the private railways whose 48-hour strike was planned for five days later, but in the circumstances called off by a settlement at half an hour to midnight the day before.

The peak passed, the norm is established. (The key percentage figure agreed is the percentage increase in total wage bill, including the cost of regular increments. Hitachi's 6.56 per cent increase in 1982, for example, was made up of 1.80 per cent for annual increases and 4.76 per cent for jacking up the scales.)

Once the struggle is declared to be past its peak and the norm settled, the remaining settlements tend to follow in a rush, though there are always a few laggards, usually in embittered enclaves of industries down on their luck whose unions cannot easily accept being as far below the norm as the managers say they must be to avoid bankruptcy. As soon as the private sector norm is established the public sector mediation body announces its recommendations which are uniform for the eight major public corporations and national enterprises, including the national railways who have been in the habit of coordinating a strike with the private commuter railways in recent years; for the higher the private sector settlement, the better the public sector does also. The mediation recommendation is usually within one or two tenths of a percentage point of the private sector average. It is ritually refused by the unions and then rapidly and formally translated into a compulsory arbitration award by the same committee.

Soon all is quiet and the union leaders and personnel managers can afford to go out golfing together again. As the last stages are reached and the Spring Offensive ceases to figure in the headlines, employers in the small un-unionized firms either give their workers the same percentage increase (thereby retaining the very big size-differential structure intact) or explain to them why the firm is in such dire straits that they cannot do so, or face the prospect of an unwonted disaffection on the part of their workers which may well affect performance. The power of the norm is shown in the narrow range of deviation from it. If the 300 biggest firms are divided into 22 major industrial groups, the variation in 1982 was between 6.05 per cent in the oil refining industry – where every firm is making bad losses – and 8.09 per cent in wholesaling and retailing, with the average at 7.0 per cent.

Some pertinent reflections

Certainly, Britain is not Japan. Japanese workers and trade unions are indeed rather more willing to believe that their betters know best than British workers. And, undoubtedly, the enterprise union system does give union bargainers a stake in their firm's success which provides common ground with managers, though as plant and enterprise bargaining becomes increasingly common in Britain too, and the role of the lay shop stewards and convenors – as opposed to full-time officials – grows in importance, the difference in that respect is not so striking. In any case, one does not need identity of conditions in another country's situation in order to be able to draw lessons from it.

The lessons one might draw about incomes policies in Britain from the Japanese example are, it seems to me, primarily lessons about the nature and effectiveness of norms. True, in Japan we are talking about an *emergent* norm, for Britain we are talking about the possibility of a *set* or *negotiated* norm. But in terms of persuasive effectiveness, the difference between the two kinds of norm is not necessarily important. After all, the teachings of the churches on the one hand, and Kinsey's findings about the practices of the average, 'normal' American on the other, both have effects on human sexual behaviour in America which are not different in kind.

I would summarize the reflections that Japan provokes in me as follows:

1 Most of the British debate on incomes policy questions – and it is odd for a country which prides itself on its democratic traditions – centres on the question of how to ensure 'conformity' to 'the government's' norm. The norm itself is usually seen as something which emerges full-blown from the mists of the Treasury's secret calculations – calculations which are either too difficult for the poor public to understand, or far too unsettling for them to be made a party to. Even within the SDP, the one

party which advocates incomes policy, discussion has concentrated on the sanctions for enforcing a given percentage wage-increase norm. Various devices such as inflation taxes on employers or on employees, arbitration awards, and so on, have been suggested, and some of the suggestions (see later) are very good. But to concentrate so heavily on sanctions is like putting all one's design skills into the safety valve instead of strengthening the boiler walls. A *persuasive* norm carries its own clout. Sanctions become less crucial if the norm is endowed with some morally compelling force which reduces the impulse to deviate and bring sanctions into play.

2   To endow a norm with this morally compelling power is not impossible even in Japan: it should be even more possible in Britain with its deeper traditions of concern with fairness and equity. The last chapter has already stressed the important role of different notions of fairness in determining the pattern of wage settlements, and fairness must be a prime consideration in any incomes policy. 'Equity lies at the root of the problem', said Aubrey Jones, summing up his experiences with the Prices and Incomes Board, 'without a commanding sense of equity no incomes policy can survive'. A trade union's 'power', the clout its leaders exercise in negotiations, depends in part on how much damage union members can do to other people by striking, but also in part on how much they dare do, how willing they are to do that damage. And what provides that willingness? Except in a few notorious cowboy industries (like fitting-out exhibitions and certain areas of Fleet Street) it seems to me that greed is rarely enough to provide it. Class hatred can help, if the managers are inept enough. But, as I suggested in the last chapter, the prime motivating fuel for a successful strike in Britain is *indignation*, a sense of being treated unfairly, of not being given one's proper entitlement under some implicit *norm* of fair treatment. It is when norms, even for annual percentage increases, *are* only implicit and not made institutionally explicit that self-righteousness (for which the British have a greater talent than the Japanese) has the maximum scope for raising indignation to strike-threat levels. *To have a wage system dominated by a sense of fairness and to have no institutional means of creating a consensus about what fairness means, is a recipe for industrial anarchy.*

3 But the conditions for endowing an officially *set* norm with the morally compelling force required are exacting. They are:

(*a*) There must be widespread participation in the norm-setting, some exercise in national collective bargaining, though it must be collective bargaining which accepts the constraints of the nation's predicament a little more readily than, say, union bargainers at British Leyland (BL) are wont to accept the constraints of the firm's predicament. (And it probably will be such; the difference being that while there is always a subsidizing government behind BL, everyone would accept that there will not always be a free-lunch-providing International Monetary Fund behind the nation.)

(*b*) Over the years of such collective bargaining at norm-setting time, a consensus has to be built up concerning what are fair and reasonable principles for setting the norm. This requires that some degree of understanding of those principles and the macroeconomic relations behind them (e.g., that devaluation raises the prices of imports, and that this represents a loss of real income which should be shared among consumers as a whole) should be common currency not only within the media and among trade-union leaders, but also among the more lively and articulate of their members.

(*c*) The norm must be seen to apply to all waged (i.e., waged and salaried) income earners, with comparable checks on the incomes of the self-employed and unearned income receivers.

(*d*) The norm should not only apply *to* everybody, but apply with equal effects *on* everybody, which means above all that the erosion of money wages by price inflation should be the same for everybody. And that means that the reference period for contracts under the norm should be the same for everybody. In other words, wage increases should take place simultaneously throughout the economy.

This last factor – the simultaneous annual round – is so much the key to all the other preconditions for developing norm-setting institutions with some compelling moral force that it is worth tremendous efforts to achieve it. The disruption costs of intervening in existing bargaining institutions to synchronize the present staggered annual round would doubtless be considerable. But the long-term benefits are such that it would be worth, say – to dramatize the point by being specific – paying the value of five years' worth of North Sea oil revenues to obtain it.

4   A powerfully persuasive anti-leap-frogging norm need not preclude flexible deviation around the norm *provided* it is possible to make a clear institutional separation between discussions about what the economy can afford for personal consumption *in total* and discussion of the claims of particular workers to improve their *relative* earnings.

5   Institutions work best when they are institutionalized. The only sensible aim in framing an incomes policy is to try to create something which can be as much an accepted part of the annual round as the budget. UK incomes policies hitherto have been constructed primarily for politicians who think a week is a long time and six months an eternity. To get the temporary respite of a wage restraint to tide over an immediate crisis, almost any kind of rag-bag bundle of contradictions has been accepted as an incomes policy provided the unions will wear it. No wonder there is widespread scepticism in Britain about the possibility of incomes policies. That scepticism is justified if the only kind of incomes policy one can think of is the short-lived expedient inevitably followed by a wage explosion as soon as the patched-up deal with the unions breaks down. But experience does *not* tell us, yet, that an incomes policy actually built for durability will not endure – because *nobody in Britain has tried it.*

The case for the simultaneous annual round

Let us begin with what is probably the most important point, the simultaneous annual round. The essence of the case for its importance has already been stated. In times of high and fluctuating inflation rates (i.e., the times we live in) only if everyone's wage increase comes at the same time can an increase which has to be expressed in nominal terms be translated into the *same* real wage increase (or decrease) for everyone. If the inflation rate is declining, a firm or industry which settles in August at what has now come to be called the 'beginning' of the annual round, might see the inflation rate fall, August to August, from an annual rate of 15 per cent to one of 10 per cent. A union settling later in the round, say the following May, might during the duration of its agreement experience a May to May fall in the annual rate from 11 per cent to 6 per cent. If the same nominal increase norm applies to both there is clearly inequity, different rates of real wage increase. If one corrects for the changes in the inflation rate, current and forecasted, and gives the May settlers a smaller nominal increase in the hope of equating the real increase with that of the August settlers, then all sense of a 'norm' disappears and with it any hope of attaching moral authority to the norm.

Since the rate of inflation is rarely constant for many months at a time, all norms held constant through a staggered round have an inbuilt inequity which just cannot be avoided. Only the simultaneous settlement pattern avoids that inequity.

By the same token it also makes possible two other things necessary for successful (persuasive) norm-setting;

1 Making *some* compensation for inflation the basic starting point for norm calculation;

2 Making it possible to construct an acceptable norm formula and to get it established as the basis for annual calculation of the norm, thus concentrating the national collective bargain not on numbers plucked out of the air ('Can't be more than 4 per cent'; 'We can never get our members to settle for less than 9 per cent'; and so on, until one wears the other down), but on discrete variables that go into the formula: likely movements in the exchange rate, prospects for increased productivity, etc. Perhaps, as a result, the TUC would even get its own economic model to prepare a persuasive case, the way its Japanese counterpart Dōmei has done.

Let me elaborate on the first point: making some compensation for inflation the starting point. During the 1960s, when we first seriously got into the business of setting incomes norms, it may perhaps have made sense to start from some measure of the likely increase in national productivity, make some calculation of the increase in real incomes that could be afforded, and *then* make some adjustment for inflation. Inflation rates were still modest and not much greater than the rises in real living standards which the economy was still delivering. The last decade, however, has fundamentally altered the actual and expected balance between (now small or negative) rates of real income increase and (now high) rates of inflation. Perceptions and bargaining objectives have altered correspondingly. The central question for a trade-union bargainer is: How can I prevent my members from falling behind the inflation rate, and then, if I can do that, how much extra can I get? Indexation cover against inflation is the starting point of popular thinking, which means that it must also be the starting point for producing a norm with any hope of being *persuasive*.

At present, however, there is utter confusion as to what falling behind, or not falling behind, inflation means. Is a wage increase intended to be compensation for the previous twelve months inflation? Or a pre-emption of the inflation likely to take place in the following twelve months? Even during previous incomes policy periods everyone has conspired to leave this crucial question unanswered: the unions presumably so that they could claim it was the previous twelve months during periods of falling inflation, and the following twelve months during periods when inflation was rising; the employers and government so that they could do the reverse.

It would be funny, like a Stephen Potter story about W. G. Grace making up the rules of cricket as he went along, if it were not such a tragic example of the shamefully muddled way we British manage our affairs. Readers may recall that in the last aborted year of the Callaghan incomes policy, the announcement *ex cathedra* of a 5 per cent norm was greeted with considerable dismay. The dismay was hardly alleviated when the Chancellor, a week later, claimed, (doubtless in a fighting speech at some businessmen's lunch) that he hoped in twelve months to get inflation down to 8 per cent. So was everyone going to be 3 per cent worse off in real terms? The Treasury *might* have explained that 8 per cent over the year means that prices will be on average 4 per cent higher in the year as a whole, so that with a 5 per cent rise everyone would in fact be 1 per cent better off. But nobody to my knowledge did so explain, either because no one wanted to concede the principle that wage increases had to be set against the *next* twelve months inflation, or because 1 per cent sounded derisory and it was thought that since 'your average worker' was too dim to understand the argument anyway it might be better to leave him happily prey to money illusion and thinking only of the 5 per cent – or, again, for the very real reason that the 8 per cent inflation was *not* of equal significance to those settling early and those settling late in the annual round.

A simultaneous round provides the chance to cut through this confusion and fix the period of inflation on which demands for compensation will be based. It would be sensible to settle for the previous six months – for three or four of which the rates would be a matter of record when the bargaining takes place – and the following six months after the pay-rise date.

Before discussing the way in which norms should be arrived at, first let me finish with the simultaneous annual round by dealing briefly with the reasons why the idea is usually greeted in Britain with a tepid lack of enthusiasm. First, getting there – persuading unions to settle for less or more than twelve months to get in line – is seen as a tiresome exacerbation of a bargaining process which God knows is difficult enough already. I have already explained why I think it is worth a great deal of effort *and* expenditure. Why not, after all, lump-sum once-and-for-all tax rebates for all workers who agree to the change?

A second powerful objection would come from those managers bargaining for large organizations, and the national trade-union officials who bargain with those organizations, who have a nicely constructed annual calendar of continuous bargaining. The different bargaining units they have to deal with are inserted into a sequential array that leaves a nice space for summer holidays but otherwise justifies the full-time year-round employment of large numbers of specialist negotiators – thus creating a professional group interest which has a lot to do with the fact that the sacred words 'the institutions of Collective Bargaining' can only be uttered in Britain with bated breath. If settlements were concentrated in one part of the year, how could they cope? And what on earth would they do for the rest of the year?

These are reasonable worries, but not without an answer. In the first place, bargaining of individual units need not be so protracted if it takes place against the background of an agreed national norm, and if managers are not trying to fight a rearguard action against a grand game of leap-frog. Simultaneous bargaining within enterprises would in fact – and especially if the means of enforcement of a norm were an inflation tax levied on the wage bill of the firm as a whole – encourage the evolution of coherent enterprise wage structures and joint union bargaining systems which can only be to the good. (The last aborted Callaghan incomes policy round contained among its miscellaneous bits of *ad hoc*cery a provision to allow BL to pay over the norm in order to bribe some of its unions into a simultaneous bargaining structure within the enterprise.)

Then, in any case, there is no necessary reason why everything has to be negotiated in the last days or hours of the bargaining period. A lot of the preliminary leg-work on changes in hours, holidays, sickness pay, shifts in differentials, can be talked out beforehand, thereby settling priorities agreed between both sides, with only the *amount* to be conceded having to be negotiated after the annual norm is known (the negotiation, if there is an inflation tax, being about how far the firm can be expected to incur the tax to go above the norm). There is no need, even, for all settlements to be reached before the pay-increase date. There is nothing new about retrospective settlements. Back-pay lump-sum payments have often proved, in fact, to have a seductive attraction.

As to the problem of justifying year-round employment for the present full-time negotiators, it is not, perhaps, beyond the bounds of possibility that they might do their negotiating job better if they were to spend a good many months of the year preparing for it with reflection and data-gathering research. Japanese trade unions, for example, which employ much larger numbers of full-time officials per thousand members than British unions, enter on wage negotiations with a vast array of comparative data about the wage structures of other firms and other countries, about the financial health and investment plans of the companies they negotiate with, about the market prospects for their industry, and about the economy as a whole, than do their British counterparts. If the consequence of releasing our bargaining manpower to research purposes for six months of the year were the infusion of a slightly higher quotient of intelligent and rational argument and a little less push and shove into the bargaining process, that might not be altogether an unhappy thing.

But there is a third reason why many people in management and government are prone to snort derisively at the idea of a simultaneous annual round. What? Take on the miners and ASLEF (the Associated Society of Locomotive Engineers and Firemen), the firemen and the health workers, all at once? Issue a standing invitation to run a general strike once a year? Yes, is the answer. Yes, because when everyone is bargaining together, I'm-all-right-Jackism becomes much more difficult. The mutual jostling to get ahead – Sid Weighell's 'philosophy of the pig trough' – which is the main exacerbating feature of our present system, disappears. The firemen will find it much more difficult to claim that they have a *right* to 10 per cent and if that is at the expense of the police, too bad for the police; and likewise the police or steel workers or whatever, vice versa. If all unions collectively are pushing against the nation's ability to pay, stating a claim about the wage share of GNP, it would be harder for unions to act on the assumption that every single claim can be settled out of a bottomless government purse, as the miners or BL workers quite reasonably assume in their present one-off bargaining bids. In short, the 'open invitation to a general strike' argument is a counsel of despair, the despair of those who can see no escape from a purely adversarial approach to these matters, who believe that since 'they' will take all they can get, 'divide and rule' is the only way to keep the whip hand. 'They' are mostly reasonable men. And those who are not have a lot of reasonable members behind them whose reasonableness can be mobilized if we have the necessary institutions to bring home to them what the basic issues are.

Some issues

I have set out elsewhere (Dore, 1982) some detailed thoughts about the incentive devices which might be used to achieve synchro-pay, and the structures needed for norm-setting and enforcement. It will suffice here to indicate a few principles.

1 The best way of enforcing a norm is probably some version of the inflation tax, of the kind elaborated by Richard Layard in *More Jobs Less Inflation* (1981).

2 An incentive to line up on synchro-pay could be given by offering a tax rebate: ten points of the Pay-As-You-Earn (PAYE) tax code, say, for as many months as the settlement period has to deviate from twelve months in order to achieve the target date.

3 And in the interim the norm to which the inflation tax applies should be some sort of inflation indexing.

4 When the system gets going on a regular basis, norm-setting should be the business of a tripartite commission, or perhaps quadripartite, with explicit representation of consumers/tax-payers/the unemployed/pensioners.

5 It should work, in its early years, with a thoughtful eye for the future, seeking not just 'a figure that might stick', but to in-stitutionalize *the process of arriving at* a figure, to get agreement on as many of the elements which must enter into a norm formula as possible, thereby narrowing the scope for disagreement as to what the norm should be. For example it should agree: (*a*) the relevant period for the inflation-compensation element in the wage in-crease, as discussed above (e.g., six months before and six months after settlement date); (*b*) what elements of inflation should be fully compensated for and what should not; (for example, there is a strong argument for not compensating for inflation caused by import price rise, through devaluation or whatever. This repres-

ents a loss to the economy, a need for lowering living standards, which can be distributed most widely, and arguably most fairly, by uncompensated inflation. Again, inflation through the 'barber shop effect' – the rise of prices of services and other areas not amenable to the sort of technical change which raises productivity – represents the way in which the benefits of science and technology are distributed around the economy and not monopolized by the people who are lucky enough still to be working in the industries in which all the labour-saving, cost-cutting automation is taking place. That might have to be treated as a separate element). And (c) whether the productivity growth which supplies the only basis for real income growth should all be pre-empted by private consumption, or whether some of it should be directed towards public or private investment.

6   The – Forum, let us call it – would have to consider not only a wage norm, but the tax implications of allowing the public sector to enjoy the same average increases as the private. It would not have to look at taxation as a whole, but should look at, and accept, any tax increases which, because of public sector wage increases, its decisions make necessary.

7   Flexibility would be fostered, (a) by use of the inflation tax system as the sole *coercive* means of sanctioning the norm (by allowing above-norm increases, but making the employer pay extra tax for permitting them), and (b) by calculating that tax, as in the Layard version, on changes in *average* hourly earnings within enterprises. This provides opportunities for internal adjustments of relativities – what used to be known as 'kitty bargaining' until Clive Jenkins said that it was fit only for tabby cats.

8   There would also be need for more deliberate adjustments at a national level: no system of wage differentials can remain frozen forever. Hence there would be a need, in addition to the forum which would deal only with the macroeconomy and produce a clear-cut norm decision without any of the ramshackle super-structure of *ad hoc* exemptions of previous incomes policies, for a separate body – say a Relativities Commission – to sort out claims to special treatment for certain groups particularly in the public sector. It would have to sort out, not – as the Advisory, Conciliation and Arbitration Service (ACAS) and other bodies now have to do – a claim for extra money, but a claim for *more* extra money than other people. It, too, would probably evolve a body of

principles: what evidence of recruitment difficulty provides grounds for raising relative pay? What scope should a new government have for expressing its ideology by raising the relative pay of policemen or teachers? What should be the ratio of the minimum wage to the supplementary benefit level? Is 'rising expectations of work comfort' a legitimate argument for increasing heat and danger money or payment for unsocial hours? Is a new social recognition of the need to increase women's employment opportunities justification for a shift of available wage funds into maternity benefits? And so on. The essence of the matter is (*a*) that the public sector should have some means of achieving the flexibility in wage structures which the inflation tax and kitty bargaining would give to the private, and (*b*) that there should be a *clean separation between discussions of the norm – of how much, as a nation, we can afford to give to extra consumption – and discussions as to whether this group or that group is valued too highly or too cheaply in relation to others.* At present the issues are hopelessly jumbled. The teachers' deep sense of grievance concerns their *relatively* low pay. The government answers their claim as if only the macroeconomy – 'what the nation can afford' – were at issue.

9   In a society so lacking (compared with, say, Japan or Italy) in entrepreneurial self-employed, there would be no harm in leaving them entirely outside the scope of incomes policies, which is fortunate since there is no obvious way of policing their inclusion. Indeed, incentives to choose self-employment are much to be welcomed. But, if there were to be control over labour incomes there must also be control over property incomes. Some form of dividend restraint would be necessary, and for a lasting incomes policy it could not be done as in the short-term patch-up incomes policies of the past, simply by making companies pile up their unpaid dividends into capital reserves. (See Chapter 8 for a suggestion as to how this might be done through forms of employee share-distribution.)

To some all this may seem just too sweetly and reasonably orderly to be true: precisely what the 'realists' would have said in medieval England if told that trial by combat might be replaced by courts applying generally agreed principles. Since, given the failure of markets to regulate them, we now have to live with administered – power-determined – wages, it is in the interest of all of us that the power should be exercised according to generally agreed principles other than mere muscle-power. The case for a Relativities Commission with these wide long-term functions is that the process of getting some kind of consensus about the meaning of 'fairness' in wage differentials cannot begin until there *is* some stable institution charged with building up that consensus around consistent principles – just as the common law could not get really established until a centralized court system administering the 'King's justice' took over from the myriad jurisdictions of the manorial courts.

Once again, what the Japanese achieve by courtesy of their cultural heritage, or the late-development effect, or the accident of history (like being forced into institutional rebuilding by shattering military defeat), we have to try to achieve by taking thought and deliberately creating new institutions. It will not be easy, but the twenty-first century is probably not going to offer any other way for nations to survive as going economic concerns.

5
Authority, hierarchy and community

There is one particular 'national character' argument commonly used to dismiss out of hand any suggestion that we in Britain have anything to learn from Japan, particularly in the sphere of pay bargaining or incomes policy discussed in the last chapter. 'Synchro-pay and public debate may be a way of getting consensus over pay norms in a society like Japan. But in Britain? With our class-conscious and militant trade unions? What managerial class could fail to be successful', the argument goes, 'with such docile workers and such complaisant trade unions as Japan has? What would it gain us, except irreconcilable conflict, if we tried to reproduce that state of affairs in England? How big a mess of pottage do you think it would take to persuade *British* workers to sell their souls to their bosses and surrender all dignity and independence the way the Japanese do?'

Let me take an example from a recent American bestseller, which is intended, it seems clear, as a counterblast to all the Japanolatry now running riot through American business schools. It is entitled *The Japanese Conspiracy* (Wolf, 1984), in the best Yellow Peril tradition. I quote a pertinent passage:

> The fact is that underpinning the Japanese system are the legions of the exploited, the workers who give far more to their nation's effort than they receive. Japan's national workforce has been mobilized, trained and deployed as an industrial army. They work hard, they march to management's cadence, but they are not, as some have suggested, happy drones: . . . they are a relatively dissatisfied, if submissive army . . . The Japanese worker serves because he has been trained for just that since his birth . . . A tradition of discipline from a feudal Japan that . . . is still potent as a spiritual force (p. 216).

Hierarchy and exploitation

There is enough truth in that picture to make it silly to dismiss it out of hand. Japanese workers *are* less unionized than British workers, even if the union membership rate is higher than in the US. Japanese unions *are* sometimes ready to accept wage cuts which a British union would not contemplate. And the story about social discipline is not untrue either. Observe a group of Japanese waiting at the kerb of an empty street for the light to change to green. Observe a Japanese high school class: fifty 18-year-olds, the girls all with fringe-cuts and the boys with regulation short hair, all in school uniform. No Englishman can see the way they stand and bow when the teacher comes to take the lesson without thinking that submissiveness, obedience, have different connotations for our teenagers and for theirs. Observe subordinates – or at least some subordinates, for one must allow for a considerable range of individual differences in Japan – observe subordinates taking orders from their superiors: the bows, the audible intake of breath, the 'hai' that sounds like a military 'yessir'. Observe a group of schoolboys going home on the train and how, when members of a junior class get out before members of a senior class, they shout a salutation which means literally 'Excuse us for going first'. It is obvious that Japan is a society in which hierarchical ranking permeates personal interactions more than most.

And yet, to equate hierarchy with domination and exploitation, as the critics usually do, is clearly illegitimate. Consider, for example, the best available calculations of income distribution. By some indices Japan comes out more egalitarian than Britain, by others about the same; by all indicators it has less inequality than France or the USA. The income of company directors and managing directors in Japanese big companies, expressed as a multiple of the average blue-collar wage in those companies, is less than in Britain, less even than in pre-Thatcher Britain; the really rich in Japan are the proprietors of smaller businesses and the owners of real estate and successful authors, not the people who control the giant corporations which dominate the Japanese economy and in which the observance of hierarchy is so marked and institutionalized. It is almost an established convention in Japan that before a large company asks its union to freeze wages or accept redundancies – even voluntary redundancies – top managers take a 10 or 20 per cent cut in salary. In Britain, the two leading textile firms both gave their managing directors a 15 per cent rise at the height of the 1981 recession when both were shedding more than a third of their workforce. And the British unions made no move, as far as I am aware, to make an issue of the fact.

Even at the level of personal interaction where the bows and hisses are observed, hierarchy is no simple matter. I recall a Sinhalese engineer who returned to Sri Lanka in a state of bemusement after working for a period in a Japanese factory. He could not have imagined, he said, that such an egalitarian society could exist. It is in Japan rather than in Britain that one finds senior managers wearing the same uniforms as shop-floor workers. It is Japan which has the single canteens in factories and offices; Britain which has – still has in large numbers despite the Industrial Society's attempts to promote what it calls single status harmonization – multiple eating places segregated by rank, and in correlation with rank, by cleanliness, by comfort, by quality of food and quantity of free alcohol. Any such symbolism apart, listen to the conclusions of a pair of American researchers who compared management styles in Japanese and American firms in California. 'Japanese tend to disagree with their superiors frequently and politely; Americans less frequently and more violently' (Johnson and Ouchi, 1974).

So, clearly, the 'intense exploitation of docile workers' explanation of Japan's industrial success is not one to be handled lightly. That manual and other subordinate workers in Japan do their jobs with a spirit and efficiency which is rare – at least on any sustained basis – in Europe or the US, can hardly be doubted. The *New York Herald Tribune* carried a report recently on the experience of Westinghouse in building nuclear reactors of identical design in the USA and Japan (18 October 1984). In Japan, 2,500 workers on a single shift completed construction in 48 months. In the USA twice as many workers took more than twice as long. Japanese superiority, in that instance, may reside in part in superior techniques of management planning: longer lead times, better use of critical path analysis and so on. But it must also have something to do with the attitudes and habits of ordinary workers.

Submission and defiance

How far is this a matter of mere submissiveness, of workers merely being willing to do what they are told out of some fear of the consequences of recalcitrance, or from some sycophantic hope of advancement? Not very much, it seems, if one is to judge, for example, from the apparent success of Quality Circles in Japan – that device, now much imitated in Britain and the USA, which sets up groups of workers to take their own initiatives to improve the organization of their work; or if one is to judge from the prevalence of quality control methods which rely less on independent, external inspection and more on individuals' careful checking of their own work under the lightest of external supervision. Right, the sceptic will say, so you convince me that it is a matter of inner commitment, of efficiency which comes from a strong inner sense of responsibility to do a good job. But we all know about false consciousness.

One man's false consciousness, of course, is another man's keen sense of justice. Where assertions of false consciousness are bandied about we are usually in the presence of a clash of values. Differences in values are, indeed, a better explanation of the difference in behaviour than any attribution to Japanese managers of superior skill in 'human relations'; they seem to me pretty innocent of the manipulative intentions our personnel managers so often pride themselves on.

One major value difference relates to power and obedience. There is no doubt that between the average British worker and the average Japanese worker there are differences in the degree to which any element of organizational subordination to the will of others is seen as irksome and a derogation of one's manhood, or should I say personhood. Trollope caught the spirit of this nicely when he described the trade union activities of Phineas Finn's landlord, Mr Bunce. Mr Bunce was always 'longing to be doing some battle against his superiors, and to be putting himself in opposition to his employers – not that he objected personally to Messrs Foolscap, Margin and Vellum who always made much of him as a useful man; – but because some such antagonism would be manly, and the fighting of some battle would be the right thing to do'.

I don't want to exaggerate the importance of Buncism as a moving force in British trade unionism, but nobody watching Mr MacGregor and Mr Scargill on television in 1984 could be in much doubt as to which of them approached their confrontation with the more joyous zest and sense of self-fulfilment. It is only a bit of an exaggeration to say that if machismo in Mediterranean societies is largely about sex and conflict between equals, machismo in Britain is largely about the heroic defiance of authority. And nowadays that goes for both sexes, so perhaps one should say personismo, or machismo plus butchismo.

One must not ignore these cultural differences if one is to explain differences in economic performance. The social scientist must get as far as he can in analysing matters of this sort with his structural and cultural factors, whatever his suspicions that differences in population gene pools may lie behind them. My questions are: what general differences are there in authority relations between Japan and Britain? How far do they seem to follow, first, from the two countries' respective social and economic histories and, second, from their histories of religious and political ideas. How far are the differences concomitant with, or reinforced by, differences in contemporary institutions?

Who needs leadership?

Perhaps the shortest way of summarizing the differences in authority patterns is to say that in Britain authority is generally much more problematic than in Japan; its legitimacy is always closer to being questioned. Teachers, sergeant-majors, managers, bishops, fathers are in greater danger of being answered back. This is more especially the case in Britain in the 1980s than in the days of Trollope and Mr Bunce. The steady erosion of deference, of the willingness of subordinates to 'know their place' has affected all institutions in our society, with the changes in the formative institutions of family and school affecting the other institutions as they are increasingly manned by generations less accustomed to automatic obedience to parent and teacher. But even in Mr Bunce's day, the difference between Britain and Japan in that regard was surely great. Hence the frequency with which we, and the infrequency with which the Japanese, talk about the importance of 'leadership'. The deep voice, the broad shoulders, the steady gaze, the possession of presence, bottom, bottle, dignity, manliness, personality, magnetism, charisma – all those qualities which serve to command assent and cooperation – are important in our society precisely because the impulse to defy has so commonly to be reckoned with.

Such qualities are prized in Japan, too, and companies look for them when recruiting graduates. But even in the field of politics, where they are most prized, they are not a *sine qua non* for holding high office, as a few moments of reflection on the personalities of recent Japanese prime ministers will suggest. It is the office which makes a man *primus inter pares* in Japan, because there is a general appreciation of the need to have a hierarchy and to *have a primus inter pares*, and there is a general acceptance of the Buggins'-turn principles by which he is often chosen. The remark I quoted earlier about Japanese disagreeing with superiors often and politely, Americans rarely and violently, fits into this more general difference. In a society where authority is problematic, where a man has to work at retaining it because it depends on his personal qualities as much as on his office, a subordinate's criticism is a personal challenge, and both it and the reaction to it are likely to be emotion-laden. In Japan, where authority resides in occupancy of the office, criticism is not personal because the occupancy is not challenged; people are secure enough not to mind admitting mistakes and not to hesitate about consulting their subordinates either because they might suggest something useful or because there is a diffuse sense of the duty to develop one's juniors, or just to make their lives more interesting.

Distance

Another, concomitant difference: aloofness, physical separation, seems much less commonly resorted to as a means of bolstering authority in Japan than in Britain. The typical Japanese office is open-plan. All the directors of Honda work at desks in one huge room with numbers of their subordinates. Separate rooms on its periphery are available for meeting visitors and for committee meetings. Distinctions are observed. The locations, size and emptiness of desks permit rankings to be identified. But there is little sense that the integrity of the hierarchy will be endangered if superiors are observed to be picking their noses or nodding off to sleep in the middle of a memorandum. By contrast, where authority depends on leadership and leadership on the personal power to command, leaders cannot afford too many human frailties. Respectful deference needs to be tinged with awe.

The typical Japanese choice would be different. The lesser concern with physical distance shown in the open-plan office symbolizes the lesser concern with social distance and with emotional distance. The relation of superior and subordinate in a work organization is expected to some extent to spill over into private life. The good boss should be solicitous about the personal problems of his subordinates, ready with a speech and a large gift as presiding go-between at their weddings, and ready to go drinking with them occasionally, confident in the knowledge that none of them would be likely to let it appear that they can hold their liquor better than he can. In the so-called national character survey conducted by a government research institute every five years, a national sample of respondents is asked, 'Which would you prefer, a boss who abides strictly by the work rules and never asks for more, but doesn't take any interest in you as a person, or a boss who shows his concern for you and your personal problems but sometimes demands more than he is entitled to?'. Every five years since the survey was started in 1948, 85 per cent of the sample, and at all ages, have chosen the more intense relationship (Hayashi, 1981).

It is a long way from the contractualist assumptions which inform British employment relations and authority structures, assumptions which reflect a basic egalitarianism which is missing in Japan. The admired section chief would, in Britain, be considered paternalistic, and no manager likes to lay himself open to such a charge, for paternalism impugns the treasured sense of self-reliant independence of his subordinates.

How to explain: history, ideas, traditions

The reader should have a fairly good idea, by now, of the differences in authority styles that we are talking about. I think it likely that he will agree that: (*a*) the differences fit in with, seem like logical consequences of, the difference between the purely contractualist 'Company Law' model firm and the 'Community' model firm as set out in Chapter 3; and (*b*) it is not intuitively surprising that the Japanese Community type should have superior competitive power.

Once again one has to ask how much of the difference is 'national character' – genes which nobody can do much about, or culture shaped by institutions which change slowly only over generations – and how much is to be attributed to contemporary sustaining institutions? Let us begin with the former, with culture in fact, because there is nothing very useful I can say about genes. Figure 1 makes clear the implicit framework of explanation I'm using. The 'cultural factors' are, in effect, the precipitate of history, the flows of causal influence shown by the A arrows.

The pattern of quiet authority, unassertive leadership and acceptance of hierarchy has by no means always been the dominant pattern in Japan. In the period of turbulent feudalism from the eleventh to the end of the sixteenth century, the military rulers of Japan – or of their respective parts of it – were rather different men, even if they were not exactly as they appear in the historical fiction

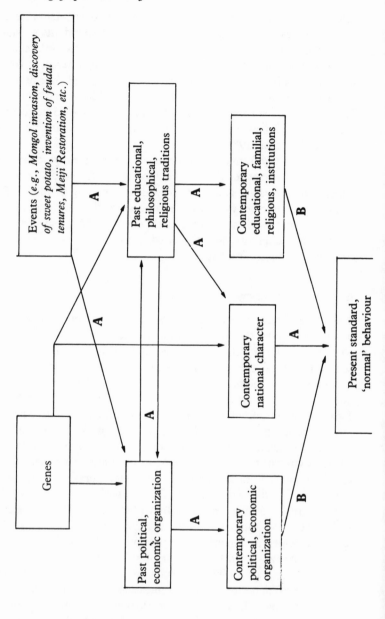

Figure 1

which is still favourite reading for Japanese managers. Their style of leadership – dominant, awe-inspiring, thrusting and predatory – was the kind of leadership equally characteristic of feudal Europe, though in Japan too, as in Europe, most admired when combined with warm personal concern for the loyal followers. But between modern Japan and that period of uncentralized anarchic feudalism intervened the Tokugawa period – two-and-a-half centuries of gentling peace. It was a period which saw a steady growth of bureaucracy in the classical rationalizing manner which so fascinated Max Weber: a gradual formalization of career patterns, careful division of responsibility, recording of precedents, filing of archives and so on. The major offices of state remained hereditary, but the actual exercise of power – largely confined to keeping law and order and collecting taxes – was in the hands of the increasingly precedent-bound, rule-bound bureaucracy.

That experience must surely have given the Japanese the basis for a very different paradigm of authority from that which history has given the British. Britain, too, saw the end of its civil wars in the seventeenth century. But Britain substituted for martial warfare the verbal warfare of politics. Politics has been the sphere *par excellence* in which we have preserved the styles of leadership and domination appropriate to an aristocratic military society. Politics has kept alive our admiration above all for strength in leadership – for bulldogs and iron ladies – while at the same time keeping alive our distrust of all those who exercise authority. Britons have become accustomed to hearing those in authority continuously denounced by their rivals for their predatory intentions or their incompetence or both, if never before so frequently and so intimately as in this television age. Tokugawa Japan, by contrast, was an administered society with no open politics. Interest conflicts were largely resolved by intrigue, cabals, persuasion and periodically cleansed corruption. The appearance of absolutism was preserved. As in the Austria described in Musil's *Man Without Qualities*, the illusion was maintained that all decisions represented the will of the appropriate competent authority, and only occasionally and desperately was there anyone to challenge the official doctrine that that will was always exercised with benevolence.

To be sure, those challenges rose to a crescendo in the middle of the nineteenth century, and the Meiji Restoration ushered in an era of Western politics, Western-style public denunciation of authority. But for the whole period since, the dominant pattern has been of a

quasi-permanent opposition group denouncing – from outside – the
authority of a quasi-permanent group of insiders which possesses a
superior claim in legitimacy. The British pattern – leaders of equal
stature, equal claims to legitimacy, denouncing *each other's* predatory abuse of authority – has never been established. 'Benevolence', a notion appropriate only to authorities whose legitimacy
does not depend wholly on elections, is still a relevant concept.

The role of ideas

And, to return to the Tokugawa period, there is some basis for the
view that, as military regimes in peasant societies go, there actually
was a little more benevolence about than is common. If so, then
some credit must be given to the Confucianism which, predominantly in the interpretation given by the Sung scholars of
China, became the dominant ideology of Tokugawa Japan and the
core of the educational system which it gradually created. In a
Western society which starts from a jaundiced, 'original-sin', view of
human nature, Acton's assessment of the inevitable corruption of
power seems naturally to follow. As a system of power-control,
democracy becomes the only possible form of government, though
the worst, because government anyway brings out the worst in men.
     By contrast, in a society which starts from the premise of original
virtue, as Confucian societies did, it is possible for things to be
different, especially since Confucian writings devote not as much
time, it is true, but some time, to underlining the duties of benevolence in rulers as well as the duties of obedient loyalty in
subordinates. They promise – though naturally emperors and
shoguns did not dwell on the fact – that a ruler who fails in benevolence will very properly be overthrown by popular revolt, for if
the people are so oppressed that they rise in rebellion then this will
be proof that the mandate of heaven has been withdrawn. The word
usually translated as benevolence, of course, does not mean welfare
paternalism, but rather a general sense of responsibility for others
and for the social order, an abstention from greed, concern for the
interests and dignity of subjects, a concern for justice, tempered
with the optimistic faith which puts more reliance on the judicious
use of rewards than on punishments.
     Two things follow from the dominance of such an ideology in a
society, especially if it is embodied in texts which form the mainstay
of that society's educational system. First, with all due respect to the

human capacity for hypocrisy and to the duty of sociologists to be cynical, some people *must* be induced by internalized norms of conscience to be more responsible in the exercise of power than they otherwise would be. Secondly, given the expectation on the part of subordinates of the *possibility* of power being exercised with benevolence, benevolence actually becomes an efficient strategy for the retention of power. In such a society, a little benevolence can go a long way to evoke trust, much further than in a society where expectations are lower and suspicion of power more deeply engrained. One can see this revealed in the patterns of revolt. For all that it was a gentler society than, say, feudal Iran or feudal Ethiopia, or feudal Britain, Tokugawa Japan was still a long way from being a model Confucian society. Authority was sometimes blatantly predatory. Some feudal lords were grasping and rapacious, their tax exactions harsh. And the peasants frequently rebelled. But the rebellions were always protest rebellions, based on the Confucian premise that rulers could be and *ought to be*, benevolent, and that a desperate life-risking protest might call them back to the path of virtue – as sometimes it did if only, in most cases, through the wholly unpredictable intervention of higher authority. It is a long way from John Ball and the egalitarian assertions of his peasant revolt, with its nostalgia for the golden age when Adam delved and Eve span and no one was set up in authority over his fellows, and with its view of political authority as mere property and of all property as theft.

In modern industry this difference in backgrounds counts. A Japanese manager finds that a little 'benevolence' goes a long way. Trust his subordinates and they may well trust him. A British manager has to go further, to overcome a suspicion of authority in general, which is often reinforced by class antagonism and sometimes, even, by John-Ball-like utopian beliefs in the possibility of abolishing managerial authority altogether and substituting workers' control.

Sustaining institutions: competence

So much for some of the historical differences which may explain the different bases of authority in the two societies. More interesting are the contemporary factors – the B arrows in Figure 1 – features of the organization of the firms themselves, and of the society which surrounds them, which serve to sustain authority patterns of such a different cast in Britian and Japan.

So far we have managed to conduct the discussion without making a distinction of some importance. It is a distinction between what one would be tempted in Britain to call intra-class and inter-class authority patterns. It is a distinction which really applies only to what I shall henceforth call 'bureaucratic organizations', of which examples are BP, the police, the Civil Service, ICI, universities, the armed forces in Britian, and practically any medium-large business firm as well as all public-sector organizations in Japan. The 'bureaucratic organization' is a sub-species of – or, if you like, a more 'evolved' form of – the 'organization-oriented type' defined in Chapter 2. For our purposes (and we may ignore most of the billions of scholarly words expended on 'bureaucracy' since Max Weber discussed it) its defining characteristics are:

1   They get employees young, for careers.

2   Career tracks are fairly predictable; certain rules define the 'hedges' on either side of each track: the best and the least you can look forward to. These usually involve age constraints: e.g., the minimum age for Under-Secretary is 38; managers get appointed to the board between the ages of 51 and 53, etc.

3   Career tracks are different for different types or grades of entrance: graduate administrator; graduate technician; clerk; technician; labourer.

4   The highest career track a person can aspire to is determined by his educational qualification.

5   The exigencies of fitting a finite number of people to a wide and changing variety of jobs, puts a premium on 'generalists': generalist administrators, generalist craftsmen, whose career progression requires them frequently to change department (and *learn* a new field of expertise) in order to edge one rank higher.

So, to go back to our distinction, which applies in Japan most clearly to bureaucratic organizations, we have on the one hand authority relations between seniors and juniors on the *same* career track, and, on the other, authority relations between those on a higher and those on a lower career track, between brigadier and lieutenant, as opposed to between brigadier and corporal. Where that distinction can be made (i.e., in bureaucratic organizations which *have* notional career tracks) it is generally the case that within-career-track authority patterns are more easily sustained both in Britain and in Japan. For all I know there may still be civil-servant

Principals who address Under-Secretaries as 'Sir' or 'Madam'. Perhaps not, but even if such overt deference has faded away in the last 20 years, few senior civil servants in Britain have reason to feel that, if they are not constantly firm and vigilant, defiance of their authority might break out among their juniors at any minute. Their relation with the clerks and secretaries, however, may be more problematic, and require more positive self-assertion.

So the fact that, in Japan, not just a few grand firms like ICI and BP, but almost every firm with hundreds rather than tens of employees *is* a bureaucratic organization in the sense outlined above, helps considerably with intra-career-track relations – the 'juniors disagreeing with seniors frequently and politely' syndrome. In a business firm in Britain with an emphasis on occupational specialization and a 'best man for the job irrespective of age' ideology, the most obvious rival for a computer manager's job is the person with whom he is expected mostly closely to cooperate – the deputy computer manager. And if there are any doubts at all about the confidence the managing director puts in the computer manager, that can be a recipe for trouble. Where, on the other hand, as in the bureaucratic organization, managers are generalists who expect to spiral upwards through successive postings in different departments, and everyone knows that it is unheard of to reach the rank of Assistant Secretary, say, or – in a Japanese firm – Department Director, before the age of *x*, *expectations* are limited, and consequently personal defeat and frustration reduced; rivalrous competition is narrowed to a band of approximate age-mates. No junior seems to be saying 'I can do your job better than you can. Why don't you make way for me?' because the *system* makes such a pretension ridiculous. I recall one particular conversation with the director of a personnel department of a large Japanese company. He was accompanied by one of his section chiefs, fifteen years his junior. Keen and as bright as a button, the section chief made all the running in the conversation. He had all the facts at his fingertips. He was the one who supplemented his chief's account with fuller and more convincing explanations of policies his chief was responsible for. All the while the director showed no obvious signs of feeling upstaged. He looked benignly on as a parent might on a child performing its party-piece. He was, presumably, secure in his senior role as a provider of general wisdom and could leave the mastery of the details to others. And he had no reason to fear disrespect from his more competent junior. I don't recall whether the director had a briefcase, but if he had, I am sure the section chief would have been quite prepared to carry it for him.

It is, of course, in inter-career-track relations – in Britain commonly perceived also as inter-class relations – that the difference between the two countries is greatest, and here again differences in organization explain some of the contrasts.

Theorists about the preconditions for authority generally stress two elements. (See, for example, Moore, 1978, p. 438.) First they stress that the person given decision-making power should have some competence which makes such a division of labour sensible, and second that he should evoke faith in his good intentions, that his use of power should be seen to be not predatory and self-interested, but concerned with the welfare of his subordinates, or of a larger whole of which both he and subordinates are part.

Let us take the competence point first. One cannot but be struck by the frequency with which British workers express doubts about the competence of their managers, and the relative rarity of such charges in Japan. There is some evidence, not least in surveys of what British workers say of Japanese managers in Britain (White and Trevor, 1983) that these assessments may be accurate, and that the difference in average competence is real. But even if there were no difference in reality, there could still be differences in perceptions, in judgements, arising from differences in the degree of trust. The fact is that it is extremely difficult for a shop-floor worker to judge the competence of a design engineer – at least until he makes a mistake that has to be rectified on the shop-floor – and even more difficult to judge the competence of a finance director. It is a safe enough generalization that as our technology and organizational and informational systems become more complex, not only do competences become more differentiated in content, they also become more widely differentiated in the intellectual ability required to master them. We are all in the hands of experts whose competence we cannot judge, and not only because we have not been trained to judge them, but in an increasing number of cases for an increasing proportion of us, because we might not be bright enough to absorb the training in the first place.

A general personality difference in the hubris-humility dimension may make Japanese workers more predisposed to accept that fact about the modern world. But there is also a difference arising from a contrast in the way competences are certified in the two societies.

Japan – thanks partly again to Confucian traditions and the strong emphasis given to education in a Confucian society – has developed what is probably the most (even if one includes its near rivals, the East European countries and the other countries of the post-Confucian sphere, China and both Koreas, probably *still* the most) meritocratic system of schooling and occupational selection in the world. It all works on the basis of what Sir Keith Joseph would have us call norm-referenced as opposed to criterion-referenced labelling. There is great national uniformity of unstreamed education for the first nine years, and then, at the age of fiteen, competitive examinations produce a rigorous differentiation of ability between those who go into high-flyer high schools, into second rank high schools, third and fourth rank high schools, and the 6–7 per cent who go to no high school at all. The 40 per cent of the age group who get to university are similarly graded at the age of eighteen by competitive university entrance examinations. From the tiny elite who make it on to the pass list for the top universities like Tokyo University, to the person of modest ability who scrapes into the Komazawa Buddhist University or the Lutheran Theological College, everyone finds his place. The top firms take their managers from the top universities, and their subordinate staff from second rank high schools (for the top high schools send all their graduates to universities); the second rank firms from second rank universities and somewhat less prestigious high schools, and so on. The fairness of the entrance examination selection system is generally accepted and so is the inference put upon the results – that academic achievement is a good predictor of the capacity to develop occupational competence through on-the-job learning. Hence Japanese shop-floor workers are likely to look on their managers as men who have performed better than themselves in a fair and relevant competition in which they were both engaged on pretty equal terms.

In Britain, where only 8, not 40, per cent of the population gets to a university anyway, and another 4–5 per cent to degree courses in polytechnics (again a categorical, two-grade prestige distinction, not a single-category gradation as in Japan), the first-line managers are far more commonly from the shop-floor and chosen for their ability to be tough, as much as, or more than, their skill with machinery or their ability to apply intelligence to the solution of problems. 'In no other country is authority less often allied to expertise' (Taverne, 1985).

Marrying authority to expertise in Britain

So what can we learn from all these British/Japanese differences in the relation of authority to competence? First let us tidy up some of the distinctions which have been introduced.

One element is the *actual* competence of the manager in direct contact with the worker in those fields of the firm's operations which the worker can judge. Cooperation and compliance are more likely to be won by a manager who understands, and even could *do* (apart from the sort of dexterity which requires long practice) the work of his subordinates *and* a lot more (can explain to them, for example, how it contributes to a larger whole or why it has to be done this way rather than that).

The second element is the extent to which initial assumptions about the competence of managers, and hence the legitimacy of their authority, are shaped by the society's person-labelling system – its system of qualifications – and the legitimacy which attaches to it. This is important, first in colouring workers' perceptions of managers' *actual* performance (it can set up a virtuous spiral of confidence and openness in the manager and favourable selective perception in the worker, as opposed to the vicious spiral of defensiveness and aloofness in the manager and unfavourable selective perception in the worker). Secondly, it affects workers' expectations of competence in more remote senior managers, the likelihood of acceptance or suspicion of their decisions, and consequently affects the whole tenor of their confidence in and attachment to their company.

The Britain/Japan differences seem to be:

1   The actual competence of front-line managers is lower in Britain, partly because the attention given to competence training is less across the board, and partly because managers, especially those promoted from the shop floor by the foreman-superintendent route, are often chosen for their ability to command and quell, rather than for their expertise.

2   Because the society as a whole places less value on formal knowledge and intellectual achievement in Britain, workers are less impressed by educational qualifications, even when they are dealing with a manager who has them and deserves them.

3   There is a second reason why educational background status is less likely to be an effective legitimator of authority in Britain.

And that is class. The difference between a university graduate and someone who left comprehensive school with two CSEs (Certificate of Secondary Education) is not primarily *seen* as a difference between someone who did well and someone who did badly in a race fairly run on equal terms, as the Japanese would see the equivalent difference. It is seen, rather, as a natural outcome of differences in class background, a reinforcement of an existing system of privilege. Japan *has* had a strictly merit entry system for its universities since 1886. Oxbridge first instituted a standard entrance examination only recently and other considerations can still override its outcome. The son of the Crown Prince, the next-but-one Emperor of Japan, wisely did not attempt to get into Japan's top university, Tokyo. But he could – and did – get into Oxford.

In terms of actual equality of educational opportunity, parents' socio-economic status has a considerable effect on children's educational success in Japan, too: *actual* social mobility rates, if we had decent comparable measures, might not look much greater in Japan for the recent generations than in Britain. (And how far our societies are similar in this respect for genetic-IQ reasons, or because of socio-economic factors, is one of the great questions overshadowing the twenty-first century.) But *perceptions* of the matter are coloured by the fact that Britain is a class society in a much deeper sense. In Britain, the educational-qualification difference between a graduate manager and a CSE worker is likely to loom less large in the consciousness of either than the difference in their accents, bearing, leisure tastes and values. Japan's is a relatively homogeneous culture: a predominantly rural society with a rural/feudal stratification system, rapidly shaken up into a quite new modern industrial pattern in the course of three generations. It has little of Britain's cultural separateness, bred out of original feudal divisions, confirmed through the slow, painful industrialization process in generations of segregation of middle-and working-class life-space in the industrial towns, and sharpened in the last century by the public/private divisions of the school system.

Some tentative proposals

So what *can* be done in Britain to anchor authority in expertise, thereby to enhance respect for expertise-authority, and to reduce the tensions, the resentments, the macho defiance, the 'humour the old bugger then quietly sabotage' strategies which are such a drag on Britain's industrial efficiency?

Central to everything, of course, is a re-evaluation of expertise, of learning, of training. We cannot afford our philistine belief in amateur muddling-through, bringing in 'one of those boffin johnnies' only when necessary. All this takes us back to Chapter 2.

But there is one particular part of the discussion in Chapter 2 which needs underlining in this context. Bureaucratic organizations, as here defined, are much more likely to be learning organizations because the generalist administrators or craftsmen are constantly being posted to new jobs which require expertise they are not expected already to possess. There is no danger of the 'You can't tell me to go back to school; I'm properly qualified, I am; I've got my degree' syndrome which is liable to prevail when people stick to their specialisms and have only their specialisms – not their flexibility, adaptability, willingness to learn – to sell in the market. There are good reasons here, then, for accelerating the transformation of British enterprises into bureaucratic organizations.

One particular institutional device, borrowed from Japan, is of special relevance for the attempt to anchor authority in competence and expertise: namely the Quality Circle (QC). There is quite a QC movement in this country and, although sometimes excessively large claims are made for Quality Circles (characteristic of the hot-air sales talk to which the personnel-management/training profession is unfortunately given), in firms with the right atmosphere – like Wedgwood's, for example – they have been quite effective in mobilizing workers' ideas for improving production methods, in making their work more interesting, in enhancing general cooperativeness, and so on. (A Quality Circle is a group of production workers who are encouraged to get together to study where improvements could be made in the production process, and to make proposals for doing so.) Most attention has been focused on the effects of Quality Circles on *workers*, however. There is little discussion in the QC literature of beneficial effects on managers, or manager-worker relations *except*, significantly, frequent remarks to the effect that 'supervisors and managers sometimes feel threatened by QCs and it requires tact to overcome this'. Tact be damned. Whether a manager feels threatened or not is an excellent test of his competence and his confidence in his expertise. Why not make this an explicit feature of the movement, proclaim it from the housetops, and create an atmosphere in which a manager who felt threatened by the possibility that he might not be competent to judge the technical feasibility of a Circle's suggestion, or that he might not be able to defend current practices, would be ashamed of betraying the least evidence of defensiveness and driven, instead, hastily to repair his lack of expertise, to make himself more competent? How about this as a slogan for the Industrial Participation Society which has taken up the QC cause: 'Introduce QCs, and shame your middle managers into competence'?

As for the second part of the equation, the respect for educational qualifications, one must begin by drawing a distinction between two kinds of 'respect for qualifications':

1   Qualifications seen primarily as a record of achievement – a certification of what a person has learned to *do*.

2   Qualifications seen primarily as a signal indicating the kind of person their possessors *are*.

A driving licence is the archetype of the first kind; being 'a graduate' or being 'an Oxbridge graduate' is, in terms of its social uses, primarily of the second type.

Now Britain never has been particularly deficient in respect for qualifications of the first type. Indeed, as I suggested above, there has perhaps been rather too much unquestioned respect, of a mutually protective kind, for claims to specialist expertise: I don't question your competence as a certified XYZ (optician, economist, haemotologist, etc.) and I don't expect you to question mine.

It is the second, the 'what kind of person you are' type of qualifications which we traditionally have not had much use for, firstly because meritocracy never really has triumphed in Britain over backdoor family influence, though it is getting there slowly (and if one sees the horrors of Japan's thorough-going meritocracy – the examination-hell which I shall touch on in Chapter 11 – one wonders how much *that* is a good thing), and secondly because differences in educational record were so much overwhelmed by, and intermingled with, class characteristics. Much better to have gone to Eton and the Guards than to a provincial university. If being an Oxford graduate earns respect, it is not so much for the meritocratic reason that only bright people get into Oxbridge and therefore those who did so must be bright, as for the class reason that those who were at Oxbridge were likely to have picked up the airs and graces, the confidence and bearing, which are associated with top people.

What I think *is* happening is – trend one – that the *second* type of qualification is becoming more important than the first, and – trend two – that in reading qualifications in that second manner, class-culture elements and intellectual–excellence elements *are* being slowly disentangled, but very, very slowly.

To take the first trend first, the second type of qualification is becoming more important than the first, partly because the growth of bureaucratic organizations makes personnel managers more interested in what the people they recruit (for careers) *are* (and can presumably learn subsequently to *do*), than in what people can, at the moment of recruitment, already *do*. And secondly, the growth of higher education and the development of a spectrum of prestige and abilities has made everyone aware that – the driving test and the Bar exam and one or two externally tested qualifications apart – there is no such thing as a standard certificate of what people can *do*. No one believes that a degree in engineering from Cambridge has the same significance for what a person can do as an engineering degree from Irontown Polytechnic. But the difference is not in what they were taught nor in how *well* they were taught, but lies in the distinction between those who get the four 'A' grades at A-level which admit you to Cambridge and those who get into the polytechnic with a 'B' and two 'E's: in short a 'what sort of person' distinction. So, inevitably, attention is drawn more to the latter.

And – to come to trend two – the development of that prestige/ability spectrum on the basis of A-level scores (it is basically only in the last five years that the practice of ranking universities and polytechnics or particular faculties by their entrants' average A-level point score has become at all widely known) is slowly making intellectual achievement more salient than class-cultural characteristics in the 'what kind of a person' interpretations which people put on educational records.

Now one might expect that a furtherance of this trend – greater respect for intellect; less for bearing, fluent articulacy, self-confidence, style – would bring us closer to the Japanese, be conducive to the marrying of authority to expertise which seems so necessary. And so, doubtless, it would, but it is a slow process. It is only twenty years since entrance examinations were introduced for Oxbridge, and they are still not the sole determinant of Oxbridge entry. Moreover, independent schools still dominate in the Oxbridge entry, and middle-class children overwhelmingly dominate. Hence, the correlation between intellectual achievement and class-cultural characteristics remains very high. Hence the power of an educational qualification to legitimate authority meritocratically – purely through respect for presumed intellectual competence – is still much diminished.

It should, therefore, be an object of educational policy to disentangle the values of intellectual excellence, together with those 'middle-class culture' characteristics of *universal* value like honesty and curiosity and concern for personal relationships, from those other historically accidental characteristics of middle- and upper-class culture with which they often get mixed up. There isn't much you can do about loud voices and arrogant manners *à la* Sloane Ranger. But there *is* something the University Grants Commission (UGC) can do about Oxford and Cambridge, and the way they serve to perpetuate the association of intellectual excellence with:

1 An expensive life-style – all the pomp and flummery of high table, May balls, etc., not much in keeping with Jowettian notions of plain living and high thinking;

2 Archaic status orders – deferential standing for high table processions, the assumption that young ladies and gentlemen must have domestic servants, for instance;

3 Anti-industrial ruralism – see Wiener's (1981) delightful denunciation: *English Culture and the Decline of the Industrial Spirit*;

4 The '*surtout pas trop de zèle*' sort of deprecation of seriousness, of a concern for usefulness. The celebration of the *jeu d'esprit*, the preference for *amusing* displays of intellect – a po-faced treatment of the question: 'Was Lady Chatterley taken by her gamekeeper missionary-wise or from behind?', for instance – over, say, any *boring* inquiry into the causes of inflation;

in short, with all the elements of what one might call 'traditional upper-class culture'.

Of course Oxbridge is highly diverse; it contains many who reject all these characteristics and exemplify very different values in their work. But they are probably a minority. The precipitate of history is a powerful thing; the saturation of these two universities with these hangover upper-class culture elements is too complete to be easily altered – as long, that is, as their intellectual excellence serves to give them high prestige, and allows them to claim lions' shares in every UGC hand-out. How much more lucky the societies able to concentrate their brains in an *Ecole Polytechnique*, a *Technische*

Hochschule, a Berkeley, a Tokyo University, which did *not* inherit a traditional function of turning upper-class adolescents into upper-class gentlemen.

The only thing that could break the chain is for the UGC to make the detachment of intellectual excellence from accidental upper-class cultural accretions an explicit object of policy. It could do so. It is now moving further down the road of explicit invidious judgements of quality and worthiness to receive research funds. If it operates according to its announced criteria, then Oxbridge will be further confirmed in its pre-eminence. If it were, however, to take aboard 'detachment' as a policy objective, it could start a sort of Brasilia movement – a deliberate move to shift the intellectual capitals of Britain to new locations – London, Manchester and Edinburgh being the obvious candidates. The crucial measure, however, would be to offer premium studentships not to Oxbridge students (as now, on the grounds that maintaining an Oxbridge style of life is more expensive than living up in Hull or Exeter) but to students at the target universities. Then those universities can have the pick of the best students, and where the best students go, there the best teachers would eventually follow – though *that* transformation could take decades. Since, on one plausible view, what students learn at universities depends much more on their hours in the library and with each other than on their hours with their tutors, that might not matter so much.

This all sounds like fantasy, perhaps, and I must confess that social engineering on this scale, and for these ends, does seem even further beyond the probable agenda of any British political party than abolition of the independent schools. (That *could* help to stop reproduction of the association of intellectual excellence with upper-class culture trimmings, depending on how it was done. Turn the schools into state institutions with meritocratic scholarship entry, for instance, and you would be likely to find much the same children getting there but this time at the state's expense instead of their families'!) It seems improbable. On the other hand, it would be wrong to underestimate the envy of Oxbridge waiting there in provincial universities (whose representatives have a majority on the UGC) ready to be mobilized, if only enough plausibility could be given to the 'detachment' objective to make it a decently principled cloak for baser motives.

Company Law model versus Community model again

I said there were two conditions usually advanced for acceptance of the legitimacy of authority: competence, which I have discussed at length, and a belief in the good intentions of the person in authority, a belief that he is not just self-interested, but concerned with the welfare of his subordinates or of a larger whole of which both he and subordinates are part.

Of those two conditions 'concern with welfare of subordinates' cuts less ice in Britain than in Japan. It smacks of paternalism which, in an egalitarian Britain, we do not like to be accused of practising and feel demeaned to be the recipient of. (I suppose one can still say: 'A good officer looks after his men', but 'A good officer is like a father to his men'?)

But 'good faith in being concerned with the welfare of the whole' is still a valid concept. It is a fundamental characteristic of a democratic leader. It presupposes, however, as in the nation, that there is a concept of 'the whole' (e.g., 'the nation') to which people attach value.

And how far, in the British firm, is that the case? In the Company-Law-type firm as we defined it in Chapter 2, not at all. 'The company' within which trust relations are supposed to prevail consists of its members (shareholders) and their agents, top managers. The employees are hired hands kept at arm's length in a contractualist quasi-adversarial relationship. It is only in firms of the Community type that it makes sense to talk about the managers' devotion to the shared goals of the group as a precondition for effective authority.

Undoubtedly the authority patterns described at the beginning of the chapter would not be viable or possible in Japan if managers and their subordinates did not both have a quite strong sense of shared 'membership' in an entity to which they attach value – in which they had a little emotional capital, a little loyalty, invested. So the question arises, again, how can we create effective Community-type organizations in the UK too? Chapter 8 will be addressed specifically to that question. Meanwhile the next two chapters look at other implications of the Community model – the ability to make long-term investments when shareholders are downgraded in importance, and the balance between tendencies towards bureaucratic rigidity and flexible capactiy for innovation.

6
Long-term thinking and the shareholders' role

The last chapter suggested that there was an intimate relation between the Community type of organization and the viability of certain kinds – the most efficiency-inducing kinds – of authority relations. When the notions of the Community model and the Company Law model were first introduced in Chapter 3, I defined the contrast between them partly in terms of the role of the shareholders. In the Company Law model the firm is seen, the way the law sees it, as the property of the shareholders; the managers, as their agents, are required to get as much work for as little money as possible out of the workforce. In the Community model the firm is seen as a kind of community in which the managers are the senior members, and the shareholders are among a number of groups 'the firm' has to keep happy.

In this chapter I want to look in more detail at the role of shareholders, and the way in which the financing of firms affects their ability to plan for the long term, to invest in projects the profitable returns of which may take years to arrive, to spend on training and research and on building up a general reputation for quality, expenditures for which the pay-off may be intangible and long-delayed. The question becomes increasingly important as more and more international trade is in branches of production which are research-intensive, where lead times are long, and where non-price factors like quality and product innovation determine competitive success.

Japanese firms are often said to be unusual in the degree to which they do 'think for the long term'. Thus a *Financial Times* journalist wrote recently:

> 'When things look dicey, US manufacturers immediately suspend capital investment, because there is a lot of pressure on them to stay profitable and show good earnings,' says Karen Mavec, an analyst in the Tokyo office of stockbrokers, Jardine Fleming. 'Japanese firms can take a long-term view: they don't have to

please shareholders by worrying about earnings if, in five years' time, they are sitting on a hot product. The Japanese approach is to spend even through a down-turn.' (22 November 1984)

Now the Community-type syndrome as a whole has a fairly obvious relation to this propensity to invest in the long-range future. Managers employed on lifetime-employment assumptions have more obvious and certain reasons for being concerned about the long-term future of their firm than a manager who is working to a system of incentive bonuses tied to his department's half-yearly results and who regularly, as he scans the head-hunting advertisements in his Sunday newspapers, contemplates the very real possibility of going to work for a rival firm.

But there is another set of institutions which are important both for permitting Community-type firms to develop, and more directly for fostering a long-term view. This is the financial structure. At the heart of British capitalism, as of American capitalism, is an 'efficient' stock market, one where share prices are thought accurately to reflect the considered expectations of well-informed analysts concerning a company's likely profitability, *especially* its profitability in the short run – a run which very rationally gets shorter the higher interest rates go, i.e., the more the future is discounted.

Japan has a rather different form of capitalism, in which shareholders and the stock exchange play a much smaller part. It is worth while considering the details of Japan's system of company finance. It has some unusual features.

Debt and equity

The first, of course, is the well-known high gearing of Japanese firms. All the qualifications have to be made. Asset undervaluation and other accounting practices much exaggerate debt-dependency (Elston, 1981). Some of the most successful firms like Toyota and Matsushita have long since been free of debt, and the number of such firms is growing. Average debt-equity ratios fell from 6:1 to 5:1 between 1979 and 1983 and continue to fall. Nevertheless, by world standards, 5:1 (even the 3:1 ratio in manufacturing) remains high.

It is not, however, so much a precarious situation as it might seem to be in Britain, but part of what Japanese writers have termed the 'multi-umbrella system' of cooperative support and risk-sharing which characterizes the Japanese economy (Nakagawa and Ota, 1981). The banks who provide the debt are as dependent on the firms as the firms on the banks; both are staffed by graduates of the same faculties of the same universities; banks provide long-term investment funds as well as short-term funds; they tend to be over-borrowed from the Bank of Japan as the firms are over-borrowed from them, and consequently are much subject to 'window-guidance' concerning the placing of loans with larger firms, the directions of which tend to fit the more long-term strategic thinking of the Japanese bureaucracy. They devote considerable resources to analysing the internal affairs of the firms they lend to and are generally not hesitant about feeding back advice on long-term strategies, though opinions differ as to whether they do this as well as the German banks reputedly do. In a system generally inimical to the notion of 'outside directors' – the board of a typical Japanese firm is more like a council of elders of the enterprise community – bankers are the most common exception. (They are, however, 'imported directors' rather than 'outside directors'. That is to say they have 'moved into the firm', probably after acquiring an intimate knowledge of it as bankers, with the blessing of the personnel department of their bank. This commonly happens when they are disappointed near-miss candidates for a directorship in the bank itself. They often become executive, not just advisory directors.)

The smaller importance of equity in the total financing picture moderates the pressure on managers exerted by the stock exchange and share price fluctuations. They need to retain the confidence of a limited group of known individual bankers, rather than a host of faceless shareholders. What insulates them even further is the second institutional difference: the structure of shareholdings, and the constellation of interests of the share-owners.

Stock markets

In the classically functioning textbook capital market the holder of equity has, in Best and Humphries' phrase (1983), 'liquidity without commitment'. He can switch to gilts when gilts look more profitable; if he thinks he can work out the implications of new information about a company faster than other people and get into the market with his rational expectations ahead of them, then he buys or sells its stock and plays his essential role of shifting its price up or down to its new equilibrium. If he is particularly lacking in risk-aversion he may invest in a small growth company or a venture capital fund, which offer the gamble that the returns in several years' time *may* be such that the yield in present values sufficiently exceeds alternative yields to compensate for the danger of corresponding losses. And he can realize gains from his adventurous foresight at any time by selling his stock, if subsequent information, reinforcing even more bullish expectations, sends the share price up.

But there *are* shareholders who do not behave in quite such a rationally calculative way – shareholders who sacrifice liquidity and accept commitment. There are, for instance, most' obviously the holders of the stock of family firms; there are individuals – and perhaps fund managers – who have subscribed capital to back a man they personally know; there are employee shareholders; there are cathedral-town spinsters who would never dream' of selling the shares which father held for so many years in undying loyalty to the Imperial Widget Company, and so on.

Both kinds of shareholders want the companies whose shares they hold to do well. The rational liquid textbook shareholder exercises pressure on managers in that direction primarily by, in Hirschman's classification (1970), the 'threat of exit': through, that is to say, managers' knowledge that if shareholders' returns seem about to fall, holders of the stock will sell, share prices will go down, capital will be more difficult to raise, possibilities of managericidal takeovers will increase. The 'committed' shareholder, by contrast, is more loyally willing to wait for better times when the company is in difficulties; but to make sure those better times actually come, he is more likely, not to 'threaten exit', but to 'exercise voice': to complain, cajole, offer constructive criticism or loony suggestions, at shareholders' meetings and elsewhere.

Best and Humphries suggest that most shareholdings were of the 'committed' kind before the end of the nineteenth century, and that it was the development of the 'efficient' stock market without trust and commitment – particularly the nature of the new issues market – and the failure to create investment banks as a substitute, which was a contributing factor in Britain's industrial decline.

But Japan still has (even – if not especially – the oldest and most bureaucratized of large firms still have) a large number of committed shareholders. Let us look, first, at the statistics of shareholdings. The statistics shown in Table 3 are defective because of nominee problems, but there is no reason to doubt the general picture they show.

Table 3   Ownership of shares quoted on the London and major Japanese stock exchanges (%)

	UK (1981)	Japan (1983)
Individuals	28	27
Stockbroking companies	—	2
Pension funds	27	0
Insurance companies	21	17
Banks	0	18
Investment trusts and other financial companies	10	3
Industrial and commercial companies	5	26
Public sector	3	0
Foreigners	4	6
Charities	2	—
Total	100	100

Source: Stock Exchange Fact Service, *The Stock Exchange Survey of Share Ownership*, 1982; Zenkoku Shōken Torihikisho Kyōgikai, *Shōwa-58-nendo Kabushiki Bumpu Jōkyō Chōsa*, 24 July 1984; and Okumura (1984) p. 55. Both are nominal value figures. The distribution by current values changes the figures in both countries by 1 or 2 per cent only.

Hosomi and Okumura (1982), describing the context of Japanese industrial policy, have said that corporate executives in Japan are able to be 'growth oriented since they are rather free from constraints exerted by short-term-profit-oriented shareholders because of a general and secular decline of strong individual ownership'. But if that were all there is to it, the rise of financial institutions in Britain should have the same effect. There are, however, several crucial differences.

First, the pension funds which play such an important part in Britain are, in Japan's lifetime employment system, disaggregated into separate reserve funds *within* the financial structure of the companies with whom the prospective pensioners do their lifetime service. Secondly, Japan has seen only a limited development of investment and unit trusts (the source of a lot of short-term volatility in Britain: the Wilson Committee cited evidence that unit trusts turned over nearly half their portfolio per year in 1973–77 compared with 19 per cent for the insurance companies (*Financial Institutions*, June 1980, para. 653)). Thirdly, the banks and insurance companies primarily hold the shares of companies they lend money to and whose businesses they insure – and whose employees are urged by their managers to have their deposit accounts and life insurance with them. And fourthly, over one quarter of Japanese shares are owned by (non-financial) industrial or commercial companies, most commonly by the suppliers or customers of the firm whose shares they own. Very commonly holdings are mutual: Nissan owns a billion yen's worth of Hitachi shares (1979) and Hitachi owns four billion of Nissan's.

Shareholding patterns, in other words, in the world of obligated long-term trading relationships which Japanese businessmen inhabit (see Chapter 9) tend to be, in Rodney Clark's words (1979, p. 86), the expression of some other business relationship, not so much a relation in itself. A high proportion of the holders of Japanese equity have more to gain from the other business they do with the companies whose shares they hold than from profits or capital gains on the shares themselves. They are 'committed' in interest terms because they have a stake in the actual long-term growth of the company. They are committed in practical institutional terms in that they hold the shares by arrangement with the issuing company and it is hardly thinkable that they could dispose of the holding without consulting that company's managers.

If one assumes that pretty well all the holdings of non-financial corporations, three-quarters of the banks' and a half of the insurance companies' are of this kind (the last have the strongest motive for seeking profits from their shareholdings), then the average Japanese quoted company has nearly half of its shares in the hands of such 'committed' shareholders.

Origins

The story of how this pattern of shareholding emerged is roughly as follows. In 1949, as industry was completing the immediate first phase of post-war reconstruction, individual holdings were nearly 70 per cent of the total. The reforms of the anti-trust law in the early 1950s, diluting the pure milk of American anti-trust thinking embodied in the Occupation legislation, made it easier for companies and banks to hold shares, and the purchase of each others' shares was one way in which the old *zaibatsu* conglomerates reconstituted themselves as more amorphous, acephalic 'groups'. Then came a period in the late 1950s and early 1960s when shareholding became a popular form of investment and shares were bought and sold across the counter in every department store. But two things happened to stimulate further transfers from individuals to comapnies in the late 1960s. The first was that trade and capital liberalization threatened to bring foreign firms into Japan. The fear of takeovers by predatory Americans prompted what was called a 'shareholding stabilization strategy'. Firms sought to get a substantial share of their equity into the hands of other firms which could be relied on for support.

This was accelerated by the stock exchange slump of 1965, a product partly of the business cycle, partly of the fact that rising stock prices had been accompanied by dividend levels commonly held to a fixed percentage of par values. The resulting fall in yields prompted many small investors to realize their capital gains and switch to higher-yielding bank term deposits. The resulting fall in share prices both made the acquisition of shares by the corporate sector easier, and gave firms added motives for persuading their trading partners to buy their shares to get the price up.

This trend was accelerated at the end of the 1960s and in the early 1970s by the rapid and widespread adoption of the practice of issuing new shares at market value. Until then the common procedure for raising new capital had been to make rights issues at par. This had offered some mitigation of the low dividend yields. With this gone, the attraction of shares to the individual investor fell further. (As a proportion of household financial assets, equity shares went down from 21 to 8 per cent between 1960–64 and 1975–79. Bank term deposits correspondingly went up from 27 to 47 per cent (Maru, 1983, p. 313)). Share prices, however, were kept up by the corporate demand. The new practice of market- value share issues gave corporations added incentives to raise their share prices by pressing their business associates to buy their stock, and a situation of high share prices, with very low yields and exceptionally high price – earnings ratios has become stabilized. There are several very distinctively Japanese ingredients in that stable equilibrium.

Distinctive features

1   Dividends remain conventionally set in terms of a percentage of par values, rather than of current profits. So set are the conventions that one of the quarterly stock exchange handbooks provides a list of 'companies which have altered their dividend payment' – in 1983 only about one sixth of the 2,000 listed (Nikkei, 1984*a*).

2   And those dividends are set at very low levels, typically 6–12 per cent of par which means dividend yields on current values which are frequently well below 1, and not often above 2 per cent. The sum of 3,300 billion yen allowed by the tax authorities as entertainment expenses to the managers of Japanese firms in 1981 was some 40 per cent greater than the total dividend payment those managers elected to give their shareholders (Okumura, 1984, p. 67). Shareholder demand for higher dividends is weak. Corporate shareholders are not particularly interested – especially the partners in mutual shareholding arrangements – and banks more concerned to get their interest payments. This is very good for investment, of course. A comparative study of Japanese and American firms showed that in the US the proportion of post-tax profits paid out in dividends remained around 30 per cent for firms which returned better than 15 per cent on capital, however much better the returns were: shareholders shared proportionately in higher profits. In Japan, the dividend ratio continued to fall as profits increased, to as low as 10 per cent for the average firm which was returning 40 per cent on capital (Okumura, 1984, p. 73).

3   Nor does a strong demand for higher dividends come from individual shareholders. Dividend expectations play a very small part indeed in the calculations of the stock-dealing companies, the unit trusts, and the remaining individual owners (those, that is, who are not 'committed' family, company director-holders, etc.). They are there for capital gains, as are the British and American unit trusts and pension funds which since 1978 have raised their share of Japanese quoted firms' equity from 2 to 6 per cent in nominal terms and from 3 to 9 per cent in market values. (Foreigners, of course, can also count on the superior strength of the Japanese economy as a whole producing long-run exchange-rate gains.)

4   The dedicated pursuit of capital gains produces strong motives for manipulation in any stock market where the rules and the prevailing morality permit it. And in Tokyo permit it they do. Manipulation and rumours of manipulation are rife, insider dealings reputedly commonplace. Most spectacularly, fringe groups of full-time speculators, closely linked with leading politicians, have been responsible for a number of 'blackmail takeover threats', carried out by a combination of secret acquisition of a

large percentage of a vulnerable firm's stock and strong-arm (though these days rarely lethal) thuggery, ostensibly in the name of ultra-Right political principles. The threatened firm (firms are forbidden by law to acquire their own shares) then has to persuade its business associates to buy the shares at a premium – the premium being, of course, at its own expense. (Lesser fry in the same profession act as 'AGM operators', blackmailing firms by threatening to disrupt shareholder meetings with astounding revelations obstreperously pursued, though efforts have been made to clean up these practices in recent years.) Overall turnover ratios on the Tokyo stock exchange are a good deal higher than in New York or London, and individual speculators are responsible for a high percentage of it (Maru, 1983 p. 330).

5   The stock exchange has never been a very savoury place in Japan anyway. Confucian doctrine always did put 'the merchant' at the bottom of the social hierarchy, inferior in usefulness to the peasant and the artisan. When ex-samurai wanted to industrialize their country they had to invent a new word for the 'businessman', the man engaged in adventurous, risk-taking productive enterprise, to distinguish him from the 'merchant' engaged in something-for-nothing speculation. The shenanigans just described only serve to reinforce the image of the stock exchange as a haunt of anti-social speculators, and this low moral tone has an important consequence. It means that the corporation manager is not inclined to take his share price seriously as a comment on his 'performance', as a signal of 'the best judgement of his best informed peers'. It may be a factor of *some* consequence in his financial management, but it has no *moral* force. It is not the sort of thing which makes him feel chuffed or hang his head in shame. A semi-popular Japanese businessmen's magazine has a lengthy account of Sony's stormy 1984 annual meeting which created a record by lasting 13½ hours. Much of the article concerns the 'AGM operators' responsible for the relentless pursuit of managers, but it lists in detail the substance of their attacks: product development failures, loss of market share, mismanagement, slow turnover growth, profits 43 per cent down. But, incredible as it may seem to anyone familiar with the British business press, the whole article contained no reference, in its account of Sony's bad year, to movements in its share price (Mutō, 1984).

6 Another consequence of the low moral tone of the stock exchange is that the best and the brightest do not go to work there. They are more likely to go into industrial and commercial companies, or more respectable financial companies in banking or insurance.

7 Even in practical terms, Japanese managers do not have to be too worried about their share price. The only form of takeover known in Japan is the rare takeover blackmail threat just described – the ordinary word for 'takeover' is the same as the word for 'hijack'. A formal takeover-bid procedure with stipulations of notice requirements, permissible time elapse, and so on, exists on the statute books, but remains unused. A recent *High-Tech Dictionary* has an entry under 'TOB'. It describes American practice and goes on: 'Japanese law was changed in 1972 to permit similar bid proceedings in this country, but the idea of taking over a company merely by the power of money seems too *dorai* (dry) to us Japanese, and in practice it never happens' (Nikkei, 1984*b*).

8 No takeovers means also no conglomerates. Negotiated mergers certainly take place, but are usually attempts at production or marketing rationalization, not attempts to diversify. Firms do diversify, but usually by internal fission, setting up project teams internally, sending younger employees off for extensive retraining, and so on. The option of buying technology by buying a firm that has it is not generally considered. Firms do, and accept that they have to do, their own research and development. Investment decisions are taken by directors, a high proportion of them engineers and scientists, who have spent their lives in the industry in which they invest, not by a conglomerate holding company directed by financial experts.

'The idea of taking over a firm merely by the power of money seems too dry to us Japanese'. The remark is very revealing of the way the enterprise is perceived in the Community mode. The low effective power of the shareholder – the dominance of shareholders who have no particular reason for exerting pressure for short-term profits – is both effect and cause of the 'firm as community' ideology, and also of the lifetime employment system which reinforces it.

And Britain?

The contrasts with Britain, blessed with a stock exchange which is at once more 'efficient' and more honest, do not need a lot of spelling out. In Britain, the Stock Exchange is not the appendix or gall bladder of the body economic, but its very heart. Perhaps there is something symbolic about the titles of the newspapers the two societies' businessmen read. Japan's premier business paper, which prides itself on its political and cultural pages as well as the business pages, is called not the *Financial Times*, but *The Economic Times*, and it is followed at some distance by four others, three with a rather more technical, one with a rather more popular bias, called respectively *The Manufacturing Times*, *The Industrial Times*, *The Stock Exchange Times* and *The Industrial and Economic Times*. It is not too much to strain after epigram to say that Britain's is a financier-dominated, Japan's a producer-dominated form of capitalism.

The difference manifests itself in various ways: the ease with which 'merchant' banks and stockbroking companies in Britain, with their high salaries, can attract the brightest talent – latterly, also, the brightest engineering talent – away from industry and the public service; the predominance, as measured by column inches of the business press, of news about takeovers, intended, thwarted and accomplished, presumably reflecting the dominance of such concerns among managers; the fact that you make your name as a captain of industry more easily by a bold, if not swashbuckling, acquisitions policy, than by howsoever spectacular a plan for long-range research and development. The fact that 'the judgement of the Stock Exchange' does command a considerable degree of respect combines with the very real threat of takeover for companies with low share values to make the daily share price – and the immediate dividend prospects which largely affect its short-term fluctuations – a central concern for corporation managers. Certainly, if they read what the press has to say about their company, they are likely to find half a dozen forecasts of their next term's results for every report of their long-term development plans. Strong-minded managers, of course, do not let these messages about how the world is judging their performance affect their own judgements of themselves and the way they set their objectives. What proportion of British managers are so strong-minded is a matter of dispute and a suitable subject, perhaps, for an authoritative survey by one of our business schools.

For most managers of most manufacturing plants in Britain today, the pressures to concentrate on the short-term bottom line come not directly from the Stock Market, but transmitted from the main board by the internal accounting procedures of the large and often conglomerate firms which own their plants, commonly a regime of independently accounted profit centres, tight control through monthly performance indicators, and often managerial bonuses tied to the behaviour of those indicators. A managing director may be told by his main board that he will be judged, primarily, on the quality of the development plans in his annual presentation. But he can be forgiven for thinking that those hard-quantified monthly performance figures are going to make more impact. A quite senior manager in a GEC firm recently described how he might spend a good deal of the second half of each month progress-chasing or trying to accelerate payments simply in order to boost that month's ratios at the expense of the next; planning meetings for new developments had to be in the first half of the month. And in the case of real conglomerates whose central boards probably have little expert knowledge of many of the fields in which they operate, the reliance on financial controls is even more complete.

Of course, profitable efficiency is what firms are there for, and if the discipline of the market and of internal financial controls helps to stimulate it, so much the better. But it is a question of balance, of the number of people a firm puts on to forecasting and planning the future, of the proportion of managers' time spent in changing production systems rather than just running them. And I do not just mean top managers. In the more successful Japanese firms the duty to 'change not just run', extends well down the line, even to shop-floor workers. The Quality Circles which have so many imitators in the US and Britain should more accurately be called Improvement Circles or How-could-we-do-better Study Groups.

But *is* the British manager who is nervous about his company's share price thereby unduly biassed towards short-term thinking? Increasingly, some would say, British investment funds are in the hands of highly sophisticated analysts who do not simply take the short-run view but have sufficient technical as well as financial knowledge to make some judgements of a firm's growth prospects. There are clear differences between 'good' firms and 'bad' firms. Enterprise cultures differ, as the recent American bestseller about excellent companies so vividly demonstrates (Peters and Waterman, 1984). Some do have a tradition of determined long-term innovation. Pilkington's worked through many millions of pounds over many years to produce float glass (though before it was a listed company);

Chloride persists with its new battery project after years of expensive disappointment. These are among the qualities which affect analysts' judgements and increasingly dominate the decisions to buy or sell which fix share prices.

Certainly the problem is not a shortage of capital for long-term growth projects. The Wilson Committee, considering the complaint that 'many investors take an insufficiently long-term view of the company's prospects and are too concerned with the search for short-term gains', found refutation in the ability of the capital market to find the funds for the long-term and risky investment in North Sea oil. There is certainly no current shortage of venture-capital funds in the City, and the wide variation in price–earnings ratios is clear proof that some companies' stocks are being held for their long-term growth prospects (or for sale during the next burst of optimism about those prospects).

But the very wideness of the spread in price-earnings ratios between the growth stocks (mostly smaller companies) and the run-of-the-mill stocks of the larger corporations suggests that there is a segmentation of the market. The fact that some investors back some companies for their futures does not mean that most investors holding and trading in the shares of most companies judge by the same criterion. Nor do the people at London Business School who have constructed a league table of pension-fund managers – by their annual earnings – expect them to do so. And, for all one's respect for firms like Logica, the bulk of Britain's research and the bulk of its development of new products is being done, and for a long time must be done, in large corporations.

Admittedly, the differences in price–earnings ratios between companies may be a reflection of judgements of the 'overall quality' of management as well as of immediate profit expectations. But such reputations shift only gradually, or dramatically only with dramatic changes in management. Any senior manager *in place* cannot do much about the reputation; he *can* do something about next year's profits and dividends.

And the evidence that, in framing its impressions of 'good' and 'bad' companies, the Stock Market shows much appreciation of capacities for long-term planning is not strong. Rodney Clark, in a recent monograph (1985, pp. 101–2), contrasts the legal reporting requirements for listed companies in Japan and Britain. Japanese companies are required to give details of research expenditure, royalties received and licences paid for (the terms of major contracts given in full), the number of research workers, the size of the laboratories and the types of equipment. By contrast, when Thorn-EMI was thinking of merging with British Aerospace and then with Inmos – all three of them firms which must research or perish – there was little discussion of the logic of merging research efforts or the synergies that might result. Only a few lines in Thorn-EMI's annual reports give much indication of its capacities for or policies on research, and there was little evidence in press comment that anyone on the stock exchange cared to inquire about such matters. And as if to emphasize its shorter-term concerns, the Inmos merger itself brought down the Thorn-EMI share price, and subsequent news that the depression in the chip market may reduce Inmos' *next year's* profitability immediately brought it down even further (*The Times*, 26 March 1985).

Take, again, the following *Times* account of the reasons for the fall of Sir Kenneth Corfield at Standard Telephones and Cables (3 August 1985):

> Institutional shareholders and stockbroking analysts have accused the company of being weak on short-term management and of putting too much faith in the uncertain future of its long-term strategy.
>
> A key element in this strategy was the acquisition in a deal worth £410 million a year ago, of ICL, Britain's leading computer manufacturer.
>
> Sir Kenneth said at the time that the merger would create a new force in the information technology market combining communications and computing technologies to meet the fast-growing markets for electronic business and office systems.
>
> STC's shares, which were trading at about 280p at the time of the ICL takeover, have been falling ever since. Last night the shares closed unchanged at 106p.

Implications

The static efficiency promoted by an 'efficient' stock market – channelling funds to their most predictably high-return uses given current interest rates – and the business culture which went with it, may have had a lot to recommend them in the 1890s when the British stock market was being set in its present mould. It is not so clear that they are appropriate today when:

1 More and more British companies are directly engaged in low-transport-cost competition, not with other British companies under the same financial and cultural regime, but with foreign companies under very different ones.

2 That competition, thanks to changes in the standard of living and consumer tastes as well as technology, is conducted less and less in the static efficiency terms of price and cost comparisons, more and more in terms of quality, innovation and reputation: products of long-range dynamic efficiency.

3 Innovation is no longer the work of the lonely individual inventor and the Schumpeterian entrepreneur, but the long-term product of heavily financed teams, work so risky and unpredictable that it is sustainable in the long run (the Galbraith thesis is still valid) only by large corporations with the resources to cast their bread on many waters in the calculation that they are bound to bring the ducks down on *some* of them.

4 Few investors, not even (least of all?) specialist fund managers, are capable of informed independent judgement of the prospects of individual development projects.

5 Interest rates look less and less like a social time discount rate as they acquire the dominant function of capturing hot money flows, so that accountants' discounted cash flows or net present values come to bear no relation to society's subjective utilities.

Much of the current concern with the financing of industry in Britain focuses on the provision of risk capital for adventurous small-firm innovators. What a Japan/Britain comparison suggests is the importance of an institutional regime which encourages and rewards suitable attention to the long term as well as the short term in the management of *large* corporations.

It is clear that the current reforms of the British Stock Exchange, preoccupied as they are with the twin objectives of enhanced efficiency (1890s style) through increased competition and more effective investor protection, are irrelevant to this concern. What else might be done?

First, this discussion prompts above all a rethinking of the balance in the modern corporation between the shareholder and the employee interest. The lesson to be taken from Japan is that long-term thinking and investing might be promoted if the employee interest is strengthened at the expense of the shareholder interest, thereby shifting the enterprise towards the Community pattern. This is a matter of such central importance to the discussion here and elsewhere in this book that a separate chapter – Chapter 8 – is devoted to it. There are one or two suggestions which might be made, however, specifically about financial matters.

Although new equity share issues are not the major means of financing British industry (they provided 4 per cent of new capital for industrial and commercial firms in the years 1979 to 1983, 15 per cent of externally raised funds), greater and cheaper availability of the alternative of long-term loan finance would be of particular value to companies which have low share prices (and hence high costs of raising equity) because of poor short-term prospects – perhaps because of unforeseen changes in external conditions – but have vigorous plans for long-term developments, for example diversifying into new markets. Straight interest subsidization would probably be better than the existing loan guarantee schemes which seem not to work very well (though this may be a particular problem of the small businesses to which they are at present confined). An alternative is interest subsidization with the subsidy to be repaid if the development is successful, a form of government–industry risk-sharing favoured in legislation now going through the Japanese Diet.

Some thought might be given also to devices for encouraging 'committed', locked-in, shareholders as distinct from quick-in, quick-out speculators. Stamp duties, graduated to the time elapse between sale and purchase, is one possible device which could have a particular effect on the unit trusts that have the more frequently traded holdings. The efforts of major companies to educate (as well as give perks to) shareholders (recently intensified in companies like ICI and British Oxygen) can be important, particularly efforts to persuade those who control the institutions' portfolios to inform themselves more systematically about the long-term strengths of the companies whose stocks they hold. The new Engineering Council made this the subject of its first pamphlet (1983). Sir Arthur Knight (1982) has suggested how new forms of organization might help them to do so. Moves in this direction could have a cumulative effect since, as suggested above, it is not just what the institutions do, but also what they are believed to do that counts. A change in beliefs about the criteria applied by the market leaders would have an effect on the focus of attention in the financial press and that in turn on the standards by which managers in industry judge whether they have cause for pride or self-reproach.

For the crux of the matter does remain habits of thought. How does one change a world in which people see no particular contradiction involved for, as Christopher Beauman has put it, 'a company whose Chairman is complaining about the City's short-term horizons to be in the process of sacking its pension fund advisors for under-performing by 0.1 per cent in the previous year'? It can be done partly by changing institutionalized incentives, partly by pointing out the contradiction at every opportunity: by trying to change the culture directly, by altering the consensus. Might one make an appeal to the prime creator of the British business consensus, the *Financial Times*? Could it perhaps, in recognition of the excellence of its technology page, its management page, its labour page, rename itself the *Financial and Industrial Times*? And might it try broadening its journalists' horizons too, transferring some of them from the back to the front pages, and vice versa, every few years?

All we would need then would be managers who actually read, and do not just skim the stock exchange listings in their daily newspaper.

7
Innovation, entrepreneurship and the Community model

The world has never been so technology-conscious as it has become in the last ten years. Is it just the wonders of the microprocessor and the electronic game? Or is it that the gradual unremitting acceleration of the rate of technical innovation has at last reached the critical level at which it cannot but impinge on our consciousness? For whatever reason, there has been a shift in perception of the nature of international trade competition which reflects a lasting shift in reality too. There is still a lot of international competition in standard products of standard qualities for which price is the dominant factor. But over an increasing proportion of internationally traded goods it is non-price factors that count. Success in the competition for shares in world markets increasingly goes to the innovator: to those who develop new products or old products improved in performance and quality; to those who develop new processes, cheaper or more accurate, or more reliable production methods.

The innovators, the research and development departments, are the new heroes. Theorizing about the process of, the conditions for, innovation is an academic growth industry. There is by now quite an accumulated body of propositions: about the difference between a generic and a non-generic technology, about criteria for the 'maturity' of a technology, the different trajectories of product and process innovations, the nature of the product cycle, and so on. Most of these propositions are couched in an ahistoric form: they are not specific to time, place, or type of social structure. And this is characteristic of much of the literature on innovation, and indeed much of the economics literature in general. An Everett Rogers sigmoid diffusion curve or a Boston learning curve is sometimes trotted out as if it had a mystical immutability, transcending continent and century. But this surely cannot be so. There *are* secular changes in the structure of our societies. It thus seems to be highly

improbable that there can be any 'laws of motion' of 'capitalism' *tout
court* – improbable, in other words, that generalizations of any
degree of concreteness about the entrepreneurial small-firm
capitalist economies of the nineteenth century would apply equally
well to today's post-Keynesian economies, dominated by government and large corporations. This transformation of capitalism
also implies a transformation of the innovation process – a watershed
in innovation history.

The first watershed, of course, was the one to which Whitehead
(1967) referred when he said that 'the greatest of all innovations is
the idea of innovation itself'. Small innovative improvements in
horses' snaffles and mill-gears had been happening sporadically for
Dark Age centuries before Renaissance men began to regard the
deliberate quest for innovative improvements as a desirable activity
and to establish the inventor as an accepted social role. And, one
might add, it was not until the eighteenth century (see Hirschman,
1982) that certain Frenchmen started to suggest that what could be
done with material technology could also be done for social technology – that social structure could be transformed by human will
acting under the influence of social blueprint-makers.

That emergence of the self-conscious inventor-innovator represents one discontinuity in the history of technology; his disappearance into the bowels of the corporation laboratory represents
the next. If the greatest innovation is the idea of innovation itself, the
second greatest must surely be the bureaucratization of innovation –
the transformation of the typical inventor from someone who takes
his or her chance in the market either directly, or by teaming up with
an entrepreneur, into a corporation employee, talent-scouted from
the university, enjoying considerable security of tenure in a large
organization, perhaps on a formal incremental scale, though more
likely trying to better himself by spiral mobility from firm to firm.

Parallel with that transition came three other changes: the growth
of oligopoly, raising formidable barriers to entry for new entrepreneurs, deriving from control over at least national markets. Second,
the increasing complexity of production technology itself and the
increasing complexity of the *organizational* problem of translating
new ideas into workable physical devices, and translating those again
into production systems (and the concomitant procurement, skill-
formation, accounting and marketing systems) necessary for viable
competitive production. Third, the cheapening of communications
and the intensification of international competition, compensating

for the growth of oligopoly within national economies, makes competitive viability more important even for the largest enterprises which dominate their home markets. All three, of course, interact. But the need for large markets to amortize the vast expenditures required for research and development in many industries – the central feature of Galbraith's New Industrial State and the justification for the European state-sponsored merger policies of the 1960s – lies at the root of them all.

And so the process of innovation has changed. Once, an ingenious millwright with an improved governor for a steam engine might hope to bring his product to market single-handed, using nothing but *market* relations – bought services – in the process: hiring capital, hiring labour, hiring salesmen. Today, even the very idea-generating process of invention is likely to be the joint effort of organizational colleagues. This is even more the case in the whole post-invention part of innovation: the process of developing a new product to the point of commercial viability, or of introducing even small incremental innovations in the production process.

It is not hard to find statistical confirmation of this thesis. Look, for instance, at the figures given in Table 4 (overleaf) which show the proprietorship of patents owned or (in 1981) applied for in the United Kingdom.

The trend in patent profiles is unmistakeable *and* seems to have been moving faster in the last thirty years than in the previous thirty. Moreover, the likelihood is that the statistics underestimate the change. The very high proportion of 1920 company patents for which no inventor is named quite probably reflects the continuing dominance of the entrepreneurial company: the inventor was the company owner. The naming of inventors by companies increases over time, but apart from the eclipse of the entrepreneurial company it is hard to say what factors determine this, since there are clearly industry differences in the nature of inventions and also national differences. (The latter may be related to differences in the legal right of employees to claim a share in any substantial gains accruing to their employers a right established in Britain by the 1977 revision of patent law, but existing earlier in the Netherlands, Austria, Germany and Norway (van Empel, 1975, p. 94). But there must also be local company traditions which affect these practices too. If one takes the large chemical firms registering several hundred patent applications in 1981, no inventor was named for 88 per cent of the patents of Hoechst, whereas for other firms the figures were 50 per cent for Ciba-Geigy, 87 per cent for BASF, 8 per cent for Bayer, 1 per cent for Du Pont, 9 per cent for Asahi Kasei, and 3 per cent for ICI. In the electrical field, the figure was 75 per cent for Siemens, 39 per cent for Philips, 21 per cent for Hitachi, 7 per cent for IBM and for Sony, and as little as a fraction of 1 per cent for GEC and Xerox and none at all for Westinghouse, Western Electric and Toshiba.)

Table 4   Owners of United Kingdom registered patents

	Individuals (%)			Companies (%)					Total
	Total	Single individuals	Two or more individuals	Total	No inventor named	Single inventor named	Two or more inventors named	Other institutions (universities, research laboratories) (%)	(Sample size)
1920–1	77.7			20.7				1.7	100
	(100)	98.5	1.5	(100)	78.2	16.1	5.7		(421)
1950–1	54.9			42.4				2.8	100
	(100)	98.8	1.2	(100)	42.3	37.5	20.0		(566)
1981	23.0			73.0				4.0	100
	(100)	84.2	15.8	(100)	19.9	39.8	40.3		(496)

Source: Names Index, UK Patents. I am grateful to Katherine Woolley and Lesley Crossley for compiling this table.

One might expect, as an extension of the organizational incorporation of invention, that there would be some increase over time in the number of inventions for which it was extremely difficult to specify an inventor: 'factory inventions', the product, as one writer puts it, of 'big research units where internal know-how by far exceeds the state of the art by which patentability is measured' (van Empel, 1975, p. 98). Certainly, the figures in Table 4 show that, where inventors *are* named, it is increasingly the case that more than one person gets the credit. The same trend – the increasing need for cooperative effort – is apparent among the unincorporated inventors. While they were almost exclusively loners until 1950, by 1981 16 per cent of their applications were the product of joint work.

A venture-capital revolution?

To some people this is all very old hat. Fair enough: Table 4 tells a true enough story, some would say, the sad story of the twentieth century up to 1980. But now the age of the large corporation has given way to the age of venture capital. Partly because of (rather mysterious and ill-specified) changes in the nature of current waves of innovation, partly because of the change in the political climate – the Threaganite rediscovery of the virtues of the market, the new wave of social approval for hungry single-mindedness in the pursuit of profits –, for a variety of reasons, we are now thought by some to be entering a post-Galbraithian world, a much more fluid and exciting world.

How much truth is there in this thesis? How much room still does remain – or is being newly opened up – for the independent Schumpeterian innovator-entrepreneur with his flash of inspiration (or alternatively his ability to tell an inspired boffin from a science-fiction writer), his drive, his market flair and his capacity for creative destruction: that strange combination of personal characteristics which cannot easily be explained or measured and which Schumpeter suggested you had just to accept as something some people had and some did not, just as some people can sing and some cannot? How much room do our economies have for such people?

The question is of very great importance for the theme of this book. I have been expounding the thesis, partly of the inevitability of the onward march of the organization-oriented firm, partly of its virtues, not least in favouring a Community type of ethos. Can it be that innovation is the Achilles heel of the organization-oriented Community model firm, and that there is no reason to believe either that it *will* become the dominant norm in Britain, or that, if we are to remain competitive, it should?

Several people have assembled the evidence regarding the relative capacity to innovate of large and small firms (Freeman, 1982; Rothwell and Zegveld, 1982). They point to the fact that, while in every country there is increasing concentration of research and development activities in large enterprises, in some countries (and the variation between countries is considerable) small- and medium-sized firms can be as innovative, even radically innovative, per unit of research and development expenditure, per employee or per pound of share capital, as large firms. At least they can be in certain industries; for example, in scientific instruments, in electronics, in textile machinery, and in bio-technology; less commonly in pharmaceuticals, petrochemicals, aerospace or aluminium smelting, the determinants being primarily the nature of scale economies and the relative newness or maturity of the technological field.

Certainly the rapidly growing proportion of employment in small firms in this country, and the increase in new-firm start-ups (20 per cent more in 1982 than in 1981, according to Binks and Coyne (1983, p. 39)), is no proof of the dawn of a new age of high-tech venture capital in Britain, as the burnt fingers of Prutec's venture-capital-fund managers can testify. However, most of these studies – perhaps inevitably, given the kind of statistical evidence available – concern small, or small- and medium-sized firms, which are by no means the same thing as entrepreneurial firms. On the one hand, some entrepreneurial firms grow rapidly but remain firmly in the grip of their founding entrepreneur (or even inventor-entrepreneur) even after they gain many more than a thousand employees. Likewise, there are on the other hand many firms with 299 employees, or even with 99, which are closer in organizational character to the large enterprise than to the traditional entrepreneurial firm: they have been in business for a long time; they have a division between ownership and technical expertise; managerial functions are specialized, formally defined, and performed by professional specialists; and so on.

Moreover, the small-firm innovating entrepreneurs in manufacturing (as opposed to services where *most* small-firm entrepreneurship is concentrated) are far from innocent of large-firm connections. If one looks at accounts of that prime field for small-firm innovation, the electronics industry of the United States in the last three decades – Route 128, Silicon Valley and all that – several things seem clear. First, the inventor-innovators who either became the venture-capitalists or joined up with them to establish the innovating small firms, got the training necessary for their intellectual breakthroughs, and their commercial breakaways, as employees in large corporate organizations, usually business firms, sometimes universities or government research laboratories. Second, many of the small firms had to seek, or at least were persuaded to seek, adoption by one of the industrial giants in order to acquire the resources to bring their ideas to competitive production. And, third, when one examines the major landmarks in the development of semi-conductor products or processes – like Webbink's list of the top twenty-five semi-conductor inventions between 1951 and 1971 which Rothwell and Zegveld (1982) quote – it is in any case clear that only a fraction are from the small firms. The giants like Bell Telephones, Texas Instruments, General Electric and RCA are those whose names recur.

This discussion is important in that we are supposedly seeing a revival of small firms in this country: new company registrations were apparently up 20 per cent in 1982 compared with 1981 (Binks and Coyne, 1983, p. 39). The vast majority of these new firms are almost certainly in services. For manufacturing, all one can say is that the number of small firms and the employment in them is declining more slowly than the total number of firms (ibid., pp. 24–5). And it does seem reasonable to assume that a number of factors have changed the nature of scale economies in favour of smaller firms: the industrial relations problems of giant firms, tax allergies, product differentiation and changes in the lumpiness of capital equipment, changes in individuals' money/leisure trade-off when the *employee* working week gets down below 40 hours, thus giving a competitive advantage to the self-employed who are prepared to work for 70, and so on.

But how many of the newly established small firms are innovating is another matter. As Britain's small firms grow, so Britain's innovation performance seems to be declining. Patent statistics are not always a reliable guide in these matters, but it would be strange if the following figures did not tell us *something* significant about relative national performance. They relate to the ownership of patents registered in the UK. British residents were, as will be seen, a long way from having the lion's share, even at home.

Table 5   Shares in patent registration

Country of residence of patent owner	1982	1983	1984
US	35.9	33.0	31.3
West Germany	22.5	17.9	14.8
UK	21.5	26.0	29.6
Japan	20.0	23.1	24.3

Source: Report of the Comptroller-General of Patents, Designs and Trademarks, HMSO, 1983.

Innovation and high technology

Patents are increasingly about high technology, and high technology is not everything, of course. They also innovate who stand and watch their wives/husbands and invent a new shape of kitchen knife, and those, too, who find a new way of organizing transatlantic air travel with low overheads. Indeed, such innovators may well be the ones who do better on world markets than the inventors of a new computer game or laser-guided missile, as well as contributing more to the sum of human happiness. But, unfortunately, the same applies to business innovations as applies to learned contributions to economic journals, namely that the prestige they gain for their authors varies roughly in inverse ratio to the proportion of the population capable of understanding their algebra. And we all think, when we see a kitchen knife, that we could have designed it ourselves.

It has to be said, though, that the difference between high technology and kitchen knife stuff is probably not just a matter of prestige (though it is remarkable how quickly discussion of national innovation efforts gets round to talk of Nobel prizes and the national glory that comes from having a lot of them). It is not just a matter of prestige because, in the case of business innovations, the high-prestige innovation probably also has' the greater economic growth potential. There *is* a correlation between nations' growth in share of world markets and their concentration on expansion in high-technology branches of *production*. This is *not*, however, to say that there is a correlation between growth in world market-share and excellence in *original* invention in high technology. Japan in the last ten years has indeed rapidly increased the volume of original technology produced in its corporate laboratories, but until recently was avowedly and unashamedly concentrating on catching up with American and European technology. Its innovators were primarily diffusion-adopters taking over, if frequently adapting and improving, technology imported from abroad and paying for it, but on the whole paying a modest price. Between 1951 and 1981 Japan spent some $16 billion on technology imports, including royalties, outright purchases and dividend payments on joint-venture equity. Those are year-by-year current dollars, but if doubled to convert approximately to 1981 dollars, the total is *still* only as much as the United States spent on research and development in a mere six months in 1981.

So, if you can have high economic growth by other means, who needs to be the maker of original discoveries? This is a highly complex matter to which statistical records can give ambiguous answers. I would be inclined to base my response on the observation of Carter and Williams (1957, ch. 16) twenty-five years ago that technical progressiveness is a function of all-round managerial quality. A firm that has the qualities which make it good at production will also *want* to be good at innovation, so that the option of just being good at production and letting someone else do the path-breaking is not really a practicable one, except for a society like Japan in the 1960s, very self-consciously catching up and unpretentiously accepting its role as pupil to the rest of the world.

So I conclude that to sustain the pace of economic growth as we need to do in order to solve our distributional problems and not feel too uncomfortably envious of other richer countries, we do need innovation, especially innovation in the production of tradables (i.e., predominantly manufactured goods), and we do need a good deal of it to be based on invention at the high-technology end of the spectrum.

And, to summarize this discussion of small-scale entrepreneurship and venture capital, I see no evidence for believing that the long-term trend for innovative activity to be monopolized by large corporations is about to be reversed. It is a trend common to all industrial societies, but with marked differences *between* societies in its salience. The United States, the home of the venture-capital-fund idea and of Route 128, is the country where the small entrepreneurial firm presents the most plausible challenge to the big corporation. Japan, despite the existence of a small number of successful venture businesses, is the country where it presents the least, where the dominant role of the big corporation is least in question.

Can that be because Japanese large organizations are better at innovating? It is a question of some interest. If we have to rely on our large corporations for innovation, how is one to ensure that the large corporations are in fact innovative?

The innovating organization

There is a common idea that the large organization is inimical to creativity. One American creativity expert wrote, mostly from his experience in United States industry, that a check on the people who had produced the best money-spinning ideas found that they were for the most part on the verge of being fired just before they produced the big idea. The highly creative person, he claimed, is likely to be alone and lonely. He generates a lot of conflict, because he is always coming up with ideas to challenge common sense and accepted practices (Taylor, 1972, p. 8).

However, that particular author was one of those ebullient post-Sputnik entrepreneurs who did rather well out of shocking the American government and business into devoting large sums of money to their research enterprises by denouncing the anti-creativity of American institutions. Quite apart from that, I am a little sceptical of such accounts: our individualistic society loves legends of individual determination. We make folk-heroes of our Frank Whittles, impervious to the rebuffs of the philistines as they hawk their revolutionary engines from door to door. We never get to hear of the shy ones who get an idea but only really convince themselves that it will work when reassured by someone else's enthusiasm for it. Do we really know how our creative organization innovators divide between the two types?

One thing of which we can be relatively sure is that the creative innovator has a harder time in what Burns and Stalker (1961) called the mechanistic organization, devoted to efficiency in routine production, than in an organization specifically geared to continuous innovation. Some of the devices for such gearing-up are surely of universal, cross-cultural, efficacy. In large organizations, creating (and giving central importance to) research and development departments, research and development budgets and programmes, or having a 'new business' manager whose specific task is novelty, are examples. Even in small organizations there are ways of creating numerous symbolic occasions for reminding people that innovation is a good thing and that there ought to be more of it. The only one of some twenty British pump firms I have visited in recent months which was planning to take on new workers was also the most consciously future-oriented company. It operated a rolling five-year plan which in itself was fairly uncommon, but it also held, at annual plan-time and on other occasions in the year, meetings of the dozen or so middle-to-senior managers which were called expressly for the communal exercise of divergent intelligence (what I suppose I would just call 'brain-storming' but for some prissy British distaste for the American-style 'rah-rah' enthusiasm associated with the word), meetings to ask who had had any good ideas for new projects lately, what possible extensions might be made to particular product lines, what could be done to exploit the potential of particular types of equipment more fully, and so on. It was, as might be guessed, an American-owned firm, though staffed entirely by – apparently enthusiastic – British managers.

Keynes was surely right in suggesting that only animal spirits could explain the willingness of men and women to innovate in spite of the promptings of prudent rationality in the face of uncertainty. Animal spirits are infectious. Hiring bright, animal-spirited people is one thing. Making an animal-spirited organization is another, and a probably more effective route to innovativeness.

There is a flourishing branch of science called organization theory, originally founded by people who believed that there were universally valid principles which should govern arrangements for human organization and which were as knowable as the principles of mechanics. Given the organization's objectives, it was a purely technical matter to discover the optimal form it should take. Organization theory has now advanced far beyond that point. Students of the science now speak of what is known as 'contingency theory'. As I understand it, contingency theory holds that there are an awful lot of variables determining the shape that organizations actually take, or ought to take, to achieve their ends. The proposition seems unassailable, though a discipline which can call such a proposition a theory has still, perhaps, some way to go! One of the major problems is that its practitioners concentrate primarily on formal structures, arrangements which determine who talks to whom, who reports to whom, and who bears responsibility for what, without having much to say about motives and the way motives interact with the formal structure on the one hand and the rest of people's lives on the other.

And it is, clearly, to the level of motivation that one needs to penetrate if one is to say anything useful about the will to innovate, and the conditions which foster it.

Which brings us, once again, to the distinction introduced already between a Company Law model firm with what I defined in Chapter 2 as a market-oriented employment system, and a Community model firm with what I called an organization-oriented employment system.

The Company Law firm is one which uses for motivating purposes the basic pattern of any pure market interaction: the stand-off bargained contract. Its archetypal characteristic is the piece-work wage system, what Marx once called the quintessential expression of capitalism. This involves the straight bargain: so much money for so much work performed, with no explicit commitments going beyond that arrangement. Systems of managerial bonuses tied to the performance of their separately accounted departmental profit centres are an American extension of the same principle. So also, in Britain, are productivity deals: a straight contractual exchange between managers who, alone, are presumed to want higher efficiency and higher profits, and workers who are presumed only to be interested in higher wages, or in maintaining demarcation lines or washing-up time privileges, or whatever.

In contrast, the Community firm drastically modifies the wholly individualistic assumptions of the market model. It starts off from the assumption that the major purposes of the organization are purposes to which all members of the organization subscribe, and that they can be expected to allow these collective purposes to supersede to some degree their own private purposes. In addition, it assumes that their sharing of these common purposes creates certain bonds of fellowship between members of the organization. From this follows a sense of community which means, first, that people are considerate of each other's feelings and seek ways, like seniority rules for promotion, to reduce the amount of interpersonal competition and hence the frequency of personal defeats; second, that people work not only for the money they take home, but also for the satisfaction of contributing to a worthwhile collective endeavour, and for the recognition and respect they are accorded for their contributions. Wages are not seen as the result of hard adversarial bargaining but as a fair share-out of the fruits of shared efforts: what was called in Chapter 3 the ESSE principle as opposed to EPEW, the market principle of 'equal pay for equal work'.

The British organizations which, like Japanese business firms, exhibit the purest type of Community organization are the armed forces. Soldiers are expected to sacrifice a lot of personal goals for the Army's collective goal of defending the nation. Piece-work is not resorted to. Prize-money and blood-money, although still paid by the Royal Navy in the Second World War, were remnants of an earlier buccaneering stage of 'booty capitalism', which had been rationalized out of a moralized and ideologized Navy by the time of the Falklands conflict. Now, there are no bonus payments depending on the number of enemy killed or even the number of bullets fired or square inches of webbing blancoed. There are only medals which represent purely symbolic recognition of loyalty and devotion to the organization's goals, medals which work as motivators because *there is* a proud sense of regimental community, and the regiment generally holds the goals worthwhile. Interpersonal competition is regulated by promotion rules with a heavy element of seniority: only corporals can be promoted to sergeant, only captains to major, and so on. Much the same could have been said of the British Civil Service too, until Rayner-like tinkerings tried to make the promotion system more competitive, and constant Thatcherite denigration damaged the elite-service pride which is an important element in making the system work.

Actual organizations: in practice and in theory

To find a British *business firm* which approaches such a pattern of Community-type organization, one has to go to cooperatives like the Scott-Bader Commonwealth, but abroad it is rather different. IBM is well known for its tradition of enthusiastic dedication, and the *average* Japanese capitalist firm, even the largest, is closer to the army version of the Community model than to Scott-Bader, at least in the matter of expecting the firm's demands to take precedence over the conveniences of private life, and in having formal and relatively predictable promotion lines based on the expectation of lifetime employment in the same firm.

But equally – although, as a recent Department of Employment study shows (Bowey *et al.*, 1982), British beliefs about the efficacy of payment-by-results systems show a remarkable resilience in spite of all the evidence about their relation to industrial conflict (e.g. White, 1981) – pure specimens of the Company Law model organization are also hard to find in Britain, or anywhere else for that matter. First, there are the deviations towards the earlier paternalistic versions of the Community model, with gold medals for long service and the talk at presentation ceremonies about the 'loyalty' of long-serving workers to the firm. Second, there are those, now more widespread, deviations that have been enforced, partly by trade-union pressure, partly by the logic of training needs, partly by movements of managerial opinion, led by bodies like the Industrial Society. I have in mind all those developments, listed in Chapter 3, which have made the ESSE principle – the fair share in corporate revenues concept – a more powerful force in wage negotiations: growth in plant-level or enterprise-level wage bargaining, in internal promotion systems, in joint consultative committees, in profit-sharing schemes, in single-status harmonization agreements, in work-flexibility agreements, in enterprise-training investments, in measures to promote 'employee involvement', and so on.

But for all these deviations, in practice and in managerial rhetoric, from the pure Company Law model in certain selected areas, most people still *think* in terms of Company Law assumptions. Politicians urge managers to get rid of over-manning and to give workers the incentive of cash rewards for harder work. They try to end the closed shop and encourage individual withdrawal from pension schemes. Managers, when it comes to detailed wage matters, can rarely think beyond the adversarial 'rate-for-the-job' bargain. 'Don't give him the impression you are pleased with how he's performing, or he'll demand an extra twopence on his rate' is a fair sample of prevailing wisdom. Trade-union leaders, largely from suspicion of the manipulative aspects of the 'involvement' movement, are deeply addicted to the Company Law model and suspicious of attempts to modify it: witness the TUC's long-standing reluctance to have any truck with industrial democracy and its final acceptance of the idea only when it was represented as an extension of collective bargaining. In the academic world, the dominant school of industrial relations experts call the Company Law model 'pluralism', which is good, as opposed to what they call the unitary view which can only mean managerial dominance and exploitation. Labour economists, for their part, have only recently, and chiefly in America, begun to incorporate in their theorizing notions of implicit contracts going beyond the immediate wage-effort bargain, and otherwise, as Solow (1980) observed recently, continue to discuss labour markets on the basis of assumptions the main merit of which is that they perform reasonably well for modelling the buying and selling of cloth.

Innovation in organizations: motivating the original inventive effort

The same assumptions frequently appear – and finally I get back to my innovation theme – in discussion of how to make people innovative in large corporations. Much thought is given to devices that try to make bureaucracies work like market-places, recreating *within* the firm the incentives and opportunities for individuals to be entrepreneurially innovative, which their nineteenth-century predecessors had in the outside market.

The clearest examples of this are in the formal intra-corporate venture systems of many large American and some British corporations. Special venture teams are set up within the company with the prospect that, if successful, they will grow into a new division. They usually revolve around a leading individual who is expected to show the same qualities of aggressive independence and drive as the traditional Schumpeterian entrepreneur. The 'intrapreneur' wrestles with the finance department for funds just as the market entrepreneur wrestles with the bank manager; he raids other departments for good people rather than raiding other firms. And, in some American companies, though not in others, he may have a contract which sets a lowish base-salary but gives him share options depending on the measured success of his venture.

These are means – most obviously so when there are formal

systems of financial reward – of getting individuals to be innovative in their own interest: of getting them to be entrepreneurial *in* the firm. An alternative – the alternative appropriate to the Community model organization – is to encourage them to be entrepreneurial *for* the firm. An interesting example of the contrast is the way factory suggestion schemes are operated in Britain and Japan. Such schemes, keenly propagated here by the Industrial Society as a means of enhancing employees' 'involvement' have been common in Britain for many years. The way they usually work is as follows: an innovative idea for the improvement of products or processes may be proposed by an employee. It is then examined by a panel of engineers who decide whether or not it is worth adopting. If adopted, the saving or extra revenue generated over a particular time period is then calculated, and the suggester is usually given 50 per cent of that sum as his share. In short, the suggestion is given its market value and bought by the firm from the employee acting as independent agent. In a Japanese firm, by contrast, there is a scale of prizes; you get a first prize, or a second or third prize, or a commendation. The cash value is generally not large, and you may not have much of it left after you have stood all your workmates drinks in celebration because of the honour. The recognition *by the enterprise community* is supposed to be the main thing.

So here are two alternative methods of motivating innovative behaviour. Both have their merits. Since innovative ideas occur in individual heads (unless a work group reaches the stage of telepathic communication), the individualism of the Company Law model, matching reward to individual innovative effort, has an obvious point. But it has disadvantages too. Much innovation nowadays requires lengthy developmental processes calling for cooperative effort among a number of people in a coordinated programme of trials. If the work is successful in a Community firm the whole group can be given the honour, with individuals being singled out for an extra-special but still quantitatively indeterminate share, only to the degree that the players who actually scored the goals have an extra-special share of the honour of a winning football team – they may be singled out to have their names recorded as 'inventors' in the patent application. If however the rewards are in money, as in the Company Law firm, more is at stake, *and* somebody has to decide how much to whom (and in the United Kingdom, since 1977, an employee can even start legal proceedings to claim a share in any 'outstanding benefit' his or her invention has brought to the firm). In these circumstances, competition between members of the team is likely to be more intense. Competition can be an excellent thing between rival manufacturers of lawn mowers. Between individuals *within* a lawn-mower firm, however, it may indeed evoke effort, but on the other hand it rarely enhances cooperation. The free flow of information which is crucial to the innovation process may well be inhibited by personal hoarding of information, and a general lack of trust may result. In the Community firm, by contrast, where one's personal reward consists of being given, in the long term, faster promotion than one's peers within the limits of certain seniority rules, cooperative information-sharing can be explicitly seen as something that earns the Brownie points which win promotion. Moreover, where individuals identify with the firm, as they would in such firms, competition in the market feeds directly back into motivation. When Bovvercut is eating drastically into Straightshear's lawn-mower market, Straightshear employees gird their loins and rack their brains for innovative ideas to beat the competition. In the Company Law firm they wonder – quite legitimately – about the chances of getting a job with Bovvercut. One case-study of continuous incremental innovation illustrates the importance of interpersonal trust, shared objectives and free flow of information. It is Cantley and Sahal's (1980) account of the gradual improvements in Coastal Command's technology for sinking U-boats during the war. They quote a contemporary who stresses how crucial it was that:

> the relation between scientists and [Air Force] staff was one of almost unblemished co-operation and trust. If this had failed on either side, Operational Research as Coastal Command knew it would have been impossible. If the scientists had not . . . sat in at [the Commander-in-Chief's] most professional and confidential conferences, but had been fobbed off at lower level discussions, they would have learned only too late of the importance of many subjects to which they made contributions of some value.

Post-innovation development

So far I have been discussing primarily the act of creation of new technology, the birth of ideas and the decision to pursue them. Commercial success depends just as much on the subsequent phases, the post-innovation phases of new-product development when the fully specified prototype is ready to be translated into a procurement system, a production system and a marketing system, and the company begins its journey along the learning curve. It is particularly at this stage that the encouragement of trust and cooperation which is the strength of the Community model of organization is likely to come into its own.

There is one other specific advantage it has which can be important in this post-innovation phase. Such firms do not *have* to be lifetime employment firms, of course. Americans seem to be particularly good at developing undying devotion to a new firm at three- or four-year intervals. Our British footballers can be sold from one team to another and be seen on television passionately hugging their goal-scoring team-mates within a matter of weeks. But the correlation between long-term career employment and other characteristics of the community model is high: witness IBM, BP, and the British Civil Service as well as Japanese firms. And where there is a carefully planned career-promotion structure specifically designed to give the high-flyers experience of all parts of the firm's business, cooperation between the various specialist functions becomes easier. So often one hears of innovations in Britain failing because of inadequate liaison between the designers, the production managers, personnel, finance, and sales. If however the design man has had a spell working in sales, and a spell working in production, he is better able to appreciate the need to consult, and has the contacts and the understanding needed to do it effectively.

There is another consequence of career employment and recruitment for general competence and lifelong learning ability, which was already briefly touched on in Chapter 5: such organizations have a lesser susceptibility to that other obstacle to communication, the 'I don't question your professional competence, so don't you question mine' syndrome. In a market system a man's self-respect, his claim to his present job and his hopes for other jobs in other firms, depend on his professional identity as an engineer, accountant or fitter. In a Community model firm with career employment, they depend instead on his history of job performance in the firm. No one needs, in order to hold on either to his job or his self-respect, to pretend that his engineering degree has made him a fully competent engineer, his apprenticeship a fully rounded fitter. This has two consequences: 'experts' can be more easily questioned and sometimes shaken out of their *ex cathedra* assumptions by 'naive' non-expert colleagues without necessarily getting defensive or hurt. Second, where no one claims to be a 'complete', 'qualified' expert, it is easier to sustain the assumption that everyone *needs* to go on learning, to maintain a 'learning environment', and the openness to new ideas and easy acceptance of change that goes with it.

Which model to recommend?

I have dwelt at length on the advantages of the Community model firm in promoting innovation because the countervailing advantage of the Company Law model – the direct appeal to individual material self-interest – is so much more obvious. Clearly, both systems work. The Company Law model made the United States a highly innovative society. The Community Model has made Japan a society which has shown its superiority in innovative incremental improvement of imported technology, and which is beginning to show signs – though some would dispute the matter – that it will soon succeed in more fundamental basic innovation now that, having reached the world frontiers in so many fields, it is beginning to give more resources to basic research.

So should one conclude with some pious platitude about societies adopting the systems appropriate to their national genius? One can, I think, go a little further and make some observations of a general nature with at least some cross-cultural validity. The first is that of the two stages discussed hitherto – securing that first flash of inventiveness in the research laboratory on the one hand, and marshalling the effort to translate a research idea into production reality on the other – it is in the second that the advantages of the Community model of incentive would seem to be more obvious. But that two-stage model is itself an over-simplification. There is also a linking stage, which needs separate consideration, this being the phase of the decision, of the entrepreneurial act of committing the firm's resources to back an idea and carry it through to production. Whether a firm with Community-type incentives tends to take quicker and/or better decisions in this phase is a matter on which the evidence is thin. *A priori* one might expect personal career security to encourage boldness because it reduced the fear of failure. On the other hand, the reduced possibility of personal reward decreases the incentive to take risks; and where security is a dominant value, caution may (reinforcing the general tendency of bureaucratic organizations to breed 'procedures') lead to endless hesitation. The received wisdom about the difference between the Japanese version of the Community firm and the American version of the Company Law firm is that decisions do indeed *take longer* in the former because so many people demand to be consulted (often because of the recognition that being consulted affords) and it takes a long time to create consensus. But once the decision is taken, implementation – precisely *because* everyone has been committed – proceeds rapidly. And, it is often suggested, the latter effect outweighs the former to give the Japanese Community firm an overall advantage (Pascale and Athos, 1981; Ouchi, 1981).

It can be argued too that, taking the three phases together, the overall advantage of a Community firm is likely to increase irrespective of cultural background. First, to take the initial phase, as the technology of production gets more complex, the scope for invention by the enterprising self-actualizing individual narrows, and there is increasing need for cooperative teamwork in both research and development, of both new products and processes. Second, in the third phase, as lead times for the production of more complex new products lengthen, and as cheaper, more efficient communications intensify international competition, victory goes increasingly to those who move most quickly in the post-innovation process, those who can get the product from the drawing-board into production fastest and then start moving rapidly along the learning curve of incremental improvement.

The popularity of Quality Circles mentioned in Chapter 5 – the organizational device to get groups of workers to spend time reflecting on the production techniques they are using and probing for possible improvements to them – is one recognition, perhaps, of the superiority of the Community model. It is a low-level form of innovation in which they deal, but a cumulatively important one, nevertheless, and the Quality Circle method of evoking it does rest on the assumption that everyone in the firm shares the common objective of making the firm successful, is prepared to make personal contributions towards that end on his own initiative, and is not going to be too contractualist in making sure that he gets exactly equivalent personal reward for all the contributions he offers. As such (although there are management consultants selling Quality Circle techniques up and down the country as a sort of add-on extra which a management can 'put in' to a basically Company-Law-type factory much as they might 'put in' CAD/CAM or work study), it is in firms which already have something of a Community-type ethos that they seem to work best.

But, given the salience of the shareholder interest in British firms, which the last chapter contrasted with the relative weakness of that interest in Japanese firms, it is rare that their income-sharing and accounting patterns *do* give plausible grounds for all the firm's employees to think that they have common objectives, that they all have a stake in the firm's success and some prospect of getting what they deem a fair share of the proceeds of that success. It is not surprising that the TUC (Trades Union Council, 1981) warns its members against Quality Circles as attempts by managers to get workers to contribute their ideas to the firm without getting paid for it: 'Trade unionists will be opposed to the introduction of QCs if they challenge in any way existing trade-union machinery or practice'; 'Management cannot expect to "claim" all the productivity and other savings generated by the work of QCs. These, like other elements of workplace productivity, are a matter for established negotiating procedures.' It is not surprising that Bradley and Hill (1983), at the end of an excellent detailed study of the operation of Quality Circles in two British firms, recently concluded: 'We believe that quality-circle experience shows the difficulty of grafting high-trust practices developed within consensus organizations onto a host organization where relationships are conducted on low-trust principles and contain adversarial elements.'

What should one conclude when one hears British managers talking grandly in Community model terms about "involvement' and 'participation', and then sees them behaving in purely Company-Law terms when it comes to the 'who gets what' questions of wage bargaining or dealing with a takeover, or discussing the cost of maintaining the senior managers' dining-room? That they are confused, wanting to have their cake and eat it, and unaware of the inconsistency? Or that they are cleverly Machiavellian, using clever words to increase the amount of cake they have and conceal the amount they are scoffing?

I suspect a bit of both, but either way the mixture is not conducive either to business efficiency nor to a decent quality of personal relations. And tha is one more reason why, in the next chapter, I shall look at the question: what might be done to edge British firms closer to the Community model?

8
The firm as community: The road to industrial democracy

This chapter has a simple thesis. On several counts the Community model firm is superior to the Company Law model firm: innovativeness, efficiency, competitiveness, the quality of life and kinds of satisfaction it delivers to those who work in it. Japan manages to have firms which are predominantly of this type, partly because they were clever enough to understand about these things, and lucky enough to have industrialized late when it was easier to do something about them; partly because the employee interest is quite strong *vis-à-vis* the shareholder interest in the Japanese form of capitalism for a variety of historical reasons; and partly because Japan is a society where authority is not *in principle* problematical, where hierarchy is more acceptable than in Britain, and subordinates are more willing to assume competence in their superiors and to accept instructions from them when the assumption appears to be confirmed.

How can Britain, with none of these advantages, get more Community-model firms? Once again, as in the case of incomes policies, we need deliberate social-engineering legislation to achieve by artifice what the Japanese enjoy largely by historical and cultural inheritance.

The central thrust of any such measures must be to shift the present balance of interest and control between employees and shareholders in favour of the former.

Ultimately, of course, this is a matter of convention, as those since Berle and Means who have analysed the divorce between ownership and control in the modern corporation have repeatedly emphasized. The relative priority of the employee interest in Japan does not rest on laws. Aoki (1984, p. 179) could find legal provisions giving (by international standards) unusual priority to the employee interest only in the procedures for custodial reorganization of companies in difficulties.

But legal rights underpin conventions, and a shift in legal rights can have a symbolic effect in shifting conventions. Even 'fanfare statements' in laws can act as reference points, as reinforcing arguments. Do not, then, despise the fact, already mentioned in Chapter 3, that the 1980 Companies Act *did* have written into it a clause which required company directors to 'have regard' to 'the interests of the company's employees in general as well as the interests of its members'. True, the clause ended with the affirmation that directors nevertheless remained legally responsible solely to the shareholders, but still, that for the first time employees and their interests were mentioned could be a springboard for advocating further measures.

Takeovers

For example, to take a matter arising directly from Chapter 6, it could be used as an argument for the regulation of takeovers. Nothing more directly makes British companies sensitive to the share price and slaves of the short term than their openness to takeovers. Nothing more disfigures the face of British capitalism than the way Britain's financial press, particularly the business sections of the 'quality' Sunday papers, give so much more prominence to the sagas of contested takeover bids – all the meritricious drama of tense boardroom scenes, the strained confrontations, the secret deals, the heroic bluffs of poker-faced financiers – than to the plans and achievements of companies which are serious-mindedly getting on with the business of making things and providing services which society genuinely values. And nothing is more destructive of a sense of community in a firm than for the employees to arrive on a Monday morning to find that the conglomerate which owns it has sold it over the weekend to another conglomerate and that all their senior managers' efforts are now devoted to a desperate fight to keep their jobs.

Takeover regulation in this country is exercised with only two objectives in view: first, to prevent excessive concentration of market power, and secondly, to prevent fraud and ensure that shareholders are adequately informed about the choices they are asked to make. There is no reason why the rules should not be framed to take aboard a third objective, to incorporate the recognition that a company is *not* like a piece of real estate, and the best and most desirable company is in some sense a community, and that the owner should have no more right unilaterally to dispose of a company than a landlord under the Rent Act can unilaterally end his contract with a tenant. In practical terms this would mean some form of mandatory employee consultation, probably in the form of a ballot, before a bidder is allowed to take up acceptances of his offer. Where there is a clash between the expressed wishes of employees and shareholders, an independent arbitrator could be appointed, and allowed, or required, to add into the equation the interests of customers, of suppliers and of the macroeconomy, when taking his decision.

Profit-sharing: the dividend connection

Profit-sharing schemes of one kind or another have been around for a very long time, and the budget concessions in the late 1970s have done a lot quietly to spread their adoption, particularly in the financial and commercial sectors. More recently the MIT economist Martin Weitzman's *The Share Economy* (1984) has had a considerable vogue among those with a social engineering bent (what unkind people would call gimmick-hunters) especially in the SDP, particularly because of his claims that payment of a substantial proportion of labour income in the form of a profit share rather than a fixed wage could have a substantial effect on employment, a belief based on the curious view that you can make firms more efficient by giving their employees a sense of participation without the employees' representatives actually wanting to participate in, say, decisions about recruiting extra workers.*

What seems never to have been tried is the tying of the employee profit share to dividends. This has one obvious technical advantage of clarity: profits can be a highly malleable concept, whereas a dividend payment is unambiguous. It has the symbolic advantage of stressing the parallel interest – the equal stake – of shareholder and employee in the success of the firm. It reminds the employees that the firm *does* need to have risk capital, at the same time as it reminds shareholders that their rewards depend on the efforts of employees. It might be objected that the only result of widespread adoption of such a scheme would be a lowering of dividends and an inflation of reserves as shareholders decided to take their rewards in the form of capital gains instead. This is rather unlikely. It would seem rather foolish, surely, having set an employee profit bonus at a level which is supposed to be an effective motivator, then to try, by devious means, to reduce it below that level.

* *Since this was written, of course, Mr Lawson has stolen the SDP's clothes.*

Employee share ownership

One alternative to shifting the shareholder–employee balance of power is, of course, to remove the distinction between them, to turn employees *into* shareholders. That this can be an effective way of creating a Community model enterprise – at least when the firm becomes wholly employee-owned and has a robust enough constitution to handle the authority/expertise problems which often beset cooperatives – seems to be demonstrated by firms such as the John Lewis Partnership and Scott-Bader. Employee buyouts of ailing firms have also shown a surprisingly high success rate in the US (see Bradley and Gelb, 1983) and have had some notable successes (e.g., the National Freight Consortium) in Britain.

More common are schemes under which share distribution is simply the preferred method of profit-sharing, where employees are expected to, and often do, sell their shares, and the employee-owned shares are never expected to amount to a substantial controlling interest. Marginal though might be the power conferred on employees by such shareholdings, it is unlikely that they would have no effect on the regard for employee interests shown when crucial boardroom decisions are taken.

There is one particular use of employee share distribution which might be developed in the context of an incomes policy such as was outlined in Chapter 4. If there were a national norm for the annual increase in employee incomes – with an inflation tax to discourage any firm from increasing its average wage by more than the norm – the necessary moral authority could never be mobilized behind the norm unless there were also control on dividend payments.

What sort of control might this be that would be effective both in promoting Community-model assumptions and as a viable part of an incomes policy built to last? Clearly it cannot be the kind of dividend restraint of earlier British incomes policies which could only be a temporary expedient, not part of an enduring set of institutions. It could only be temporary because profits not distributed in dividends simply go to swell reserves and capital values and probably produce a dividend bonanza as soon as the incomes policy explodes from its own internal stresses.

So what would a permanent set of arrangements look like? One possibility might be the following:

1   The policy to apply only to bigger firms where there is a pretty clear division between ownership and control, perhaps all firms

quoted on the Stock Exchange or all firms capitalized at over £X. Such a restriction is justifiable for two reasons: because there is a case for stimulating the risk-bearing enterprise of genuine owner-managers, and because owner-managers can simply switch funds between profits/dividends and their salaries at will anyway.

2 Select a base year, presumably the year before the first incomes policy year, which will also provide the base year for wage settlements. Calculate an 'allowable base year dividend' for the eligible companies in such a way as not to penalize companies which have declared low dividends in that year, perhaps for the highly laudable purpose of making long-term investments. Perhaps, taking at its face value the claim of the Stock Exchange that the share price represents the best evaluation through a consensus of the most informed objective observers of the intrinsic worth and efficiency of the company, a reasonable way would be to set the base as a given rate of interest (say something between the building society deposit rate and the average earnings yield of shares on the Stock Exchange) paid on the average share price, over the base year, of each company's stock.

3 Thereafter, the 'allowable dividend payment' to be increased annually by the same percentage as the wage increase norm.

4 To encourage companies to invest in the long-term future, 'dividend payment entitlements' can be carried over from year to year for a fixed number of years, i.e., any company which pays a smaller dividend than is allowed in one year can make up the shortfall by an equal amount over the allowance in any of the following, say, five years.

5 Post-tax profits over and above the dividend payment would not simply go into reserves attributable to existing shareholders. Herein lies the crucial difference between a 'temporary expedient' incomes policy and an incomes policy built to last. It is the steady swelling of profit reserves in profitable companies (or rather the continuing attribution to shareholders of those reserves; the retention of earnings within the firm is itself highly desirable) which has made a cosmetic and short-lived nonsense of earlier dividend restraint. One might instead suggest the following: the reserves would be converted into equity share certificates.

The distribution of these shares could be handled in various ways. One suggestion might be: one third to the existing shareholders (in proportion to their holdings); one third to employees; and one third to a national fund rather on the lines of the Swedish Meidener arrangements. Equality of treatment of shareholders and employees would, like the linking of employee profit-sharing bonuses to dividends, be a way of affirming the equal stake both parties have in the company. Contribution to a national fund would be justifiable on the grounds that the benefits the firm receives in the form of extra profits from a technological breakthrough which it temporarily monopolizes, or from some other kind of monopoly position in the market, or just from its general efficiency in production, *ought* to be shared with the community at large, and if that is not done by lowering prices then it should be done in some other way. (It can also be justified from another point of view which will be discussed in Chapter 11.)

Industrial democracy

But, clearly, any kind of substantial shift of shareholder rights from existing shareholders to employees can only come about as a result of a wealth transfer of very considerable proportions. And if such a transfer of wealth is possible, it is by no means self-evident that the transfer should be to those who are employees (and in the 1980s one has learned to say 'are lucky enough to be employees') in firms with large capital assets. Chapter 11 will argue for alternative directions for wealth redistribution which the future may well make increasingly necessary.

There remains, then, if the Community model is not going to be easily created by turning employees into shareholders, the question of what can alternatively be done to give employees a stake in their firm by giving them a share in the shareholders' controlling power, and giving it to them *qua* employees. What, in other words, should be done about industrial democracy?

Debate about industrial democracy in Britain must surely be due for a revival, nearly a decade after the abortion of the last attempt to introduce some measure of legal compulsion (the Bullock Report (1977) and the subsequent White Paper). In practically every country in Europe some form of limitation of the shareholder interest in favour of the employee interest has been on the statute books for many years. West Germany built the post-war miracle on a structure of co-determination, a part of the landscape of German society for the best part of four decades.

And what do we have in Britain? A government dedicated to undying opposition to the European Communities' draft Fifth

Directive which would make shareholder–employee power-sharing mandatory. And elsewhere a deafening silence. The managerial optimists of the One-Nation Tory/Alliance/right-wing Labour centre are silent because still discouraged by the Bullock debate. The Labour Party is silent because the trade unions are not interested. And the trade unions are not interested because they have other fights on their minds.

One trade union, the Electrical, Electronic, Telecommunications and Plumbing Union (EEPTU), has taken a decisive step towards endorsement of the Community model firm. The pattern has, significantly, been worked out in deals with Japanese subsidiaries in this country: one single all-embracing plant-based union; pendulum arbitration without strikes or lock-outs; wide-ranging works-council consultation; factory-wide grading schemes; elaborate management –union contracts incorporating all basic factory rules. The recognition agreement at the Hitachi Hirwaun factory says, in its second clause:

> In this joint approach, the company and EETPU recognize that there is a common objective to continue to ensure the efficiency and prosperity of the Company for the benefit of its members, its customers, its shareholders and its community.

Note the order, with shareholders in third place. 'Members' here means employees. EETPU represents 'all company members below middle management level'.

The EETPU, possibly to be followed by the Amalgamated Union of Engineering Workers (AUEW), is of course very much a minority element in the union movement. Its acceptance – advocacy even – of what is regarded by many TUC members as an attitude of abject collusion with the capitalist enemy is not likely to become dominant TUC strategy for some years yet. It represents, however, through its acceptance of an organization-oriented (see Chapter 2) employment system, an approach to the Community model by the Japanese method, quietly elbowing the shareholders aside, accepting 'management' not as shareholders' agents, but as trustees of the interests of 'the company and all its members', allowing the potential for adversarial division to arise only from possible differences between 'short-term-interested subordinates' versus 'long-term-vision seniors and experts', and in any case making sure that this opposition is muted by an ideology of basic identity of interest.

That Japanese method can work fairly well in the wholly owned subsidiary of a Japanese multi-national because the 'shareholders' who come number three on the interest group list are, in fact, the managerial colleagues in Tokyo of the 'managerial members' running the subsidiary in Britain. Will it work as well, will the shareholders be as willing to be elbowed aside, when 'the share-holders' means, say, a Tiny Rowlands, a Charles Ronson, a Robert Maxwell or some other of our City buccaneers?

For the average British firm it is unlikely that the EETPU-type Japanese approach to the Community model will get very far. But there is little interest, indeed some hostility, in the trade-union movement to the alternative route by which a more Community type of firm might be reached: the traditional 'industrial democracy' route of power sharing between employees and shareholders within the board structure of the firm. The TUC's antipathy to such arrangements was overt until the early 1970s. The creation of Com-munity-type enterprises is not good news in the least for unions who see their *raison d'être* as lying precisely in the adversarial relations of the Company-Law-type enterprise. The unions were persuaded to go along with the establishment of the Bullock Committee only because they believed that industrial democracy could be an ex-tension of collective bargaining. And so it would have become if the Bullock arrangements, giving unions pre-eminent control over the selection of employee representatives on company boards, had been carried into effect, thereby preserving Company-Law stances and producing little pay-off in efficiency or cooperation. Opposition was understandably great; there was a long delay; a White Paper which again shirked the essential issues, and the matter was dropped to general relief.

Industrial democracy eventually inevitable?

But the issue will not go away. There are good reasons for thinking that industrial democracy is 'on the cards', bound to come. What I see those reasons as being I summarize in Fig. 2. The Bullock Committee itself hinted at something of this underlying logic when it spoke of a higher material standard of living having made people less tolerant of poor safety and health conditions, redundancy and un-employment (Bullock, 1977, p. 22). It identified as other trends:

1   More education, and particularly education which stimulated independent and questioning approaches to authority.

2   The slow-down of growth and diversion of aspirations to other

153

Figure 2 Industrial democracy and job restructuring: some structural factors behind increasing interest

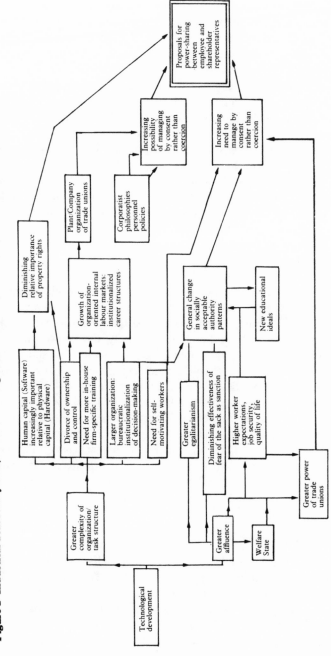

fields. (A kind of 'sublimation' variant of the Maslow thesis of a hierarchy of needs from lower-level physical ones to higher-level needs for autonomy and self-actualization, a hierarchy up which societies and individuals move with increasing affluence and security.)

3   Increasing complexity of business organizations, remoteness and concentration of decision-making power, calling forth countervailing forces and calls for business corporations to recognize general social responsibilities.

4   Accelerating pace of invention and concomitantly increasing role of innovation in competition leads to increasing need for adaptability in the workforce.

5   This adaptability can only be speedily obtained with the consent of workers, given the increasing power of trade unions (Bullock, pp. 20–3).

Underlying secular trends and their technological roots

Apart from the second, these are all long-run evolutionary, rather than short-run cyclical changes. They relate, that is to say, to the one trend in the history of Europe's last four centuries which has been cumulative and unidirectional, namely the growth in scientific knowledge and in the sophistication of material – and also partly social – technology. (Sophistication being measured, perhaps, by the length of time it takes a person of given mental ability to learn it.) If one probes deep enough, all theories of social evolution have the accumulation of technology as their starting point or central spine, or power-pack, or whatever metaphor one prefers. Figure 2 is an attempt to systematize a number of arguments concerning the intermediate variables which explain why the growing sophistication and complexity of industrial technology should lead to a concern with industrial democracy.

Affluence and the Welfare State

For the most part Figure 2 is, I hope, self-explanatory, but a few elaborations of its arguments may be in order, starting in the bottom left-hand corner with the implications of higher standards of living. That the growth of state welfare and the rising level of the welfare minimum diminish the disciplinary power of employers by making the prospect of job loss less disastrous is an obvious argument, but one countered to some extent by the manifest increase in the strength of unions' concern with job security in countries like the UK in the last few years. The latter, however, can best be seen as a consequence of the enlargement of expectations and definitions of what a worker has a *right* to expect. As, in the European mixed economies at least, the involvement of the state in industry grows, so the expectations of job security are consolidated by the assumption that it is the state's job to keep firms in business if they are in danger of leaving their workers without jobs. The London *Economist*, anxious about market imperfections and sluggish supply response in the UK economy, may deplore the immobility of British labour and its unwillingness to move to the parts of the country where jobs are still to be had. But the *Lancashire Evening Telegraph* (16 April 1980), representing local working-class sentiment conditioned by two de-cades of regional development grants, will attack *The Economist* for unfeeling economism and declare that people have a right not to be forced out of their homes and friendship networks merely to find work.

The diagrammed relationship of 'higher worker expectations' (and enhanced definitions of rights, etc.) to the strength of trade unions may not be immediately obvious. It relates to the point made in Chapter 3 about 'fairness' and its relation to trade-union power. It is his members' sense of indignation which gives a trade-union leader the potential to call them out on strike, and their sense of indignation is a function of the gap between their expectations and the treatment they are offered, which can grow as much from a raising of ex-pectations as from a worsening of treatment.

Egalitarianism

The sources of growing egalitarianism are, of course, far more complex than the mere near-universalization of schooling and middle-class living standards. Theoretical equality is implicit in the legal and market institutions necessary for (nineteenth-century) capitalist economies to work. And it has been a major theme of modern history to trace the way the principle works through from the legal and economic sphere to the political – rapidly in a United States born out of an individualistic view of the state as the guarantor of individuals' rights to life, liberty and the pursuit of happiness, more slowly in European states with a European-type feudal heritage, even more slowly in some respects in Japan with a

Japanese-type feudal heritage. Sociologists, intermittently, have tried to improve on Tocqueville's agnosticism about the causes of egalitarianism ('a sign of God's irresistible will') and on the historians' assumption that it is basically a matter of the spread of ideas, by analysis of institutional differentiation and the segmentation of spheres of life and the way in which status incongruence – the ranking of individuals in one sphere of life being reversed in another – dilutes the rigidity of *any* status order.

Whatever the sources, the erosion of automatic deference *either* to ascriptive superiors *or* to superiors of higher rank in a functional organizational hierarchy, the diminution in the absolute 'volume' of authority which status superiors can expect to wield, is a matter of common observation in those societies – Europe and the American south – where the vestiges of earlier status orders have been important elements guaranteeing the stability of organizational hierarchies. Fathers can no longer expect from children, teachers from school pupils, bishops from worker priests, nor managers from workers, the same automatic obedience as they once rightly expected and considered as their due. The erosion of deference is a double process of subtle interaction: obedience depends partly on the confidence with which authority is exercised, and the confidence of those exercising authority depends partly on the expectation of obedience. The erosion of authority relations in school and family predisposes new generations against automatic deference to superiors in factory and army, and the resultant changes in the work world feed back on the organization of schools and behaviour in the family.

Some organizations hold out against these processes more successfully than others, by selective recruitment, more coercive structures of rewards and sanctions, more automatic regulations for enforcing them, or simply the weight of tradition. Army officers get away with an imperiousness not allowed to factory managers. A professor at an Oxford college still phones his porters' lodge and says: 'Jones, this is Professor Smith'. A professor at a new British university is more likely to say: 'Bill, this is John Smith'.

The general drift, however, is unmistakeable. The aloofness, awe, respect/fear recipe for authority becomes less viable in work organizations, leaving leadership charisma, if you are lucky enough to have it, demonstrated superior competence and/or (the opposite of aloofness) constant consultation as the only recipes left.

All of this is ground well trodden in Chapter 5. There I was primarily concerned with differences in levels of deference and acceptance of subordination between Britain and Japan, the differential incidence of 'Buncism', the automatic tendency to challenge authority as a matter of manly honour. National differences may be wide, but they are not immutable, and undoubtedly there were more 'Japanese' attitudes towards authority about in Britain a hundred years ago than there are today.

Organization-oriented tendencies

Several times in the course of this book I have talked of the pressures, ultimately stemming from technical and organizational change, which push business firms towards an organization-oriented (see Chapter 2) structure. The link between these pressures and the development of more constitutional forms of management by consent, is the concern of the top half of Fig. 2. Most of the arguments are familiar: from Berle and Means about the divorce of ownership from control, from Galbraith about the need for planning and bureaucratic decision-making as the range of functions to be controlled increases in complexity, from Doeringer and Piore (1971) about firm-specific technologies, training needs and the growth of internal labour markets; one is tempted to say, also, from McGregor (1960) and Herzberg (1966) about the need for self-motivated workers, but by and large the relativist position does not come easily to the prophets of management who are more likely to see their doctrines as just truer and better than anything that has gone before, rather than as better adapted to the new conditions of a new age.

The development of plant/company organization of trade unions is an essential part of any British account of this process (the growth of plant and enterprise bargaining is one of the processes listed in Chapter 3 as contributing to the drift towards the Community model). It is so because in no other country do craft unions oriented to the local labour market rather than to work-places remain as strongly established, not just in a few minor areas like construction and printing as in the US, but in mainstream manufacturing too, though the movement towards enterprise-based forms – not least in the EETPU agreement mentioned above – is clearly apparent.

The erosion of a sense of the absoluteness of property rights varies, of course, from society to society, and is promoted not only by the factors featured in Fig. 2, but also by the 'creeping socialism' of state regulation and a growing body of environmental and other legislation which reflect assumptions about the public character of enterprise. British and American managers still firmly frame their annual reports to the shareholders in terms of what has been happening to 'your company', not, as in comparable Japanese reports, to the affairs of 'our company' (Sogo, 1981). But the business creed reflected in Rotary Club lectures on the social responsibilities of American business, or in the speeches of business representatives of Britain's National Economic Development Council (NEDC), already reflect a less absolute sense of property rights.

What can be done practically?

However, it is a considerable step from asserting that *some* form of power-sharing between shareholder and employee representatives is bound to come, to spelling out, in detail, how, in a country like Britain with Britain's cultural and institutional legacy, it is going to be possible to design institutions which work, which will *ensure that shared power adds up to efficient authority.*

A constant theme in the chorus of management criticism which greeted the Bullock Report was the argument that trade-union representatives on the board would contribute only delay and inefficiency. (They were, it will be recalled, to be equal in numbers to shareholders' representatives with a minority of neutrals to hold the balance: the $2x + y$ formula.) I do not recall reading any half-way analytical account of why this should be so – these, after all, were still the days when a certain hangover of wet Toryism prevented even the Institute of Directors from being too insulting about trade unionists as a category – but the implicit reasons were, presumably, that:

1 Trade unionists would not have acquired the necessary experience to understand the complex issues on which boards have to take decisions. Probably true, but do the politicians, retired admirals and ambassadors on the boards of our companies understand, say, the electronics industry in which the companies whose boards they adorn operate?

2 The admirals, diplomats, and so on, are intelligent, quick learners, aware of what they understand and what they do not understand, capable of contributing useful reasoning power and freshness of mind to problems (as well as experience-based 'feel' for the way organizations work). Trade unionists will be less intelligent, less able to contribute. There was absolutely no reason

to suppose this to be the case in the generation of Ernie Bevin, when highly intelligent people were leaving school for a milk-round at the age of 12, and dunderheads were leaving Wellington for a successful army career. With the increase in equality of educational opportunity, the argument becomes increasingly plausible.

3 Employee representatives elected through trade-union channels would be lifelong trade unionists, the people most suc-cessful at the militant prosecution of the *sectional* interests of the groups within the firm whom they represent, trained to give the reflex action 'that's your problem!' to any attempt by managers to invoke in argument the interests of 'the company as a whole'. (And quite rightly in the Company Law model firm, where the rules of adversarial bargaining should forbid sympathetic con-sideration of 'the other side's' problems.) It is too late in life to expect them to change and suddenly, as board members, begin to take a 'for the good of the company as a whole' point of view. They would tend to sit silent through all discussions about the desirability of breaking into this or that market, developing this or that product, and spring into life only when an issue directly affecting workers' wages or well-being is discussed.

There is a good deal to be said for arguments 2 and 3, (though 3 is an exaggerated caricature of the truth: pure Company Law firms are rare in the private sector, and a good many works' convenors are in fact closer to the Community model in the way they perceive their role). There really is a problem of ensuring, on the one hand, that decisions are taken by those most *competent* to take them (in terms of their grasp of details, ability to do the reasoning which predicts the consequences of alternative courses of action, and so on) and, on the other hand, that they are *accountable* to the employees of the firm for their responsibility to try to work for the 'good of the company as a whole' (i.e., not to sacrifice the common interest of all parties for the disproportionate interests of one group, e.g., the managers, or the shareholders). Competence is necessary if the firm (and the economy) are to survive and prosper; accountability is necessary if the effort-evoking, cooperation-evoking, properties of the Com-munity model are to be achieved.

Getting the right balance between competence and accountability is extremely difficult for at least three reasons. First is the problem already discussed apropos of the Bullock proposals: how can the men and women likely to be most effective as accountability watchdogs on behalf of the manual-worker majority (those least able to understand difficult boardroom decisions) have, not only the trust of those they represent, but *also* the competence to understand what is going on?

Second is the sheer time and effort problem. Time spent being accountable, explaining decisions and the considerations on which they were based, demonstrating good faith, persuading, is time which cannot be spent on gathering the information and doing the analysis necessary to make decisions better.

And thirdly, there is the balance in the accountability devices between suspicion and trust. All forms of accountability – from the parliamentary question to the audit of the tennis club books – are forms of institutionalized suspicion. If the suspicion is too overt, if the checks are not just the conscientious following of the audit rules in the expectation that all will be in order, but a relentless 'they'll get away with anything if you don't keep your eye on them' pursuit of incriminating evidence, then the motivations which make decision-makers competent will be destroyed. Their effort-input will diminish and so, more definitively, will their willingness to take initiatives and to back risky entrepreneurial ventures. In order not to destroy competence, accountability has got to be based 90 per cent on trust, only 10 per cent on evidence that the trust is well placed.

Choosing the right 10 per cent, and making sure that the channels by which the evidence is gathered and diffused are right, is what all the debates about the correct forms of industrial democracy are about. The German model supervisory-board/executive-board hierarchy is one way of achieving the 10 per cent/90 per cent division and keeping the accountability watchdogs out of the top managers' hair for most of the time.

I would suggest an alternative to a hierarchy of boards which has the advantage of specifying more clearly *which* 10 per cent of the array of top-level decisions the accountability devices should focus on. It seems fairly safe to assume that the crucial decisions are the 'who gets what' decisions and that the quickest way of changing gear from a Compnay Law mode to a Community mode is to set up a system whereby *workers' representatives have as much right to a say in determining managers' pay and conditions of work as representatives of management now have in determining workers' pay and conditions.*

This could be done by a system of parallel boards with divided functions. Let the main board be dominated by senior executives as it is now (with perhaps some changes in the other members to be considered later). But let there also be established what one might call a Fairness Council. (Recall the arguments in Chapters 3 and 4 about the crucial role of the concept of 'fairness' in British industrial conflict.) This should be made up of representatives of shareholders and various groups of workers, *including managers as one interest group among others.* (Consumers might also be represented in some large firms.) The Fairness Council (hereafter FC) would scrutinize, and within certain limits have veto powers over, all decisions of the board which have implications for the *distribution* of the rewards given to, and the burdens placed on or contributions expected from, the groups represented. Members of the Board (*not* the manager interest group representatives on the FC itself) would be in attendance at meetings of the FC in order to 'sell' the Board's proposals to the FC, but would not vote. The chairman of the FC might well be independent – one of the outside directors, perhaps, chosen by the other FC members by unanimous vote.

This suggestion rests on an attempt to do what, in its sketchy couple of pages on the subject, the Bullock Report notably fails to do: namely to think through what boards actually *do*. One way of categorizing the decisions they take is in terms of their:

1 *Efficiency implications*: the bearing of the decision on the firm's capacity to grow, increase its operating profit, its market share, value-added per employee, or whatever is accepted (by the FC) as being a reasonable measure or set of measures of the success of the enterprise, i.e., a reasonable definition of the *common* objectives of everyone involved;

2 *Equity implications*: their meaning in terms of the likelihood of increased income or fringe benefits, the possibility of redundancy, harder or less pleasant work, etc., for members of the enterprise.

A wide range of management decisions (both those which do and those which do not normally reach board level) involve both kinds of implications: wage settlements (primarily an equity matter) affect the firm's ability to get efficient people in the labour market; the choice between dividends and retaining earnings involves the firm's power to raise new capital if it needs it as well as the question of what is fair to the shareholders; a new productivity-enhancing machine puts some people out of their familiar jobs and perhaps out of a job altogether; the finance manager's Rover is not only nice for the manager (equity) but possibly a determinant of his bargaining effectiveness with the banks if it is read as an indication of his status in the firm.

In the Company Law model managers are supposed to be single-mindedly concerned with maximizing the profit of the shareholders and to hell with everyone else. Most of our fly-blown rhetoric (hard-nosed conflict sociologists' rhetoric as well as politicians' and businessmen's) preserves this assumption in the talk about the 'two sides' of industry. Mainline management-school business ideology, however, has moved on from there to a rather dubious version of the Community model. Managers are now spoken of as the guardians of the interests of 'the company as a whole'. They are supposed to take decisions which judiciously weigh the differing interests of everyone involved and find the fairest point of compromise without ever, ever giving special consideration to their own *self-*interest in higher salaries, better fringe benefits, more managerial jobs, better returns on their stock options.

The suggestion made here for a Fairness Council parallel to the board rests on the view that:

1   The 'Platonic guardians' view of managers is neither wholly true nor wholly false.

2   The best way to flush out the 'managers' self-interest' aspects of (manager-dominated) Board decisions is to have managers' representatives defend them in a Fairness Council where they are *expected* to act in an avowedly self-interested way.

3   Workers' representatives, after many years of work much closer to the shop floor than most managers get (in Britain) may well have the experience and expertise to make valuable contributions to efficiency decisions. Boards ought to have some places for ex-manual and ex-clerical workers, both for this reason and as a symbolic affirmation (like suggestions schemes) that everybody's knowledge and experience counts.

4   But the people best able to contribute to efficiency decisions are not necessarily the people who have achieved prominence in the company by the firmness with which, as shop stewards, they have stood up for the sectional interests of the workers they represent. The anti-Bullock argument mentioned earlier has some truth. It *would* be a sudden and not easy transition if they were required to step outside their representative role and simply contribute expertise to efficiency decisions. They should be appointed to the Fairness Council where they could continue to do what they are good at.

5 But there are good grounds for believing that they would do it rather differently and that the atmosphere of industrial relations would greatly improve because:

(*a*) Suspicion often poisons bargaining encounters at present precisely because of the ambiguity of the managers' role both as guardians and as self-interest-maximizers. A forum in which everyone avowedly speaks self-interest will clear the air.

(*b*) The other thing which often poisons bargaining encounters is the status differential and the resentment it arouses, worker resentment of the fact that workers are always the supplicant proposers, managers the disposers. The symmetrical arrangement making managers' pay increases as much a matter for the FC as workers' should cure that.

(*c*) Equally it should diminish diffuse resentment directed at what are thought to be excessive management pay and privileges if the extent of such privileges were known and differentials the subject of explicit decision. The system proposed might in fact alter the distribution of rewards in our society over time; it would almost certainly 'harmonize' status-linked differences like length of holidays, pensions and sick-pay rights, hours of work, free lunches, and so on. But one might expect that it should generate a sufficient atmosphere of respect for reality for differentials not to be reduced to the point at which there is a large-scale brain-drain of able managers to other countries.

6 The dynamics of small groups are such that the FC should build up a certain *esprit de corps*. The sentiments which its members might come to feel (of attachment to the FC, and by extension to the corporation of which it is part) might not be easy to achieve simply by the mutual pursuit of rationally calculated self-interest.

What would such a system do to collective bargaining? The short answer is: extend it. Additional matters will be brought within the scope of trade unionists' influence, such as dividend payments and managers' salaries. Much of the mainline pay bargaining will take place *within* FCs (and may evolve into an annual company kitty-bargaining procedure). The articulation of this with industry-wide bargaining procedures and the national trade-union structure (what Donovan's Royal Commission called the 'formal system') will present some problems, but they can be resolved as they have been resolved where conventional company bargaining structures have been set up: at Ford's or at Pilkington's or at British Leyland.

There will remain two sorts of industrial disputes to be dealt with 'through procedure', possibly involving use of the strike weapon. The first will arise over matters dealt with by the FC, when the FC itself fails to reach an acceptable compromise and an overruled minority digs its heels in, or when members of one of the representatives' constituencies repudiate his acceptance of an FC decision. The procedures for such disputes will have to involve some outside mediation or arbitration and it should, presumably, be a sub-committee of the FC (drawn from the overruling majority in the case of a matter unresolved in the FC) which acts for 'the company' in the dispute. The second will be disputes arising from the day-to-day decisions of managers within their delegated powers. The FC itself would play an important part in the procedures for the second kind of dispute.

It all sounds a bit bizarre, perhaps, a bit too neat and tidy for an industrial world brought up to respect the illogicalities of 'custom and practice'. 'Fairness Council' perhaps sounds a bit soppy. Well, 'equity commission' might sound a little more pompous and proper, but there is no great harm in trying to persuade people to talk frankly of underlying realities and to do so in the language of everyday discourse.

Some, I know, will disagree: 'A bit of pompousness, a bit of fudging, a bit of illogical respect for custom and practice are really the only ways you ever get anything done in this world. All this attempt at neat, rational, separation of the issues will never work in Britain. It is precisely because what you call the efficiency issues and the equity issues *are* mixed up and *stay* mixed up that we manage to get the compromises that keep things ticking over. Your Fairness Council will only sharpen up differences that could be papered over with an appeal to the interests of the whole. You've got to have people accepting a lot of blurring at the edges; you can't have *every* management decision questioned from a 'so what's he going to get out of it' point of view; it's going to erode what little authority management's got left, and when that's gone we're going to be really in the soup. You can't run industry without some sort of authority.'

My answer to that is twofold. First I would challenge the conception of authority which such criticism implies, on the grounds set out in Chapter 5. Authority does not *have* to rest on status ascription, or on some 'aura' which impresses the groundlings. It can be rooted in subordinates' perceptions of managers' competence, in their recognition that the competence is being directed to common, shared purposes not to private purposes, in their judgement of managers' honesty, fairness and concern for other people. Secondly, I think beliefs about the limits of rationality are overdone. I see no reason why the ability to reach compromises through rational argument – by separating appraisal-of-fact questions from interest questions – should somehow be a monopoly of people like the Swedes.

II
The linking institutions

9
Goodwill and the spirit of market capitalism

Part I was about the structure of enterprises and the way share-holders and employees get their rewards out of enterprises. Its message might be crudely summed up as follows: don't expect too much of either labour markets or financial markets. A very important kind of efficiency (in the end, much more important than the allocative efficiency which comes from putting resources to their highest-rate-of-return uses) is that which comes from personal commitment to one's job, from human cooperation, mutual trust and goodwill, especially between managers and their subordinates, or between those who set guidelines for incomes policies and those who have to refrain from attempts to subvert or evade them. And to secure that kind of cooperative goodwill one often needs institutional arrangements designed to modify the working of market forces in the interests of what – given the values prevalent in the society – is considered to be 'fair'.

Part II follows the same theme with respect to economic relations outside the enterprise: in this chapter, those linking enterprise to enterprise; in the next, relations between government and enterprise; and in the last, those linking the people who have a role and a stake in the wealth-creating sector of the economy with those who do not.

One of economists' favourite Adam Smith quotations is the passage in *The Wealth of Nations* in which he sets out one of his basic premises:

> It is not from the benevolence of the butcher, the brewer and the baker, that we expect our dinner, but from their regard to their own interest. We address ourselves, not to their humanity, but to their self-love, and never talk to them of our necessities but of their advantages.

I wish to question that sharp opposition between benevolence and self-interest. Perhaps, so that he should be alert for signs of possible bias, the reader should be warned that a prolonged soaking in the writings of Japanese eighteenth- and nineteenth-century Confucianists at an early age has left me with a soft spot for the virtue of benevolence, even a tendency to bristle when anyone too much disparages it. At any rate I wish to argue, apropos of benevolence, or goodwill, that there is rather more of it about than we sometimes allow; further, that to recognize the fact might help in the impossible task of trying to run an efficient economy and a decent society.

I say goodwill rather than benevolence because benevolence, in my Confucian book, though not I think in Adam Smith's, is something shown in relations between unequals, by superior to inferior, the reciprocal of which is usually called loyalty. Goodwill is more status-neutral, more an expression of Hobhouse's 'principle of mutuality'. And it is that broader meaning which I intend. A formal definition of my subject might be: the sentiments of friendship and the sense of diffuse personal obligation which accrue between individuals engaged in recurring contractual economic exchange. (By 'economic', I mean only that the goods and services exchanged should be commonly subject to market valuation.)

Goodwill, of course, is a term of art in the commercial world. In the world of petty proprietorships, familiar to most of us, if you are selling a corner store you set a price on the premises, a price on the stock and a price on the goodwill. Back in the old Marshallian days when economists took their concepts from everyday life rather than trying to take everyday life from their concepts, goodwill meant the same thing to economists too. Palgrave's (1923) dictionary of economics defines goodwill as:

> The expectancy of a continuance, to the advantage of a successor in an established business, of the personal confidence, or of the habit of recurring to the place or premises or to the known business house or firm, on the part of a circle or connection of clients or customers.

The next economics dictionary I find, McGraw-Hill's, exactly half a century later, has a very different definition of goodwill:

> An accounting term used to explain the difference between what a company pays when it buys another company and what it gets in the form of tangible assets (Greenwald, 1973).

Samuelson (1980), to his credit one of the very few textbook writers in whose index one will find the word goodwill, illustrates the concept with J. P. Morgan taking over Carnegie's steel interests, making it clear that Morgan paid a premium well over the market value of the fixed assets primarily because he thereby advanced significantly towards a monopoly position. In other words the goodwill concept is extended to cover not just the benefits accruing to the purchaser of a business from the affectionate or inertial habits of its customers, but also those accruing out of his consequent shift from the position of price-taker to that of price-maker – his en-hanced ability to hold those customers up to ransom. To be fair to the economists who have adopted this use of the term, and partially to retract my earlier gibe, one could say that the standard definition of the term has changed because everyday life has changed. A world in which the terms appropriate to the small owner-managed business formed the dominant norm, has given way to a world dominated by the large corporations and their accountants' terms. Certainly, if anyone wanted to write an Old Testament Prophet-style de-nunciation of modern capitalism *à la* Marx, he could hardly ask for a better illustration than the corruption of the concept of 'goodwill', that primordial embodiment of basic social bonds, into a term for some of the more ugly anti-social forms of profit-seeking.

The disaggregation of factory production

A good place to study the role of goodwill in economic life is the small town of Nishiwaki in western Japan whose industry is almost wholly devoted to the weaving of ginghams, chiefly for export to Hong Kong to be made up into garments for Americans to wear when square-dancing in the Middle West. This is an area where hand-loom weaving goes back some centuries. Power-looms came in during the late nineteenth century and they brought with them the factory system as they did everywhere else. And twenty-five years ago although many small weaving establishments had survived, the bulk of the output was accounted for by larger mills, many of which were part of vertically integrated enterprises with their own cotton-importing, spinning and finishing establishments.

By 1980, however, the picture had changed. The larger mills had closed. The integrated firms had retreated, as far as direct pro-duction was concerned, to their original base in spinning. Most of them were still, either alone or in collaboration with a trading company, producing their own brand cloth, dyed and finished. But they were doing so through the coordination of the activities of a large number of family enterprises. The key family business was that of the merchant-converter who contracted with the spinning company to turn its yarn into a certain type of cloth at a given contract price. The converter would send the yarn to another small family concern specializing in yarn dyeing, then it would go on to a specialist beamer who would wind it on to the warp beams in the desired pattern and also put the warp through the sizing process. Then it would be delivered to the weaver who might do his own weft preparation and the drawing-in (putting the harness on the beams ready for the looms) or might use other family businesses – contract winders or drawers-in – for the process; and so on to the finishers who did the bleaching or texturizing or over-printing.

What is the reason for this fragmentation? What changes in Japanese society and the Japanese economy account for what most orthodox notions of the direction of the evolution of modern economies would count as a regression – the replacement of a system of production coordination within a vertically integrated firm by a system of production coordination between a large number of fragmented small firms; the replacement, to use Williamson's (1981) terms, of coordination through hierarchy by coordination through the market?

I can think of four possible long-term secular trends which might help to explain the change.

The first is the rise in wages and the shorter working week of employees in union-organized firms. Wages are commonly lower in small firms – especially in Japan where the privileged position of the large enterprise elite has become firmly conventionalized, and inter-scale wage differentials are very great. But that is not all. Family enterprisers themselves are often willing to work much longer than 40 hours a week for what may or may not be a larger *total* income than wage workers get, but for an *average* return per hour of labour – hence wage cost per metre of cloth – which is below the employee's wage. If you like, family enterprisers are now willing to exploit themselves more than the unions or the law permit employees to be exploited, a condition which did not hold when *employees* were already working close to the human maximum, a 70-hour week for a subsistence-level wage. The clear superiority of the factory system at that time may have been lost since.

Second, the secular trend to high taxation and higher levels of taxation-allergy make the family enterpriser's advantage in both tax avoidance and tax evasion more attractive – *vide* the growth of the secondary 'black' and quasi-black economy in many other countries.

Third, there is a technical factor: the capital lumpiness of some of the new technology. For example, expensive, large and fast sizing machines can hardly get the through-put necessary to make them profitable within a single firm. Inter-firm specialization becomes the best way of realizing economies of scale.

Fourth, much higher levels of numeracy and literacy mean a much wider diffusion of the accounting and managerial skills necessary to run a small business, the prudent ability to calculate the rentability of investments, and so on.

These are all features common to societies other than Japan and may well be part of the explanation why the woollen industry of Prato has also moved to a fragmented structure in recent years. But there is another factor which applies especially in Japan. The reason why the dominant trend in the West seems to be in the reverse direction – away from coordination through the market towards coordination through the hierarchy of a vertically integrated firm – is, as Oliver Williamson (1979; 1981) is never tired of telling us, because of the transaction costs entailed, the costs arising from the imperfections of markets with small numbers of buyers and sellers in which the bargaining transactions are made difficult by what the jargon calls 'impacted information'. These features so enhance the bargaining power of each party that, when there are no significant economies of scale to be gained by their mutual independence, one party (usually the strong one) buys out the other to put a stop to his 'opportunism' (rapid response not only to price signals – which of course is always admirable – but also to information about vulnerable weaknesses of the other party).

Relational contracting

Here is another of those timeless generalizations concerning 'capitalist economies' about which Japan gives pause. Transaction costs for large Japanese firms may well be lower than elsewhere. 'Opportunism' may be a lesser danger in Japan because of the explicit encouragement, and actual prevalence, in the Japanese economy of what one might call moralized trading relationships of mutual goodwill.

The stability of the relationship is the key. Both sides recognize an obligation to try to maintain it. If a finisher re-equips with a new and more efficient dyeing process which gives him a cost advantage and the opportunity of offering discounts on the going contract price he does not immediately get all the business. He may win business from

one or two converters if they had some *other* reason for being
dissatisfied with their own finisher. But the more common consequence is that the other merchant-converters go to their finishers
and say: 'Look how X has got his price down. We hope you can do
the same because we really would have to reconsider our position if
the price difference goes on for months. If you need bank finance to
get the new type of vat we can probably help by guaranteeing the
loan.'

It is a system, to use a distinction common in the Williamson
school, of relational contracting rather than spot-contracting
(Goldberg, 1981) or, to use Williamson's (1979) recent phrase,
'obligational contracting': more like a marriage than a one-night
stand, as Robert Solow (1980) has said about the modern
employment relation. The rules of chastity vary. As is commonly the
case, for those at the lower end of the scale, monogamy is the rule. A
weaver with a couple of dozen automatic looms in a back-garden
shed will usually weave for only one converter, so that there should
be no dispute about prior rights to the fruits of his looms – no clash
of loyalties. Specialists with faster, larger-volume through-puts, like
beamers – scarcer, more attractive, more in demand, therefore – may
have a relation *à trois* or *à quatre*. For the converters themselves, at
the top of the local hierarchy, there have grown up curious conventions rather like polyandrous concubinage. The Japan Spinners
Association is dominated by the so-called Big Nine firms. None of
the Big Nine will tolerate one of its converters taking cotton yarn
from *another* of the Big Nine. However, one rank below the Big Nine
are the so called New Spinners, and below them the post-war up-
starts, the New New Spinners. A Big Nine spinner will tolerate its
converters having relations with them, though, of course a New
Spinner will not tolerate a relation with another New Spinner. So the
converter can end up with one of each – a first husband, and a
number two, and a number three husband, as it were.

As in nearly all systems of marriage, divorce also happens. That is
why I said that a finisher with a cost advantage could attract other
converters who happen for other reasons to be dissatisfied with their
finisher. When I use the analogy of divorce, I mean traditional
divorce in obligation-conscious societies, rather than the 'sorry I like
someone else better: let's be friends' divorce of modern California.
That is to say, the break usually involves recrimination and some
bitterness, because it usually has to be justified by accusing the
partner of some failure of goodwill, some lack of benevolence or, as

the Japanese phrase is more often translated, 'lack of sincerity'. It is not enough that some external circumstances keep his prices high.

I have made these relations sound like the kinship system of a Himalayan village, but of course the specific patterns of who may trade with whom are of very recent origin. What are entirely traditional however are, first, the basic pattern of treating trading relations as particularistic personal relations; second, the values and sentiments which sustain the obligations involved, and third such things as the pattern of mid-summer and year-end gift exchange which symbolizes recognition of those obligations.

But how on earth, the economist will want to know, do the prices and ordered quantities get fixed? The answer seems to be that, once established, prices can be renegotiated at the initiative of either party on the grounds either of cost changes affecting either party, or else of changes in the competitive conditions in the final market in which the brand cloth is sold. There are also fringe spot-markets for cotton yarn and grey cloth, and the prices ruling in these markets and reported in the daily textile press provide guides. To further complicate the issue there is some collective bargaining. Both the weavers and the converters in Nishiwaki have their own cooperative union and guide prices may be agreed between them; alternatively, in some other textile areas, the weavers' cooperative sets a minimum contract price which its members are not supposed to undercut, though there is general scepticism about the effectiveness of such an agreement.

Relational contracting between unequals

The basic principles on which these price and quantity negotiations rest appear to be threefold: first, that the losses of the bad times and the gains of the good times should be shared; second, that in recognition of the hierarchical nature of the relationship – of the fact that weavers are more dependent on converters than converters are on weavers – a fair sharing of a fall in the market may well involve the weaker weaver suffering more than the converter, having his profits squeezed harder; but third, the stronger converter should not use his bargaining superiority in recession times, and the competition between his weavers to have their orders cut as little as possible, to drive them over, or even to, the edge of bankruptcy.

It is in the interpretation of these principles, of course, that ambiguity enters. Benevolence all too easily shades into exploitation when the divorce option – the option of breaking off the relationship – is more costlessly available to one party than to the other. There is, even an officially sponsored Association for the Promotion of the Modernization of Trading Relations in the Textile Industry in Japan which urges the use of written rather than verbal contracts in these relationships and is devoted to strengthening moral constraints on what it calls the abuse – but our economic textbooks would presumably call the legitimate full use – of market power. As for the nature of such abuse, surveys conducted by the Association show that suppliers with verbal contracts are more likely to have goods returned for quality deficiencies than those with proper written contracts (Seni kindaika, 1980). Weavers will wryly remark that returns become strangely more common when the price is falling (and a rejected lot contracted at a higher price can be replaced by a newly contracted cheaper lot).

The work of the Association is an interesting illustration of the formal institutionalization of the ethics of relational contracting, doing perhaps for contracting what the post-war labour reform did to transform the employment system of large firms from manipulative paternalism into something less exploitative and better described as welfare corporatism – a process which I have described elsewhere (1973). All one can say about the contemporary trading reality is that those ethics appear to be sufficiently institutionalized, to be sufficiently constraining on a sufficient number of the firms and families in Nishiwaki textiles, for the pattern of trading I have described to be a stable and viable one.

That pattern is repeated in many other areas of the Japanese economy – between, for example, an automobile firm like Toyota and its subcontractors. Here again, the obligations of the relationship are unequal; the subcontractor has to show more earnest goodwill, more 'sincerity', to keep its orders than the parent company to keep its supplies. But equally the obligatedness is not entirely one-sided, and it does limit the extent to which the parent company can, for example, end its contracts with a subcontractor in a recession in order to bring the work into its own factory and keep its own workforce employed.

I have been taken to task by Okumura (1982b), the Japanese economist who has written most interestingly about these relationships, for speaking of the 'obligatedness' of a firm like Toyota as if a corporation was, or behaved like, a natural person. But I still think the term is apt. The mechanisms are easy to intuit, if ponderous to spell out. First of all, there are *real* personal relations between the purchasing manager of Toyota and the manager or owner-manager of a sub-contracting firm. But, of course, managers change frequently, particularly in firms with a bureaucratic career-promotion structure like Toyota. It is part of the commitment of such managers, however, that they identify with their firm and their department. If it were said, therefore, in the world outside, that Toyota, or its purchasing department in particular, had behaved badly by playing fast and loose with its subcontractors, the manager responsible would feel that he had let his firm down. If the accountants in the costing department urge a tough line with sub-contractors, he may well tell them that they are short-sighted and even disloyal to the firm in underestimating the importance of its reputation. These seem to me readily understandable mechanisms by which the patterns of obligation between individual owner-managing converters and weavers in Nishiwaki can be duplicated between corporations.

I have discussed two cases of obligated trading relationships which are explicitly hierarchical. If there is any doubt as to who pecks whom in the pecking order look at the mid-summer and year-end gifts. Although it may vary depending on the precise nature of the concessions sought or granted in the previous six months or anticipated in the next, the weaver's gift to the converter will usually cost more than vice versa – unless, that is, either of them miscalculates the gift inflation rate, the point of transition, say, from Black Label against Suntory Old to Napoleon brandy against Dimple Haig.

Relational contracting between equals

But these relations are not confined to the hierarchical case. Even between firms of relatively equal strength the same forms of obligated relational contracting exist. Competition between Japanese firms is intense, but only in markets which are (*a*) consumer markets and (*b*) expanding. In consumer markets which are not expanding cartelization sets in rather rapidly, but that is a rather different story which does not concern us here. What does concern us here are markets in producers' goods, in intermediates. And for many such commodities markets can hardly be said to exist. Take steel, for instance, and one of its major uses for automobiles. The seven car firms buy their steel through trading companies, each from two or three of the major steel companies, in proportions which vary little from year to year. Prices, in this market, are set by the annual contract between the champions – Toyota on the one side, New Japan Steel on the other.

It is the concentration of such relationships which is the dominant characteristic of the famous large enterprise groups, known to Japanese as *grūpu*, and to foreigners, usually, as *zaibatsu* or *keiretsu*. There are six main ones of which the two best known are Mitsui and Mitsubishi. These groups are quite distinct from the hierarchical groupings of affiliates and subsidiaries around some of the giant individual firms like Hitachi or Matsushita or MHI. The Mitsubishi group, for example, has no clear hierarchical structure. In its core membership of 28 firms, there is a certain amount of intra-group share ownership – on average about 26 per cent of total equity widely dispersed throughout the group in 3 or 4 per cent shares. There is a tiny amount of interlocking directorships – about 3 per cent of all directors' seats. And most of the firms have the group bank as their lead bank, and bank of last pleading resort, but that bank provides on average less than 20 per cent of all loan finance to group firms. The only thing which formally defines the identity of the group is the lunch on the last Friday of the month when the presidents of every company in the group get together, often to listen to a lecture on, say, the oil market in the 1990s, to discuss matters like political party contributions, sometimes to hear news of, or give blessings to, some new joint venture started up by two or more member firms, or a rescue operation for a member firm in trouble Okumura (1982c.)

But the main *raison d'être* of these groups is as networks of pre-ferential, stable, obligated *bilateral* trading relationships, networks of relational contracting. They are not conglomerates because they have no central board or holding company. They are not cartels because they are all in diverse lines of business. Each group has a bank and a trading company, a steel firm, an automobile firm, a major chemical firm, a shipbuilding and plant engineering firm and so on – and, except by awkward accident, not more than one of each. (The 'one set' principle, as the Japanese say.) Hence, trade in producer goods within the group can be brisk. To extend earlier analogies, it is a bit like an extended family grouping, where business is kept as much as possible within the family, and a certain degree of give and take is expected to modify the adversarial pursuit of market advantage – a willingness, say, to pay above the market price for a while to help one's trading partner out of deep trouble.

The preference for relational contracting: Cultural sources?

The starting point of this discussion of relational contracting was the search for reasons to explain why it made sense for the spinning firms producing brand cloth to coordinate production neither through hierarchy in the usual Williamson sense of full vertical integration, nor through the market in the normal sense of continuously pursuing the best buy, but through 'relational contracting'. It was, I said, because such arrangements could be *relied on* in Japan more than in most other economies. There is one striking statistic which illustrates the extent to which it is in fact relied on. The volume of wholesale transactions in Japan is no less than four times as great as the volume of retail transactions. For France the multiple is not four but 1.2; for Britain, West Germany and the USA the figure is between 1.6 and 1.9.

How does one explain the difference between Japan and other capitalist economies? Williamson has 'theorized' these 'obligational relationships' and explained the circumstances in which they will occur – when the extent to which the commodities traded are idiosyncratically specific (such that the economies of scale can be as easily appropriated by buyer or by seller), and the extent to which either party has invested in equipment or specialized knowledge for the trading relationship, are not quite such that vertical integration makes sense, but almost so. He also asserts, that in such relationships quantity adjustments will be preferred to price adjustments and price adjustments will be pegged to objective exogenous indicators (though he allows, in passing, for the not very 'relevant' or 'interesting' póssibility that 'ad hoc price relief' might be given as an act of kindness by one party to the other (Williamson, 1979)).

Perhaps Williamson has evidence that this is the way it is in America and the fact that his argument is couched in the terms of a timeless generalization merely reflects the tendency of American economists to write as if all the world were America. (Just as British economists write microeconomics as if all the world were America, and macroeconomics as if all the world were Britain.) Or perhaps he does not have much evidence about America either, and just assumes that 'Man' is a hard-nosed short-run profit-maximizer suspicious of everyone he deals with, and allows everything else to follow from that. At any rate Williamson's account does not provide the tools for explaining the difference between the Japanese and the British or American economies. There is nothing particularly idiosyncratic about the steel or cloth traded in many of the obligated relationships, little specialized assets involved (though there are in automobile subcontracting). Nor is there clear avoidance of price adjustments: weaving contract prices, in fact, look like graphs of nineteenth-century business cycles.

Clearly we have to look elsewhere for an explanation. Try as one might to avoid terms like 'national character' which came naturally to older generations of sociologists, in favour of the scientific pretensions of, say, 'modal behavioural dispositions', it is clearly national differences in value-preferences, or dispositions to action, with which we are concerned. And, as Macfarlane (1978) showed, when he looked into the origins of English individualism, to attempt to explain *those* takes one on a long speculative journey – at least into distant ill-recorded history, even if, for ideological reasons, one wishes to rule out genes. But it is legitimate and useful to ask: what are the concomitants of these dispositions? What do they correlate with? Are they an expression of more general traits?

One candidate explanation is that the Japanese are generally very long-term-future-oriented. At this moment, for example, the Japanese Industry Ministry's Industrial Structure Council is already composing what it calls a 'Vision' of the shape of the world economy in the mid-1990s. The economist is likely to seize on this explanation with relief, because it will allow him to ignore all dangerous thoughts about benevolence, and accommodate the relational contracting phenomenon in the conventional microeconomics of risk aversion and low time-discounts. Any sacrifice of short-run market advantage is just an insurance premium for more long-term gains.

And he would find some good evidence. Nakatani (1982) has recently done an interesting calculation comparing 42 large firms inside one of the large kinship groupings like Mitsui and Mitsubishi which I have just described with a matched sample of 42 loners. The loners had higher average profit levels and higher growth rates in the 1970s. *But* they also had a considerably higher dispersal around the means. The group firms were much more homogeneous in growth and profit levels. What went on in the groups, he concluded, was an overall sacrifice of efficiency in the interests of risk-sharing and greater equality.

Relational contracts, in this interpretation, are just a way of trading off the short-term loss involved in sacrificing a price advantage, against the insurance that one day you can 'call off' the same type of help from your trading partner if you are in trouble yourself. It is a calculation, perhaps, which comes naturally to a population which until recently was predominantly living in tightly nucleated hamlet communities in a land ravished by earthquake and typhoon. Traditionally, you set to, to help your neighbour rebuild his house after a fire, even though it might be two or three generations before yours was burnt down and your grandson needed the help returned.

But you could be *sure* that the help *would* be returned. And this is where we come back to Adam Smith. The Japanese, in spite of what their political leaders say at summit conferences about the glories of free enterprise in the Free World, and in spite of the fact that a British publisher with a new book about Adam Smith can expect to sell half the edition in Japan, have never really caught up with Adam Smith. They have never managed actually to bring themselves to *believe* in the invisible hand. They have always insisted – and teach in their schools and their 'how to get on' books of popular morality – that the butcher and the baker and the brewer *need* to be benevolent as well as self-interested. They need to be able to take some personal pleasure in the satisfaction of the diners quite over and above any expectation of future orders. It is not just that benevolence is the best policy – much as we say, rather more minimally, that honesty is the best policy. They do not doubt that it is – that it is not a matter of being played for a sucker, but actually the best way to material success. But that is not what they most commmonly say. They most commonly say: benevolence is a duty. Full stop. It is that sense of duty – a duty over and above the terms of written contract – which gives the assurance of the pay-off which makes relational contracting viable.

Note that this is a little different from what Durkheim (1893) had in mind when he was talking about the non-contractual elements in contract and refuting Spencer's claim that modern societies were held together solely by an organic web of individualistic contracts. Durkheim was talking about the intervention of *society* both in enforcing the basic principles of honesty and the keeping of promises, and in regulating the content of contracts, deciding what was admissible and what offended social decency or basic human rights. And in Durkheim's book it is the consciousness of an obligation imposed by society as a whole – or, on its members, by an occupational group of professional practitioners – which enforces those rules. In Japanese relational contracting, by contrast, it is a particular sense of diffuse obligation to the individual trading partner, not to society, which is at issue. To put the matter in Parsons's terms, relational contracting is to be understood in the universalism–particularism dimension, whereas the Durkheim point relates to the fifth dichotomy that Parsons later lost from sight: collective-orientation versus individual-orientation. To put it another way, the Japanese share with Durkheim the perception that contract, far from being fundamentally integrative, is basically a marker for conflict. Every harmonization of interest in a contract simply conceals a conflict either latent or adjourned, as Durkheim said. The Durkheim solution is to have universalistic social institutions contain the conflict – an engine-cooling system to take away the heat. The Japanese prefer particularistically to reduce the friction in all the moving parts with the emollient lubrication of mutual consideration.

Perhaps one should not overdraw the contrast, however, in view of the empirical fact that the Japanese, who stand out among other capitalist societies for their addiction to relational contracts, also stand out as the nation whose businessmen and trade unionists seem to have a more lively sense of their obligated membership in the national community than those of other nations. Japan has fewer free-rider problems in the management of the national economy; patriotism seems to supplement profit-seeking more substantially in, say, the search for export markets, and so on. Perhaps the common syndrome is a generalized dutifulness, or to put it in negative form, a relatively low level of individualistic self-assertion. I am reminded of the Japanese scholar and publicist, Nitobe. In his lectures in the USA in the 1930s he used to tell the national character story about the international prize competition for an essay about the elephant. In his version the Japanese entry was entitled 'The duties and domestication of the elephant'.

But there is, it seems to me, a third element in the Japanese preference for relational contracting besides risk-sharing and long-term advantage on the one hand and dutifulness on the other. That is the element, to go back to Parsons's variables again, best analysed in his affectivity/affective-neutrality dimension. People born and brought up in Japanese society do not much *like* openly adversarial bargaining relationships, which are inevitably low-trust relationships because information is hoarded for bargaining advantage and each tries to manipulate the responses of the other in his own interest. Poker is not a favourite Japanese game. Most Japanese feel more comfortable in high-trust relations of friendly give-and-take in which each side recognizes that he also has some stake in the satisfaction of the other.

All of which, of course, is not necessarily to say that the effect is genuine. Pecksniffs can do rather well in exploiting these relationships when they are in a stronger bargaining position – the point made earlier about the ambiguities of these relationships.

Employment practices and relational contracts

This is the moment, perhaps, to pause in this discussion of trading relations in markets for intermediates and capital goods to point up the similarities between Japanese practice in such relations, and the Japanese preference for 'organization-oriented' employment systems, for firms of a Community pattern. An organization-oriented employment system replaces the spot contract, easy-hire-fire assumption on which much writing about labour markets is based, by a long-term – indeed career-perspective – relation. The contract is seen, in fact, less as any kind of bilateral bargain, than as an act of admission to an enterprise community wherein benevolence, goodwill and sincerity are explicitly expected to temper the pursuit of self-interest. The parallel between relational contracting in the intermediates market and in the labour market is obvious. There can be little doubt that the same cultural values explain the preferred patterns in both fields.

Relational contracting and efficiency

But anyone looking at the competitive strength of the Japanese economy today must also wonder whether this institutionalization of relational contracting, as well as serving the values of risk-sharing security, dutifulness and friendliness *also* conduces to a fourth valued end – namely economic efficiency. Any economist, at least any economist worth his neo-classical salt, would be likely to scoff at the idea. Just think, he would say, of the market imperfections, of the misallocation and loss of efficiency involved. Think how many inefficient producers are kept out of the bankruptcy courts by all this give-and-take at the expense of the consuming public. Think of the additional barriers to entry against new, more efficient, producers. Gary Becker, in a lecture at the London School of Economics in 1980 claimed that give-and-take trading was even an inefficient way of being altruistic. In the end, he said, through greater survival power, you get more dollars-worth of altruism by playing the market game and then using the profits to endow a 'charitable foundation like Rockefeller, which I suppose is true and would even be significant if 'altruism' were a homogeneous commodity indifferently produced either by being friendly to your suppliers or by posthumously endowing scholarship.

But that apart, the main point about sub-optimality is well taken. The Japanese economy is riddled with misallocation. A lot of the international dispute about non-tariff barriers, for example, has its origin in relational contracting. Take the market for steel which I mentioned earlier. Brazil and Korea can now land some kinds of steel in Japan more cheaply than Japanese producers can supply it. But very little of it is sold. Japan can remain as pure as the driven snow in GATT (General Agreement on Tariffs and Trade) terms – no trigger prices, minimal tariffs, no quotas – and still have a kind of natural immunity to steel imports which the British Steel Corporation would envy. None of the major trading companies would touch Brazilian or Korean steel, especially now that things are going so badly for their customers, the Japanese steel companies. Small importers are willing to handle modest lots. But they will insist on their being landed at backwater warehouses away from where any domestic steel is going out, so that the incoming steel is not seen by a steel-company employee. If that happens, the lorries taking the steel out might be followed to their destination. And the purchaser, if he turned out to be a disloyal customer, would be marked down for less than friendly treatment next time a boom brings a seller's market. What distortions, an economist would say. What a conspiracy against the consumer! What a welfare loss involved in sacrificing the benefits of comparative advantage! If the Japanese economy has a good growth record, that can only be *in spite of* relational contracting and the consequent loss of efficiency.

And yet there are some good reasons for thinking that it might be *because of*, and not *in spite of* relational contracting that Japan has a better growth performance than the rest of us. We come back, again, to the distinction between allocative efficiency, and 'x-efficiency' which I made at the end of Chapter 1. The term 'x-efficiency' was coined by Harvey Leibenstein (1966) to refer to all those virtues I referred to there: the ability to plan and programme, to cooperate without bitchiness in production, to avoid waste of time or of materials, and so on. Leibenstein, theorizing about these behaviours, boils them down to two elements: effort and the pursuit of rationality, and individuals' determination of how much of each to give to their job, given – presumably – how much of each they have available to give in the first place. As a demonstration of the importance of these factors, Leibenstein tries a comparison between a measure of allocative efficiency – the estimated welfare loss from tariffs and price distortions in a number of empirical cases – and a measure of x-efficiency – the inefficiency which one can infer from the range in capital and labour productivities within certain industries as between 'best practice' and 'worst practice' firms. The welfare loss here is the extra output which would be obtained if all firms did as well as the best. Of course, x-efficiency always turns out to be the greater, but one does not have to accept that particular test to agree that the distinction between allocative efficiency, which has to do with rational responses to price signals, and all those other kinds of efficiency which raise the productivity of inputs in a business organization is an extremely useful one, and x-efficiency is as good a catch-all term for the second bundle of qualities as any other.

It is in the second dimension, in its effect in making 'best practice' better and more widely diffused, that the Japanese system of relational contracting has merits which more than compensate for its price-distorting consequences. To take the case of employment and the lifetime commitment first, the compensatory advantages which go with the disadvantage of inflexible wage costs, are reasonably well known. In a career employment system people accept that they have continually to be learning new jobs: there can be great flexibility; it makes more sense for firms to invest in training; the organization generally is more likely to be a learning environment open to new ideas. If a firm's market is declining, it is less likely to respond simply by cutting costs to keep profits up, more likely to search desperately for new product lines to keep busy the workers it is committed to employing anyway. Hence a strong growth dynamism, and so on.

As for relational contracting between enterprises, there are three things to be said. First, the relative security of such relations encourages investment in supplying firms. The spread of robots has been especially rapid in Japan's engineering subcontracting firms in recent years, for example. Second, the relationships of trust and mutual dependency make for a more rapid flow of information. In the textile industry, for example, news of impending changes in final consumer markets is passed more rapidly upstream to weavers and yarn dyers; technical information about the appropriate sizing or finishing for new chemical fibres is passed down more systematically from the fibre firms to the beamers and dyers. Third, a by-product of the system is a general emphasis on quality. What holds the relation together is the sense of mutual obligation. The butcher shows his benevolence by never taking advantage of the fact that the customer doesn't know rump from sirloin. If one side fails to live up to his obligations, the other side is released from his. According to the relational contract ethic, it may be difficult to ditch a supplier because, for circumstances for the moment beyond his control, he is not giving you the best buy. It is perfectly proper to ditch him if he is not giving the best buy and not *even trying* to match the best buy. The single most obvious indicator of effort is product quality. A supplier who consistently fails to meet quality requirements is in danger of losing even an established relational contract. I know that even sociologists should beware of anecodotal evidence, but single incidents can often illustrate national norms and I make no apology for offering two:

1   The manager of an automobile parts supplier said that it was not uncommon for him to be rung up at home in the middle of the night by the night-shift supervisor of the car factory 60 miles away. He might be told that they had already found two defective parts in the latest batch, and unless he could get someone over by dawn they were sorry, but they'd have to send the whole lot back. And he would then have to find a foreman whom he could knock up and send off into the night.

2   The manager of a pump firm walking me round his factory explains that it is difficult to diagnose defects in the pump-castings before machining, though the founders are often aware when things might have gone wrong. 'I suspect', he said cheerfully, 'our supplier keeps a little pile of defective castings in the corner of his workshop, and when he's got a good batch that he thinks could stand a bit of rubbish he throws one or two in.'

I leave the reader to guess which is the Japanese and which the British story.

How uniquely Japanese?

So if it is the case that relational contracting has some *x*-efficiency advantages which compensate for allocative inefficiencies, what lessons should we draw from all this about how to run an efficient economy and build a decent society? The first thing to do is to look around at our economies and take stock of the ways in which benevolence/goodwill actually modify the workings of the profit motive in daily practice. So far I have referred to relational contracting as something the Japanese have an *unusual* preference for. But that is far from saying that they are *uniquely* susceptible to it. If we look around us we will find far more evidence of relational contracting than we think. This is so even in America where capitalism seems generally to be more hard-nosed than in Europe. In an interesting article written twenty-years ago, Stewart Macaulay (1963) examined the relative importance of personal trust and enforceable legal obligation in business contracts in the USA. He found many businessmen talking of the need for give-and-take, for keeping accountants and lawyers, with their determination to press every advantage, out of direct dealings with other firms. Among those with experience of large projects in the civil construction industry it is a truism that successful work requires a bond of trust between client and contractor. Engineers, as fellow-professionals, sharing a commitment to the project's success, can create that trust. Their firms' lawyers can endanger it by the confrontational stance with which they approach all potential conflicts of interest. Recently I got a simple questionnaire answered by seven managers or owner-managers of weaving mills in Blackburn, asking them about their trading practices, and found a strong preference for stable long-term relationships with give-and-take on the price, and a claim that, on average, two-thirds of their business already was that way. In the British textile trade, of course, Marks and Spencer's is well known for its relational contracting, squeezing suppliers a bit in times of trouble but not ditching them as long as they are maintaining quality standards, and accepting some responsibility for helping them technically. In the supermarket world, Sainsbury's have the same reputation, supposedly very different from that of Tesco's which believes that frequent switching of suppliers encourages the others to keep the price down.

Quality, affluence and relational contracting

There may be something very significant in the nature of these examples. Try adding together the following thoughts:

1 Marks and Spencer's is well known for one thing besides relational contracting, namely that it bases its appeal on product quality more than on price.

2   There is also an apparent relation between a quality emphasis and relational contracting in Japan.

3   Sainsbury's is up-market compared with Tesco's which is for keen pricers.

4   Japan's consumer markets are *generally* reckoned to be more middle class, more quality-sensitive and less price-sensitive than Britain's. (Textile people, for instance, have given me rough estimates that if one divides the clothing market crudely into the AB groups, fastidious about quality and not too conscious of price, and the rest who look at price and superficial smartness rather than the neatness of the stitching, in Britain the proportions are: 25:75; in Japan 60:40.)

5   Japan of the 1920s, and again in the post-war period, was much more of a cut-throat jungle than it is today. Not the ethics of relational contracting, nor the emphasis on product quality, nor the lifetime employment system, seem to have been at all characteristic of earlier periods of Japanese industrialization.

Add all these fragments together and an obvious hypothesis emerges that relational contracting is a phenomenon of affluence. It is when people become better off and the market-stall haggle gives way to the world of *Which?*, where best buys are defined more by quality than by price criteria, that relational contracting comes into its own.

It does so for two reasons: first, because quality assurance has to depend more on trust. You always *know* whether the butcher is charging you sixpence or sevenpence. But if you don't know the difference between sirloin and rump, and you think your guests might, then you *have* to trust your butcher: you have to depend on his benevolence. Also, I suspect, when affluence reduces price pressures, any tendencies to prefer a relationship of friendly stability to the poker-game pleasures of adversarial bargaining – tendencies which might have been formerly suppressed by the anxious concern not to lose a precious penny – are able to assert themselves. Japan's difference from Britain, then, is explained both by the fact that the cultural preferences, the suppressed tendencies, are strong, *and* by the fact that the price pressures have been more reduced by a much more rapid arrival at affluence, and consequently a greater subjective sense of affluence.

Again there is a parallel with labour markets and employment contracts (see the cell 'affluence' in the bottom left-hand corner of

Fig. 2 in the last chapter). It is when people have become less desperate to get the money for tomorrow's bread, or even the Sunday joint, that they can begin to think of other things they want out of their job, like security and dignity. There is, then, not just a formal similarity between the growth of relational contracting and trends towards organization-oriented employment forms which we charted in the first part of this book; they spring also from the same roots.

Relational contracting, rigidites and economic policy

Economists have occasionally noted these trends, but have generally treated them as market imperfections, basically lag problems of the long and the short run, for in the end habit always succumbs to the pursuit of profit. And among imperfection problems they have found them less interesting to analyse than other kinds like monopoly. And those bold souls among them who *have* taken aboard the new phenomenon of stagflation, and tried to explain the tendency for contraction in demand to lead to a contraction in output, not a fall in price, to increased unemployment but only slow, delayed and hesitant deceleration in the rate of wage increase, have rarely recognized the importance of a general growth in relational contracting, of the effects on the effectiveness of fiscal and monetary regulators of the fact that more and more deals are being set by criteria of fairness, not by market power. More commonly, they speak of the growth of oligopoly on the one hand and on the other of trade-union monopoly consequent on statutory job protection and higher welfare benefits. They have explained stagflation, in other words, not as the result of creeping benevolence – the diffusion of goodwill and mutual consideration through the economy – but as the result of creeping *male*volence, increasing abuse of monopoly power. And the cure which our modern believers in the supreme virtues of the market have for these 'rigidities' is a deflation stiff enough to restore the discipline of market forces: in product markets to make firms competitive again and force the inefficient out of business; in labour markets to weaken trade-union monopolies and get firms hiring and firing according to their real needs.

A few people have given relational contracting and its growth the importance it is due. Albert Hirschman (1970), first in this as in so many things, described the general syndrome of voice and loyalty taking over from exit and entry as the characteristic disciplining force of advanced capitalism. More recently Arthur Okun (1981) developed before his untimely death a similarly comprehensive view of relational contracting and, moreover, explained in his *Prices and Quantities* its connection to worsening stagflation. He wrote of the tendency in capital goods and intermediate markets, and to some extent in consumer markets, for what he called 'customer markets' to grow at the expense of 'auction markets', and of the corresponding growth of 'career labour markets', employment characterized by an implicit contract of quasi-permanence – 'the invisible handshake' is one of his phrases – all adding up to what he called a 'price-tag economy' as opposed to the 'auction economy' of orthodox textbooks. What I do not think he fully took aboard is the way in which social relations in customer markets and career labour markets take on a moral quality and become regulated by criteria of fairness. Consequently, his remedies, apart from being far more imaginatively interventionist, are not so very different in kind from the more common marketist prescriptions for dealing with the rigidities of stagflation. That is to say, he also concentrates on devices to change (*a*) incentives and (*b*) expectations under the unchanged assumption that economic behaviour will continue to be guided solely by short-run income-maximizing considerations.

There is no mention of Japan in his index, and none that I have discovered in his book. But if we do think of Japan, a society which has far-more-developed forms of relational contracting than ours and glories in it, *and* achieves high growth and technical progress, we might think of a different prescription.

It would run something like this. First, recognize that the growth of relational contracting can provide a very real enhancement of the quality of life. Not many of us who work in a tenured job in the academic career market, for example, would relish a switch to freelance status. I hear few academics offering to surrender their basic salary for the freedom to negotiate their own price for every lecture, or even demanding personally negotiated annual salaries in exchange for tenure and incremental scales. And if you overhear a weaving-mill manager on the telephone, in a relaxed friendly joking negotiation with one of his long-standing customers, you may well wonder how much more than the modest profits he expects would be required to tempt him into the more impersonal cut-and-thrust of keen auction-market-type competition.

But the second point is this. Having recognized that relational contracting is something that we cannot expect to go away, and that inevitably a lot of allocative efficiency is going to be lost, try to achieve the advantages of x-efficiency which can compensate for the loss.

This prescription has a macro-part and a micro-part. The macro-part includes, first of all, maintaining the conditions for free competition in the one set of markets which remain impersonally competitive – the markets for final consumer goods. This is necessary to provide the external stimulus for the competing chains or pyramids of relational-contract-bound producers to improve their own internal efficiency. It means on the one hand an active competition policy, and on the other, where monopoly is inevitable, the organization of countervailing consumer watchdog groups. Also included in the macro-part are first, an incomes policy, since if it *is* now criteria of fairness rather than the forces of supply and demand which determine wages in career labour markets, those fairness criteria had better be institutionalized. Second, it means an attempt, if you like, to tip the ideology towards benevolence; in Fred Hirsch's (1977) term, to try to revive an 'ethos of social obligation' to replenish the 'depleting moral legacy' which capitalism inherited from an earlier more solidary age, not least by stressing the importance of quality and honest thoughtful service, the personal satisfactions of doing a good job well as a source of pride and self-respect, letting profits be their own reward, not treated as if they were a proxy measure of social worth. The Department of Industry's recent announcement of an £8 million programme of subsidies for improvement in quality assurance systems in British factories is at least a recognition of the enhanced importance of quality in the modern world, even if there are no signs of a recognition that this might entail new attitudes and values (or a new affirmation of old ones now lost), a move away from the spirit of *caveat emptor*.

The micro-part of the prescription involves a better specification of the ethics of relational contracting. Previous chapters have dwelt at length on ways in which we should, for instance, take the growth in job tenure security not as an unfortunate rigidity, but as an opportunity to shift enterprises towards the Community model and reap the production advantages which can come from a shared interest in the firm's success, from cooperation and free flow of information and the flexible willingness not to insist on narrow occupational roles. There is room for more discussion about, and perhaps prescription for, desirable patterns of subcontracting relationships. We have seen that the Japanese have created a campaign-type organization to establish codes of business practice which will prevent exploitation of subcontractors. The French, too, have been considering the regulation of subcontracting, establishing criteria for designing what constitutes unfair dismissal of the subcontractor, parallel to those for employees. Presumably they would have to make protection dependent in some way on performance criteria: the quality and conscientious timing of deliveries. Clearly, it is a field of considerable difficulty, rather less amenable to regulation than the employment relation. But it is one where regulation could pay off in improved national competitiveness, and when we again have a government which acknowledges that the state may play a positive role in national economic development, it is something which would well repay study.

It is to the role of the state that the next chapter turns.

10
Industrial policy

There is still a widespread idea that industrial policy is about civil servants presuming to pick winners and giving emergency aid, after dubious backroom politicking, to lame ducks. The Thatcher government, and especially its first industry minister, Sir Keith Joseph, was originally going to have none of it. But in fact, central government grants to industry, running at the equivalent of 6 per cent of fixed capital formation in 1977 were still as high as 5 per cent in 1982. Some of the lamest of lame ducks continue to be subsidized. The Support for Innovation subsidy scheme, after a brief moratorium caused by over-subscription, has resumed at a level much higher than in 1979. The Alvey programme is spending £250 million in the hope that Britain can remain – or once again become – a significant participant in artificial intelligence/advanced computer developments. All those forces which, as noted in Chapter 1, are turning the regulatory state into a developmental state, are not to be gainsaid, even under a government with such an extreme 'marketist' ideology as that of Mrs Thatcher.

It is worthwhile, therefore, looking at Japan, which has had a developmental state for over a century, as a comparative reference point. It is not easy to take a balanced view about Japan's industrial policy. Those who fear Japanese competition and seek every excuse for putting up protective barriers against it, are prone to offer a highly conspiratorial version of the 'Japan Incorporated' view: secret planning headquarters in Tokyo at which businessmen and officials, bent on seeking revenge for the Second World War, target certain Western industries for destruction by concerted competition. Free-market ideologues (especially Japanese free-market ideologues on the international conference circuit) are liable to suggest that the Japanese government's feeble efforts at industrial policy have contributed nothing to Japan's success, that the government has put very little money into industry, that government advice and guidance has been largely spurned.

For a more comprehensive view of the role of Japanese industrial

policy – the nature of administrative ·guidance, the research initiatives, the use of preferential interest rates on Japan Development
Bank loans, the sectoral coordination of investment in temporary
investment cartels, and of counter-cyclical market management in
recession cartels, and so on – I would refer the reader to the
companion volume to this one, *Flexible Rigidities* (Dore, 1986). Here
I shall discuss, selectively, some aspects of particular relevance to
British practice.

The civil service

One obvious place to start is with the role of government, and
especially the civil service, in consensus creation. Let us start, as in
other chapters, with the cultural factors. Japanese society is (*a*) a
good deal more culturally homogeneous, and (*b*) more future-
oriented, than Britain. The future-orientation would surely show up
in any comparative content analysis of Japanese and British newspapers and bookstores. One might divide futurological writings
roughly into two kinds; on the one hand there is what one might call
the 'gee-whizz' literature about the undated future when we are all
going to work contentedly at home, occasionally popping out to dig
the garden in between bouts of communing with our computer
terminals, our fast-food terminals, our kidney dialysis terminals, and
whatever. In the other category – of sober futurology – I would put,
say, serious attempts to forecast the structure of the British economy
in the early 1990s, attempts to find a rational basis for answering
policy questions like whether it is sensible to try to preserve a
weaving industry or aluminium-smelting industry in this country.
Perhaps the average Englishman in his magazine-reading and TV-
watching comes across a piece of gee-whizz futurology, say, once a
fortnight and a piece of sober futurology once every two months. If
you live in Japan, it is more likely to be every other day for the gee-
whizz kind and every week or so for the more sober kind.

A Canadian political scientist interested in the degree of future-
orientation of civil servants in different countries, asked a sample of
them what were the most important problems on which they were
working, and then categorized those problems according to the
extent to which they related pressingly to the present, or to the
medium- to longer-term future. The percentage of civil servants
whose chief professed concerns related to the future were: in Italy 3
per cent, in France 7 per cent, in West Germany 8 per cent, in

Sweden 9 per cent, in the United States 13 per cent, and in Japan 35 per cent (Kubota, 1980).

Newspapers are a good guide in the homogeneity dimension, too, three major dailies almost indistinguishably of – say – *Daily Telegraph*-like quality being taken in 4–8 million homes each. The absence of really class-conscious, culturally disparate class divisions, and the pattern of politics that goes with it, have a lot to do with this, of course. There is no clearly polarized political competition between genuinely alternative governments. There is, instead, a permanent majority party and a number of fringe parties which act as gadfly critics of the established power, and draw their support from various segments of the least advantaged – but nevertheless rarely totally alienated – groups in society. The dominant party, the Liberal Democratic Party, is led by politicians who specialize in charisma and interest-group brokerage accompanied by a good deal of corruption. They are not expected to be intelligent or to get much of a grip on the ministries they are awarded, basically by seniority and faction-loyalty criteria. They are not given much time to get a grip in any case. Constant reshuffling to maximize the number who get to be ministers is the way faction leaders pay their debts.

All of which are ideal conditions for technocracy. (Civil servants also handle, for example, all the detailed parliamentary scrutiny of legislation going through the Diet: the minister only has to give the initial speech and look wise for the rest of the time.) Policy initiatives generally come from the civil service rather than from party committees, and it is by taking initiatives, having ideas and pushing them, as well as being a loyal performer of the tasks assigned to him, that a civil servant gets the reputation as a high-flyer which puts him on the promotion fast track, i.e., gives him the prospect of making section chief rank at the age of 31 rather than the average age of 33–4, at being one of the 15 per cent of his contemporaries who become a bureau chief, and so on.

The public service is highly regarded in Japan. Books like *The Bureaucrat and SS Japan* (Kakizawa, 1978) – conversations on policy issues with ten early-40s high-flyers from different ministries – and *Portrait of the new bureaucrats who 'produce'* [theatrical sense] *Japan* (Sakakibara, 1977) find a ready readership. The civil service has no difficulty recruiting from the very best universities. The sort of Oxbridge science graduate who gets snapped up in Britain by merchant banks and investment analysts, lured by the prospect of being in the top 0.05 per cent of salary earners in a few years time, goes instead, in Japan to a penurious post in the Ministry of International Trade and Industry, 50 to 60 per cent of whose intake in recent years has been from science faculties.

As a vice-admiral wrote to *The Times* (2 August 1985) apropos of princely increases in public sector top salaries awarded by Mrs Thatcher to make them competitive with the private sector, Britain too used to be able to expect the cream of its cream to work for 'honour, pride, love of one's work, membership of one of the orders of chivalry, adequate but moderate pay and a pension sufficient to enable the holder to continue work without pay' – a formulation as consonant with traditional Tory values as one could wish. Five years of the Thatcherite New Right, however, and the denigration of the public service and devaluation of every motive except the pursuit of material advantage in the market, have taken their toll. The Civil Service Commissioners now find it difficult to fill administrative posts with people of the calibre they have traditionally sought. Changes of personnel practice – bringing in supposedly talented outsiders for key jobs at market rates – have had a further demoralizing effect. According to the *Economist* (12 July 1986), not a single Assistant Secretary or Senior Principal resigned between 1981 and 1983. In 1984 and 1985, 43 Assistant Secretaries and 62 Senior Principals left.

One thing that Japan ought to make us rethink, therefore, is the role of the public service in general and of the administrative Civil Service in particular. The success of the Japanese at macroeconomic management – which is clearly a consequence of the skill and leadership of the economic ministries, and their ability to maintain effective consultation mechanisms with the banks and business – and the success of Japan's long-term economic development strategy, to which their contributions are less obviously measurable but real, both suggest the following:

1   An elite administrative civil service is a highly valuable national asset. I mean 'elite' in the triple sense: (*a*) most intellectually able; (*b*) respected for their ability and their disinterestedness; and (*c*) conscious of and valuing that respect, and prepared to be disinterested in order to go on earning it.

2   Gingering up the Civil Service by bringing in brilliant outsiders, and breaking through established seniority constraints to accelerate the promotion of high-flyers, may well be (see Chapter 7) at the expense of committed dedication. The muting of inter-

personal competition, and the mutual trust and cooperativeness which stems from that, depends on people believing themselves to be respected and treated fairly and without favouritism, i.e., according to known rules, not whimsical superiors' discretion. That may go, and the loss may be a good deal greater than the gain.

Consensus

The point about the role of consensus in economic behaviour can be put this way. To a Japanese surveying the British scene, it would seem incredible that there should not be a widespread and anxious appreciation of the fact that in ten years' time the fall-off in North Sea oil yields will leave the British economy with a potentially horrendous external payments problem; that the trends in the balance of trade in manufactures are ominously set in directions that promise to exacerbate rather than cure that situation; that other long-term trends include: a declining world share in the provision of financial services, a steady increase in the proportion of manufacturing capital which is foreign-owned, a declining British share in the patent registrations in the UK, a steadily increasing share in the profits of major British companies which derives from their operations overseas, and so on. It seems incredible, that is, that there should not be a certain range of ideas and assumptions about the long-term future with which people – or to be more specific, the readers of the quality newspapers, say – are wholly familiar, the subject of sufficiently commonplace references in everyday political speech-making, that they can be referred to in shorthand words – 'the mid-90s problem', 'the manufacturing trade-balance problem', etc. – as the Japanese talk of 'the population-ageing problem', 'the structural creditor-nation problem', the taken-for-granted starting points for policy discussion.

For that is the point of this kind of consensus about the long-term perspective. It provides legitimation for measures with long-term pay-offs, especially those likely to be bitterly opposed by people – in declining industries, for example – who are likely to suffer dislocation, albeit compensated dislocation, in the short run.

The actual devices used by the Japanese to help create this kind of consensus are not complex. There is the annual Economic White Paper which is the responsibility of the Economic Planning Agency, a kind of George-Brown-type Department of Economic Affairs which has survived as a respected and scholarly, if not power-wielding department. (Part of *our* problem, of course, is not being able to respect anything which does not have power.) The White Paper has been supplemented, indeed overshadowed, in recent years, by the so-called 'Visions' which are the responsibility of MITI. These are broad-sweep looks at major world trends and how they affect Japan, published every three or four years. They are drafted within MITI, and legitimized by a large unwieldy body called the Industrial Structure Council (where trade unionists, *qua* trade unionists have about the same, almost token, representation as women's groups). It is lucidly written. Great care is taken to en-capsulate major ideas in a few pithy phrases, as one can easily do with an ideographic script. (For example, in eight characters: 'Economy-wise major country: resource-wise minor country'; or in four: 'A nation that must live by its technological expertise' – both chapter headings in the 1980 *Vision*). And it sells over 20,000 copies. (A new Vision was in gestation for 1986, but the Ministry has decided to hold off for a while. The reasons are complex, but include a reluctance to give ammunition to foreign critics of greedy Japanese targeting of the sunrise industries.)

The importance of this broadly-shared 'appreciation of the national situation' is not easy to pin down, but there must surely be some pay-off from a shared sense of the *inevitability* of certain long-term trends, those arising from the growth of Third World (and now especially Chinese) manufacturing, from the substitution of non-ferrous, non-metallic materials for steel, from the finite nature of fossil fuel reserves, from changes in demographic structure, from the need to insure against Saudi Arabia exploding in religious war, and so on. It must surely play some part in mobilizing support for gov-ernment-sponsored measures to ease structural adjustment: specially favoured treatment for growth sectors of high international com-petition, special let-them-down-gently treatment for declining in-dustries to encourage them to fade away and not make trouble.

Britain has a body purpose-built for the creation of the same sort of consensus: the National Economic Development Council (NEDC) and its staff in NEDO. And yet its impact on national life and national thinking is minimal; there are many of its monthly meetings which only the readers of odd corners in the *Financial Times* get to hear about.

Nobody can do much about the predominant structural reason for this: the fact that Japan is a consensual technocracy and Britain a competitive partyocracy with two contending class-based parties, both capable of electoral victory. This predisposes members of the Japanese Industrial Structure Council to acknowledge and emphasize the possibility of unanimity about 'the objective situation' and of NEDC to start from the initial assumption that claims about 'the objective situation' made by opposing parties are probably just tendentious manoeuvrings for some party/class advantage. The sooner the SDP–Liberal Alliance can bring Britain into an age of centrist coalitions the better.

There are perhaps other structural weaknesses. NEDO is free-floating and peripheral to the in-fighting of daily decision-making. The MITI officials who staff (guide, direct, dominate) the Industrial Structure Council are intimately involved in the day-to-day formulation of policy. An agreed statement in that body about, say, the future of the textile industry, is a reliable forecast of legislative measures to follow. Given the British tradition of ministerial control over policy it might not help much to bring NEDO into the DTI, but more NEDO–DTI or NEDO–Treasury joint working groups and reports would help to build up, at least a civil servant consensus about the range of feasible policy options. One possible way of doing this would be for NEDO to have the job of coordinating a joint Civil Service brief for Parliamentary Select Committees launching out on a major inquiry.

But there are two other features of Japanese industrial policy which deserve close attention besides the famous consensus: the role of industry associations, and the capacity for bargained compromise to protect those who suffer from inexorable economic change.

Industry associations and transparency

'Government hand-outs' will always attract scorn and suspicion as long as they involve discretionary subventions to individual firms, prompted by who knows what lobbying – overt by constituency MPs, covert by friends of friends. There have, on occasion, been murky rescues in Japan too – one famous shipyard case is well documented (Johnson, 1982). But they are rarities. Most of the industrial policy measures carried out by the Japanese government are policies for whole industries, negotiated with the industry associations concerned, or with all the leading firms of the industry collectively.

In some cases the government simply plays a coordinating role as in the 'investment cartels', legitimating what would otherwise be reprehensible collusion under the Fair Trade Act to prevent over-enthusiastic competitive investment in large plant (petrochemicals, for instance) from leading to excess capacity, or the 'recession cartels' organizing concerted and shared production cut-backs at the bottom of the trade cycle. In others, the government adds a little financing to its initiatives, as in the various research clubs which it has initiated (of which the Fifth Generation Computer project is currently the most famous), or in the plans for coordinated capacity cuts in declining industry: in shipbuilding, for example, with a development corporation to buy up scrapped equipment and vacated land, funds for retraining and rehousing displaced workers.

But in all these cases, MITI (or the Ministry of Transport, or Health, in the case of certain industries) has a reliable interlocutor; an industry association. This is not like a typical British trade association with an ex-brigadier as its secretary, a minor information-distributing and lobbying role and the membership of only half the firms in the industry. Japanese firms belong to their industry associations in the way that a Japanese farmer hardly conceives of the possibility of not belonging to the hamlet association in the settlement in which he lives. They are for the most part staffed by former managers and engineers of leading firms, and they provide common research and statistical services on a quite generous scale. Japanese firms have a lively sense, both of 'the industry as a community' and, more generally, of the need for careful thought about where to set the boundary between cooperation and competition, between free information-exchange and secrecy. The answer varies with circumstances, but in general they are inclined to favour a good deal more cooperation and free information-exchange than most British firms would allow.

The result of all this is to make the operation of industrial policy a rather more open and transparent process than it is in Britain, and one, on the whole, less surrounded by suspicion and allegations of corrupt dealing. It means that there is more careful devising of rules (yes, bureaucratic rules: it *is* the devising of rules that takes arbitrariness out of administration). An example is the elaborate set of criteria negotiated between the Ministry of Transport and the shipbuilding industry for deciding the size of capacity cuts and how they should be calculated and what level of compensation should be guaranteed. Another is the accumulated wisdom evolved for the running of part-government-funded research clubs. One problem which arises in such research is the ownership of patent rights, something which is of some concern to the Alvey project whose guidelines on the matter are seen by some to be not wholly viable. In Japan, the state owns all rights in 100 per cent government-funded research. Tricky questions arise, however. When a patentable breakthrough owes only its final topping-off to the government-funded cooperative project and builds substantially on knowledge a firm had *before* it started to put its research into the project pool, why should the state claim the whole property right? The solution the Japanese have arrived at at least puts such disputes on a firm factual basis. When they come into the project and undertake research on a particular theme as part of their contribution, the firms write down all the relevant research findings they have already achieved, on the basis of which their further research will be built. This is then put in a sealed envelope and stored in the safe of the club project's secretary, for opening if there is any subsequent dispute.

Perhaps (to stand on its head my argument in Chapter 4 and Chapters 8 and 9 that sometimes what the Japanese achieve naturally, by dint of cultural heritage, we need laws to bring about) precisely *because* Japan is a society where personal ties and obligations are so strong, it needs much more bureaucratic regulation to overcome personal favouritism and corruption than do we who are much more given to acting on universalistic rather than particularistic principles. But that would be rather largely to overestimate the reliability of gentlemanly codes of honour in modern Britain, especially after the recent scandals in Lloyd's and the Stock Exchange. We could well, here, in the matter of the meticulousness of fine-print regulation of government's dealings with industry, take a leaf out of Japan's book.

And we need, even more, to ponder seriously the role of industry associations and the need for reliable channels of transparent transaction between industry and government. We have such bodies already created in the 'Little Neddies' which are part of NEDO. Some are active in playing precisely their intended role, but even they operate with the most exiguous of staffing resources. If there is ever a government inclined to take these matters seriously again, the revitalization of the Little Neddies should play an essential role.

Taking care of the losers

The other general feature of Japanese industrial policy is that it is *not* ruthless. It *does* believe that market forces cannot in the long run be gainsaid; that there is no way Japan will become a major textile exporter again, for instance. But it is not assumed that everything has to be left to market forces. It expects and allows for a bit of delay in the operation of those market forces, a bit of protection or subsidization here and there to ease their impact. This is the (allocative efficiency) price to be paid for generating the sense of fairness which makes smooth structural adjustment possible. Thus, a lot of the detail of industrial policy measures show the state intervening to protect 'the little man'. In the shipbuilding industry reorganization, capacity cuts were graduated: 45 per cent for the biggest firms, but 15 per cent for the smaller ones. 'Administrative guidance' from the Ministry of Finance prevents the big banks from flooding the country with cash dispensers for fear of what it would do to the little banks. The spread of supermarkets is subtly control-led on behalf of the small retailer (and the allocative inefficiency is apparent for all to see in the figures for per capita productivity in the commercial sector). Ministry officials and the big spinning firms would like to see the end of the loom-registration system designed in the 1950s to discourage excess capacity in the weaving industry. They have had Industrial Structure Council sectoral committee re-ports endorsing that objective since the mid-1970s. But the small weavers and their cooperatives who derive some benefits from·the system have so far succeeded in preventing a date from being set for reaching that objective; and so on.

Admittedly the mangement of decline is easier in a country like Japan where, firstly, the general growth dynamic is such that even relatively declining areas are still receiving spill-over benefits (in social infrastructure, etc.) from general growth in the economy; secondly, many of the declining industries are in the traditional small cottage-industry sector with a high average age of proprietor and a prospect that waiting a while *will* bring a natural wastage solution, and thirdly, the declining sectors are not most vocally represented by trade unions which can add a generalized anti-establishment class antagonism to the 'defence of the losers' plea. 'The little man' who gets defended in Japan (the main losers from structural changes so far) are mostly drawn from among the 25 per cent of the working population who are self-employed. In Britain where the self-employed still number less than 10 per cent of the working population, the victims are mostly employees made redundant, who present much more intractable problems.

Nevertheless, the main point still holds. It is not the case that a distortion of market forces can never be justified *on efficiency grounds*. It can, if the loss that comes from tying up resources in less-than-optimally productive sectors is balanced by the reduction in conflict and sabotage, the eventual resigned acceptance of the inevitable which comes from demonstrating a concern for fairness, from showing that those who talk about economic policy having to promote the 'good of the whole' do include everybody in the whole.

And, to summarize the main earlier parts of this chapter: it helps to achieve these ends if you can sustain a properly organized, properly corporatist, system of transparent bargaining between government and industry, insulated from the private lobbying pressures of individual firms, individual MPs, individual 'old boys'. It also helps if the society has a general respect for the public service, sustained by the knowledge that the public service does, indeed, recruit the best and the brightest.

11
Meritocracy, employment and citizenship

I have referred several times to the differences between Japan's and Britain's educational systems. The Japanese system is one of the most single-mindedly meritocratic in the world. It is similar in that respect to those of the other post-Confucian countries – both Chinas, Singapore and both Koreas – and to Eastern Europe. But the degree of genuine equality of opportunity and aspiration – greater, probably, even than that of Czechoslovakia which approaches it most closely – and the subtle refinements in its processes of social selection make it a paradigm of social organization well worth contemplation.

Japan might well be called the most Platonic society on earth, or the Bravest New World on earth, but there is a difference. When Plato talked about the people of gold and silver and of brass, and when Huxley peopled his dystopia with Alphas and Gammas, they had inherited genetic differences in mind. So do the Japanese when they talk about the differences between a Tokyo University graduate and a high-school drop-out. But (apart from the difference that they see the social hierarchy in terms of a spectrum rather than of categorical Alpha/Beta divisions) they *talk* as if the Tokyo graduate is separated from the drop-out not primarily by genetic endowment, nor by class-based differences in opportunity (it is remarkable how little even left-wing parties talk about that), but by effort. And indeed, even if IQ is the dominant element, to the extent that one can measure these things (and don't forget the greater homogeneity of social environments in Japan, making the contribution of IQ differences to developed-ability differences even greater than would be the case in Britain), effort does play a considerable part in deciding who emerges with what kind of label from the school system.

And it is the role played by effort – effort, unlike genetic endowments, under the control of the will, of the centre of intentionality, the locus of the sense of self – which gives legitimacy to the system, creates the presumption that people 'deserve' the material and prestige and power rewards which, by virtue of their

qualification label, society accords them. The way the system works
is roughly as follows.

Nowadays Japanese children are educated until the age of 15
wholly in mixed-ability classes in mixed-ability schools. At 15, competitive entrance examinations sort them out into five or six grades of
high school each of which draws on a very narrow segment of the
ability range. There is the universally acknowledged 'top school' of
the district which gets a lot of its graduates into the top universities;
there may be one or two second-rank schools which get their
children into medium-rank universities; then third-rank schools,
many of them vocational, which get few of their graduates into any
university at all but a lot into junior colleges, and so on down to the
bottom-rank schools where morale is lowest, drop-out rates highest,
and subsequent prospects the least hopeful. Ninety-four per cent of
the children completing compulsory middle school now go on to the
three-year high schools, and any child can take the entrance examination for any school in the district. But amazingly, despite the
strict limitations on numbers and strict competitive entrance
criteria, very few children fail to enter the school they apply for.

This is thanks to a highly efficient system of commercial mock
tests, two or three of which every child takes in middle school. The
secret lies in the fact that the marking of these tests in each subject is
standardized on national population norms. The results of these
tests, plus informal quota diagnostics in counselling, ensure that each
high school gets just about its quota of applicants from the right
ability range. The same process sorts out the 18-plus age group
between the universities of different rank. Once, Tokyo University,
at the peak of the hierarchy, used to get seven or eight applicants for
every place; today only two or three and these quite clearly the *crème
de la crème*. Those who have little chance now know that fact ahead
of time, for the mock test firms will tell you on the basis of last year's
out-turn what sorts of standard scores are needed for entrance to
which faculties in each one of the 500 universities in the land.

It is all about people 'learning their place'. Thanks to the mock
tests and their national-population-norm standardization, people do
learn their place because the tests' story about their place does not
change all that much. Year after year it says: for maths you're a 50-
per-center, for Japanese language a 60-per-center. The 5 or 6 per
cent of children who leave school at the age of 15 rather than go to
high school had been told that they have no place in the meritocracy,
and must make out as best they can in the shadow world of family

enterprise, the low-paid menial employments which remain. It is not surprising that the Japanese Prime Minister should have gained popularity by setting up a high-powered commission to study the whole educational system, what the Japanese call, disparagingly, a system of mock-test-standard-score education.

But the system works. The last piece of the institutional complex is job recruitment. The top firms recruit their managers from top universities and their lower-ranking workers from the best of the third-rank high schools whose pupils do not go on to university, the second-rank firms from the second-rank universities and so on. The gradation is clear, not only in recruitment patterns, but in business indicators. In many industries there is a clear hierarchy, made relatively stable partly by the differential recruitment of bright people itself, partly by all those factors which tend to make oligopolies stable in any society. Take airlines, for example, where the state regulatory system adds extra stability to the market-share ranking. Number one airline gets the pilots with the highest scores in pilot school, the most attractive stewardesses. Everyone assumes that most of those working for airline number two would have preferred to be working for number one, but just did not make it. Number one can afford to pay more; it has the more entirely stable workforce, because once in it few want to leave. As noted earlier, lifetime employment, the key element in Japan's Community model firm, developed in the elite firms of Japan's early industrialization precisely by such mechanisms. To revitalize its workforce, number one airline can get away with earlier retirement ages than number two or number three airline, precisely because many of its former employees can go to work for numbers two and three for a few years after they have retired. And as with airlines, so too – even more so – with universities and in other business sectors, though the division is often more categorical, as between the Big Five and the rest in the steel industry, for instance.

Lifetime employment is obviously a pivotal part of this system. The link between school performance and initial recruitment becomes a definitive determinant of life-chances because of the lack of mobility. The fact that recruitment *is* recruitment for a lifetime career makes recruiters' concern with general ability rational. And school performance is the best indicator of general ability available to them. The fact that any given firm with a given place in the hierarchy recruits a relatively ability-homogeneous group of employees from its appropriate place in the school-output spectrum, means that a seniority-constrained promotion system, not differentiating too much between high-flyers and plodders, makes good sense.

Of course, Japanese society is not as rigidly structured as I have suggested. There are industries – particularly consumer goods industries – where the hierarchy of firms is not stable. And even in Japan the cognitive abilities measured by school achievement tests are not the only determinant of individual careers. Other qualities – the drive and determination and dynamism which Lydall (1976) once called the D-Factor: a sense of responsibility, physical stamina, personal presence and ability to impress others – all play a part. Those qualities too, however, are incorporated into, tamed by, the bureaucracies, public and private, which claim the bulk of those in the top half of the ability spectrum. They are accommodated by the discretionary leeway left in their promotion systems. They are precisely the qualities expected to differentiate the high-flyer on the seniority-promotion fast track from the plodder (perhaps of identical or even better school record) on the slow one. Only in those (to be sure, not inconsiderable) sectors of the economy dominated by small-scale entrepreneurship are these qualities of prime importance, making it the one fluid sector of Japanese society where social destinations are not easily predictable from educational qualifications.

The pattern of our future?

Is Britain going the same way, towards just such a type of society? At many points in this book I have suggested that perhaps we are. Chapter 3 discussed the 'spectrumization' of employment, with wage levels graded – within the same occupation – by the size, prestige and power of the employing organization and the presumed ability level of the worker. It set out all the indications that Britain, too, might be moving more towards a Community model of the firm with reduced mobility, more internally structured promotion systems and consequently more careful checking of ability potentials for recruitment purposes. Chapter 6 discussed the increasing tendency to ground authority in competence certified by educational levels, and tendencies towards stricter meritocratic selection within the educational system itself.

It seems a paradox. We once had a highly hierarchical society. Feudal England was a place where some were born villeins and some were born knights and lords of the manor. Legal rights, social honour, every aspect of life-chances, differed between those of high and those of low estate. Gradually, for six centuries, society has become more fluid as it has become more affluent. The story of recent centuries is the story of increasing egalitarianism, a story succinctly encapsulated in T. H. Marshall's lectures, *Citizenship and Social Class* (1950). It is a story, in his version, first of the establishment of equality of civil rights, equality before the law, then equality of political rights with the extension of the suffrage, and finally equality of social rights with the establishment and gradual raising of a welfare minimum, received not as a charity but 'as of right'. Can it be that this trend will reverse itself, that we can now look forward to a New Hierarchical Order; one, this time, in which high and low estate is determined, not by birth but by educational achievement (with the possibility that, for genetic as well as social reasons, the correlation between birth-class and educational achievement, between parent's occupational 'level' and child's occupational 'level', will become increasingly high)?

There are some non-trivial reasons for thinking that might be so. The persistent trend towards greater egalitarianism is clear. It can, almost certainly, be traced to the social and economic changes which have resulted, over the centuries, from the accumulation of scientific knowledge and the transformation of production techniques. But there is one other enduring trend, even more directly a consequence of the accumulation of scientific and technological knowledge. It may be enunciated in a general form as follows: the more sophisticated the technology a society uses, the more salient becomes the *awareness* of differences in natural talent – especially of the kind roughly measured in IQ tests – and the more social arrangements are likely to take account of them.

Paradoxically, in other words, the more egalitarianism has grown, the more inequalities – the ineluctable inequalities of genetic endowment – have come to count.

I cannot give correlated time series in proof of this proposition; I can only appeal to commonsense perceptions. In pastoral societies almost anyone could master the arithmetic needed for the simple purposes to which arithmetic was put, like counting sheep. Even calendrical arithmetic was simple enough that few astronomers had sons who were not able to grasp the secrets of the trade over a long childhood training. With only primitive voice-training techniques, most people could manage acceptable standards of yodelling. Today, only tenors whose sophisticated training shows them to be gifted get listened to. And the skills required to run an atomic power plant or a jumbo jet, to design an integrated circuit or an experimental corrective institution, are such that it is not within the capacity of all, or even of a large percentage, of the population to acquire them in a reasonable period of time. And it is very much in the interests of the rest of us, firstly, that those who do these jobs should have acquired those skills, and secondly, that people should not embark on the lengthy and expensive training to acquire them unless there are strong reassuring indications that they will succeed. And among the various dimensions of talent – musical and athletic talent, telly-personality charm, and so on – it is the general all-purpose mental talents, measured by IQ tests, which are most widely seen as relevant.

The economy of this kind of talent, in other words, becomes of increasing importance for social efficiency, and through a variety of institutional initiatives, partly by government, partly by those in charge of work organizations, and partly by those looking after the interests of occupational groups, the devices for channelling talent begin slowly to accumulate. China started two thousand years ago, of course, but in Britain the first formal ability tests for jobs came with the East India Company in the nineteenth century, then for the home Civil Service, finally even for the Foreign Service. The forerunner of the British Medical Association started in a modest way, selecting recruits by general academic ability in 1851. The ICIs, the Unilevers and the Anglo-Burma Oils – eventually even the Vickers and the English Electrics – started recruiting bright university graduates for special management career tracks in the early decades of the century.

Today, job opportunities differ starkly for those who have done history or engineering at Oxbridge (entered by a good performance in an especially difficult entrance examination, or by getting three or four As at A-level), compared with those who have followed an identical syllabus at a redbrick university (entered with, say, two Bs and a C) and those coming from a similar course at a polytechnic (entrance: a B and two Es). Further down the spectrum, for the last 30 years since the creation of the CSE, not just the top 25 per cent of the age group but every child has left school with qualifications – or with a significant absence of qualifications – which enable employers to 'place' them roughly in the general ability spectrum. And the new unified 16 + General Certificate of Secondary Education, albeit in some senses a continuation of the continuing egalitarian trends in education, is designed to be if anything more efficient in this proxy ability-measure function.

Employment in the future

Once again, looking at Japan as Japan is, can help us to see Britain as Britain might be becoming. Suppose that all these signs of the times do indeed point in a Japanese direction. Should we be applauding – as I, by and large, have endorsed – all the trends which seem to be promoting the development of Community model forms? Or should we be drawing back in horror? And if so, to what? If we see a New Hierarchical Order emerging as the given end-product of the growth of meritocracy, should we then let Oxbridge admissions be determined once again by family pull or by money?

I imagine not. But we should, at least, be a bit more aware of what is happening, of the long-term consequences of present trends, and of correctives to some of those consequences, correctives which may need preparing for, long before their problematic aspects become acute.

I have in mind particularly the consequences for employment patterns and, consequentially, for our notion of citizenship and basic citizen equality. What is implied by the fact that the increasing sophistication of our technology – including our systems for gathering and sorting and evaluating information and processing it into decisions – makes native ability, learning capacity, trainability, call it what you will, more important? If one can imagine a scale of the intellectual demandingness of jobs, to be measured, say, by the number of weeks or years it takes a person of given intelligence to master it, then the intellectual demandingness of the average job is continually rising. And the pace of change is fast. In my boyhood there was almost nothing around the house whose workings I could not understand except the radio, and I had friends who knew all about that. Today the house is full of devices I would not have the hubris to remove the lid from. Is it possible that we shall move, or have already moved, into an era when there will be too few bright people to do competently all the difficult jobs that need doing and too few jobs for the less bright people to do?

This was a fear freely and openly discussed some thirty years ago, before the more recent manifestations of egalitarianism made it seem like pushing people below the dignity minimum even to single out 'people of low ability' as a category. Norbert Wiener (1950) in the late

1940s already spoke of the first industrial revolution destroying the jobs which required physical labour and the second industrial revolution destroying the more routine jobs requiring manual and clerical skills. Kurt Vonnegut in 1952 wrote a splendid and disturbing novel depicting the New Hierarchical Order which results. In his *Player Piano* world, measured IQs alone determine the individual's allocation in a centrally controlled occupational hierarchy. But only the top two or three deciles of the ability range are needed for genuinely productive jobs. The rest of the population are either in the army where, although they have no weapons, they can 'hide their hollowness beneath twinkling button and buckles, crisp serge and glossy leather', or else, more dispiritingly, they are in the makework Reconstruction and Reclamation Corps – 'the reeks and wrecks' – enjoying, as they used to say about Camden Housing Department, 'leisure on the rates'. The *welfare minimum* is high and rising. But what one might call the *dignity minimum* – that basic modicum of respect which each accords to all by virtue of their shared citizenship – has plummeted. And what is more, the elite's concern with the dignity minimum has disappeared. A 1985 Englishman cannot read Vonnegut's description of how that happened without a shiver of recognition. The older generation of engineers and managers, he records, had been through the war and they knew that valour and comradeship and decency and good feeling were values for judging men as important as smartness. So they were always slightly sheepish about their eliteness. But not so the younger generation: now, he says, 'this elite business, this assurance of superiority, this sense of rightness about the hierarchy topped by managers and engineers – this was instilled in all college graduates, and there were no bones about it'. He might be describing the transition from the wet generation of the late Earl of Stockton to the generation of the hard young men of Mrs Thatcher's circle.

Certainly, fiction is no infallible guide to reality, but the reasoning which led Vonnegut – and many of his contemporaries – to make such predictions in the 1950s bear thinking about today in a Britain where not even the most hopeful growth projections for the economy have unemployment falling to 10 per cent before 1990. Can there be any connection between the development of the New Hierarchical Order (HNO) and the persistence – what appears to be the structurally in-built nature – of unemployment?

Japanese unemployment

Japan would suggest not. Japan combines the capitalist world's most developed version of NHO with one of the capitalist world's lowest unemployment rates – less than 3 per cent by the official figure and not more than a percentage point or two higher if the data are recalculated with American definitions. Among the major reasons for Japan's low level of unemployment are:

1 Japan's economic managers (see Chapter 4 on incomes policy) have got a grip on inflation and also insulation of their interest rates from hot money flows. They can afford to maintain a high level of domestic demand.

2 The Japanese manufacturing sector has shown itself adept at innovating, not only in labour-saving production processes, but also in producing new products for itself and the rest of the world. Contrary to the situation in countries like Britain which adopt all the new labour-saving machinery which destroys jobs, but rely on imports for a lot of that new machinery – and other new consumer products too – in Japan productivity increases in manufacturing have been exceeded in several of the last five years by output increases, i.e., numbers working in manufacturing have actually increased.

3 Japanese levels of state-guaranteed welfare are lower than in Britain. Although there is minimum-wage legislation (currently about £1.50 an hour) jobs can be offered at wages which are a lower percentage of the average wage than in Britain. Hence, a wider range of jobs – jobs yielding a lower added-value at market valuations – are viable and on offer.

4 To the financial deterrent to reliance on welfare is added a much stronger social-stigma deterrent than in Britain.

5 There is a much larger sector of self-employment/family enterprise employment in Japan (about 25 per cent of the working population) which absorbs (into involuntary low-income work-sharing, in effect) many of those who would otherwise be unemployed.

So far, so good. But the danger of growing unemployment is coming to be increasingly talked of in Japan. Though the unemployment rate is still low, it shows a slow secular trend of increase. And unemployment is beginning to show some of the same characteristics as in European countries, namely, concentration among younger age groups (*getting into* a job in the first place is the difficult thing in a lifetime-employment economy), and concentration among those who, by the standards of the New Hierarchical Order, are judged to be of lower ability, lower employability.

Structural trends and employment: the arguments

The vast majority of economists in this country would deny that the increase in British unemployment over the last decade (in fact it has been steadily increasing for over two decades) has anything to do with such phenomena as an employability threshold or an ability range. It is adequately explained, they would say, first by the fact that the unholy tail-chasing cousins of cost-plus pricing and price-plus wage demands have made inflation endemic, and this Government knows no other means of inflation control besides deflation.

Secondly, they would say, it is, indeed, in part a consequence of technical change. Labour-saving capital goods have, to be sure, destroyed jobs. But past experience shows that this is a temporary state of affairs which cures itself in two ways. On the one hand, the improvement in productivity creates new wealth, which makes a demand for new goods and services which creates jobs. But all this takes time. If the wealth it creates takes the form of profits which are then invested in South Africa, it may take quite a lot of time – particularly if the wealth-holders consume a lot of their accruing income in Barbados or Tuscany – but in the *long run* it will happen. On the other hand, part of the increase in productivity has been taken, in the past, in the form of increased leisure rather than increased goods and services, and shorter working hours, longer annual holidays, have produced an aggregated job-sharing effect. That's also bound to happen again, but that also takes a considerable adjustment time. But there is no reason at all to suppose that we won't eventually get back to full employment.

The contrary thesis is that, while the added-value of a job performance is in part a function of the capital with which, and the organizational structure in which, it is performed, there are – at any given level of technology – upper limits on the contribution any individual can make, depending on the skills to which he has the ability to be trained; secondly, there *is* therefore such a thing as an employability threshold, defined as the capacity to be trained to do a job which, at market prices, produces an added-value greater than, and so can yield a wage greater than, the welfare minimum; and thirdly, while this threshold shifts according to the aggregate level of demand and its effect on market prices, these cyclical shifts apart, there is a trend for the 'threshold at maximum feasible demand' to rise over time as a combined result of (*a*) the selective elimination by labour-saving technology of low value-added jobs, and (*b*) the raising of the guaranteed welfare minimum.

That argument suggests a demand-side inhibition to the process whereby, hitherto, work has been shared through the introduction of shorter hours and so on. Employers will be reluctant to let hours contract and to take on extra people, because they will find it harder to get people of the requisite ability for the jobs that remain. There are also, possibly, supply-side inhibitions to the work-sharing process. Preferring more leisure rather than more pay – which a lot of people have to do, for the shorter working week/longer holiday/ earlier retirement means of redistributing work opportunities to operate – is less likely when people are working only 35 to 40 hours a week than when they were working 60-hour weeks and had one week's holiday a year. And, today, there are more powerful trade unions to enforce any preference workers may have for more money rather than more leisure. Add to this – on the demand side again – the preference many employers exhibit (because of training costs, employment protection, and so on) for giving their existing workers overtime rather than taking on extra workers.

An economist with neo-classical equilibrium economics bred in his bones will have none of this. Sooner or later, the job structure will adapt to the skills and talents available: market forces may work imperfectly, but they do work in the long run to get the best use out of all the resources to be employed. The remoteness of that ideal theoretical world from the one we live in should be apparent to anyone who takes a train journey through the northern parts of England and Scotland. Is every piece of land productively adapted to its most profitable agricultural or recreational use? Doubtless it would be *if* all the landlords depended on income from their land for their livelihoods, and *if* Britain were a closed economy. But (the analogy to the 'welfare minimum' effect) if the owner of a bit of Northumberland gets by well enough on the income from his stocks and shares, why should he not keep his estate in fallow wildness for his own enjoyment, rather than trying to grow carrots on poor soil, in an English summer, to compete with those Spanish and Italian juggernauts coming nightly across the Channel?

It is all too easy to see the mechanisms whereby unemployment first becomes concentrated among the least able, and then can become an inbuilt feature. One needs to separate a recession effect and a technical change effect. For contemporary British unemployment one needs to understand both.

First the recession effect. Let us simplify reality by using Phelps Brown's (1977) notion of an 'ability to work' (ATW). While recognizing that different kinds of jobs require a wide range of different abilities, let us assume that one can crudely subsume them in a single ATW dimension because there is a significant degree of inter-correlation between them, much as one can crudely subsume in a general measure of 'intelligence' individuals' scores on a variety of measures: of memory, of spatial imagination, of verbal ability, ability to calculate, and so on. Suppose that the working population falls into one of five ATW grades and these correspond with job grades. Suppose that there is full employment and, roughly, ATW Grade 1 people are in Grade I jobs, Grade 3 people in Grade III jobs and so on. Recession hits all along the line. People are made redundant in every grade. The unemployed are, in ATW Grade terms, a faithful cross-section of the population.

But suppose that the recession goes on and on. People cling to their jobs in recessions, but there is still a good deal of job-quitting, some sacking, some filling of vacancies. Grade 1 people – both those made redundant and the new Grade 1 youth – naturally apply for Grade I jobs, but there are not enough to go round because of the recession. After six months they become dispirited and start applying for Grade II jobs. Employers with Grade II jobs are glad to have them, and give them preference over Grade 2 people. And that means that even more Grade 2 people are 'bumped down' into Grade III jobs, and still more Grade 3 people are bumped down to Grade IV jobs, while the number of Grade 4 people bumped down is almost enough to take up *all* the new offerings in Grade V jobs, leaving the unemployment concentrated among the Grade 5 people plus a few 'resisters' in higher categories who refuse to take jobs below their 'proper level'. Some Grade 5 people who were in jobs before the recession may keep them; the new Grade 5 youth entrants have no chance of getting a foot in the door.

The technical-change effect which overlies this slightly complicates the story. Grade I jobs expand. There is no bumping down from Grade I to Grade II. Quite the contrary, there is a sucking up, and there might well be a good deal of less-than-fully-competent performing of Grade 2 people in Grade I jobs. (Though whether one needs to go to the lengths of paying Laszard Brothers several million pounds to find someone competent enough to run a steel corporation, as Mrs. Thatcher did to hire Mr. McGregor, is a different matter.) But there is an over-and-above-recession contraction in the number of jobs available from Grade III downwards. And the contraction in Grade V is the greatest. Again, since jobs disappear by abstention-from-replacing more than by bankruptcy or actual sacking, it is the young would-be entrants who suffer.

Evidence

And is there evidence of these processes? Yes, a certain amount.

The rise in unemployment is not new. There has been a steady rise in the numbers unemployed at the peak of each business cycle since the mid-1960s, long before our present monetarist era, which argues some kind of structural change.

The same is true of the change in the relation of vacancies to unemployment. In the 1960s, pretty regularly, as one would expect, the number of vacancies went up when unemployment went down and vice versa. But not now. Between the second quarter of 1981 and the fourth quarter of 1983, vacancies rose by 65 per cent from 90 to 160,000. Simultaneously employment fell and unemployment increased by over half a million.

Another recent tendency is that as the length of incompleted terms of unemployment has increased with the increase in the number of long-term unemployed, as the economy picks up, the length of repeated terms of unemployment has decreased. There seems to be a sharpening difference between the 'discouraged unemployed' who find it difficult to get into any job, and the 'mainline participants' who find it easy, as soon as they lose a job, to find another.

Unemployment is increasingly concentrated in families. Only 31 per cent of unemployed men had a wife or child working in 1983, compared with 61 per cent of employed men, a gap which had widened by 11 percentage points since 1976 (UK Central Statistical Office, 1985).

The people whose employability is most obviously in question – handicapped people, people with severe learning difficulties – find it increasingly difficult to find the 'sheltered employment' they used to find. The sorts of jobs in which they could make *some* contribution even if not one quite worth their wage, are just not there any more.

Exacerbating factors

Let me make it clear what I am not saying.

I am *not* saying that unemployment levels are a wholly supply-determined phenomenon, given by the levels of employability of the workers available. Unemployment can exist above as well as below the employability threshold. And, although one defines employability as a characteristic of *people* it can only be measured in relation to the job structure available at any time. Clearly, if we were weaving our own cloth instead of importing it from Hong Kong, if we were willing to spend more money on fast foods and less on video recorders, if we were willing to tax ourselves more to hire more hospital aides and prevent the National Health Service from running down, the employability threshold would be much lower down the ATW spectrum than it is now.

Secondly, I am not saying that employability is a function of genes in any straightforward way. Employability is a function of the interaction between, on the one hand, the quantity and the job structure of effective market demand for labour, and on the other the developed capacities of the labour force. And the developed capacities of the labour force are a function of the effects of the family, school and general cultural environment acting on basic genetic endowments. Clearly, for any given demanded job structure in this country, the employability threshold would be lower if our educational system were more effective, if it gave better drilling in basic mental skills. Prais' (1985) and Postlethwaite's (1985) recent studies of school attainments in Britain and Germany over the whole of the compulsory education span, show that there is little difference in the top half of the ability range. It is the below-average performers in Germany whose achieved standards are so much better than *our* below-average performers. It is the slower learners who are cheated in our school system.

Nor is there any doubt that the concentration of unemployment in the younger age groups represents another environmental influence working disastrously to change the capacities side of the supply-demand interaction in ways likely to raise the employability threshold. Nothing is better calculated to reduce a person's mastery of tenuously acquired skills than a prolonged period without the occasion to practise them, nothing so destructive of the self-confidence and sense of responsibility which are also crucial ingredients of employability.

And in our proto-NHO, there is now an additional element in

youth unemployment, besides sheer idleness, which is particularly destructive of self-confidence – an element produced by the same trends as concentrate unemployment among the young in the first place – all those elements of the shift towards the Community model which increase the emphasis on job security and reducing turnover and cause unemployment more and more to take the form of a lengthening queue of starters waiting to get in. It also means that employers are no longer recruiting even low-wage manual workers quite as casually as they once did, now that employment commitments are more serious, employment contracts less easily broken. And as employers become more carefully selective in recruiting starters, what do they use for selection – what else *can* they use – but school records?

The evolution of the Youth Training Scheme (YTS) is a case in point. Some employers who took a mixed batch of YTS trainees in the first year of the scheme in a spirit of social service, and then found themselves under strong moral pressure to keep all of them in employment at the end of the year, often decided to be more selective even of their YTS trainees the next time round. And by these processes a kind of *recognized hierarchy* of 17-year-olds appears. Those who are able and/or well enough off are in further or higher education. One step down are those in apprenticeships and traineeships and jobs with a promotion future. Then come those who have a regular job, whether dead-end or not. Then come those on employer-based YTS schemes, and ITech Centre schemes, and then come those on other Mode B YTS schemes, community programmes and the like. With local variations, some pattern of that sort seems to be emerging. I call that pattern a 'recognized hierarchy' because there is general agreement on the preference order, and who should envy whom. Few youngsters on Mode B YTS community programmes would not prefer to be on employer-based programmes with better final job chances. Hence, if the *world* presumes that the Mode B boys and girls were deemed not good enough by Mode A training providers, it does so with some justification. Hence the grading provides a non-haphazard basis for accepted social labelling. Hence, because so founded, the labels can hurt. And it hurts the very youngsters who are most likely to have found school a self-confidence-destroying experience of failure and frustration and dignity denial. Once, leaving school and finding a job was a release from those experiences, a liberation which put them above the dignity minimum. Now – one more sign of the shaping of the NHO

– even the labour market is structured to prolong their disadvantaged status.

And if, as I suggest we have good reason to fear, a number of them – a growing number of them – find themselves relegated to permanent membership in an equally socially recognizable unemployed/unemployable status, what happens to our concept of citizenship? What happens to the dignity minimum? What happens to the basic fictions which sustain our democracy?

False hopes

Let me deal, very briefly, with two quite spurious solutions. First there are those who say airily that the solution is simple and lies in an adjustment of our mistaken values. It is only, the argument goes, in societies which falsely identify work with social worth that there is any problem of dignity deprivation for the unemployed. Technology has made such a value system outmoded. It is time we realized it, time that we put our schools to educating people for leisure. Do that, our value systems will change, and we shall have no problem of dignity deprivation for those without work.

The fallacies of this argument are, alas, all too obvious. There is still going to be a lot of complex, challenging and interesting work to be done in our society, and the chance of doing it is still going to be highly prized, not just for the money, but also for the power that goes with the decision-making jobs, and the work satisfaction that goes with all the problem-solving jobs. The distribution of work and leisure is getting more and more skewed, it seems to me, at both ends. Not only is the growing aggregate volume of leisure increasingly concentrated in the involuntary leisure of the unemployed; work, too (defined here as activity which has a money reward) is getting increasingly concentrated among a minority of the gainfully employed – the workaholic moonlighters and 70-hours-a-week executives and civil servants and barristers who are either able and ambitious, or, like the author and those who will read this book, have so many opportunities in their work for choice and what Maslow (1954) called self-actualization, that the whole distinction between work and play is blurred. In the schools, the pupils with prospects of such jobs will be the bright ones, the teachers' favourites, the ones it is most rewarding to teach. It is their prospects and ambitions and preferences which will dominate the ethos of the school. The new leisure ethic – self-cultivation and all that as a superior alternative to getting and spending – is not going to have much of a chance.

There are signs, indeed, that the work ethic might get stronger rather than weaker in industrial countries, at least in laggard countries like Britain, as a result of the dilemma we face in trying to run an international free-trade system on the one hand while maintaining national sovereignty in economic policy on the other. The stridency with which we are increasingly urged in Britain to restore our ailing economy to competitiveness is evidence thereof. It is another consequence of technological change. The cheapening of transport and communications has so intensified international competition that we are forced to pull our socks up. We can no longer afford the hangover effect of our old aristocratic versions of the leisure ethic, let alone cultivate a new one.

The second spurious argument is the political one, sometimes heard on the Left. There should be no problem about the dignity of the unemployed. All we have to do is to give them political education, to make them see that it's not *their* fault they are unemployed; it's all because of the rottenness of society, the mistaken monetarist (or other) policies of the government. It would be an insensitive argument, even if it were never used by the (employed, salary-earning) activists of the intellectual proletariat to mobilize baton fodder among the easily led. Supposing you *do* convince an unemployed man or woman that 15 per cent unemployment is the result of the government's wickedness. That does not solve his dignity problem which is: why should it be me who is the one in ten rejected and not the other nine, especially if, in the New Hierarchical Order, the answer 'it's just pure luck' becomes less plausible.

Among one group, however, the dignity problem *can* be solved by such arguments, and that is among blacks who have, of course, the greatest incidence of unemployment and prospects of long-term unemployment. If they can see themselves – with good evidential support – as the victims of unfair discrimination, not of personal deficiencies, their despair can be turned into anger against the discriminators rather than paralysing dissatisfaction with themselves. This therapeutic effect of increasing black militancy and hostility towards the majority society is not greatly consoling, however, to those who are prejudiced in favour of social harmony and fraternity.

It is probably also true that the growth in unemployment paradoxically eases *that* problem. If you are the one in ten who is rejected, that is dispiriting. But it is not so dispiriting as being the rejected one in fifty when the other forty-nine all get jobs. But it is *more* dispiriting than if you're part of, say, a 50 per cent unsuccessful minority and only one in two get jobs. The *Economist* (4 December 1982) was puzzled by a survey which found the unemployed to be feeling 'less ashamed, less depressed, less useless and less bored' in December 1982 when their numbers were reaching 3 million than two years earlier when they were half that number, perhaps already a sign of that principle at work.

But nobody who reads Vonnegut's *Player Piano* and remembers his comfortable, philistine, welfare-benefit underclass, would look in that direction for a solution to the problem of maintaining the dignity minimum in a society with large numbers of people who cannot claim a share of the jobs that are going. And I, personally, must declare my attachment to the Protestant work ethic. Abolish acquisitiveness if you like, but I would not like to live in a society which did not honour those who perform socially useful functions.

A new basis for the dignity minimum

So one looks for ways in which the dignity minimum *can* be maintained because everyone has the chance to perform socially useful functions, everyone has a job. James Meade (1984), in his fascinating T. H. Marshall Lecture, has pointed the way. We need, he said, some means of lowering the real wage, while raising real incomes, by increasingly managing the distribution of the gains of technical progress in ways independent of the price and wage mechanisms. One possible device which he considers – and which has been around a long time – is the idea of a social dividend paid to everyone. This takes care of the dignity minimum problem, first by making the payment universal, and given as of citizen right, and no longer a means-tested contingency fall-back when what is seen as a 'normal' wage income fails. It does so, secondly, by making all wage income an extra supplement to the basic citizen wage, by drastically lowering the feasible minimum wage, the minimum value-added that performance of a job function must yield, thereby lowering the employability threshold, and enabling almost everyone to have a job.

As for the financing of the dividend, Meade suggests that, if machines are going to do more and more of the work and men less and less, then allocative efficiency probably requires that the wage share in national income should fall in relation to the capital share. If the state acquired a sizeable share of this increasingly significant capital stock through a capital levy or wealth tax, the social dividend could then be financed from the growing proceeds of this collectively owned capital; more and more of our income would be property income and less and less labour income, while maintaining not too unequal shares.

The trouble is: how to get from here to there, how to make feasible the financing of the social dividend on a scale big enough to count; how to make a capital levy of the necessary size politically as well as administratively feasible; how to bring about the wage reduction that is a necessary part of it.

An immodest proposal

The scheme I am about to outline takes off from the Meade ideas just noted. It tries to deal with the transition problem and in a way that takes account of the concentration of unemployment among the younger age groups. First of all, to begin with the least important part, why not build up the state patrimony, the capital fund from which the social dividend is to be paid, gradually and in kind – by the process of capital dilution. Companies dilute their equity by giving the fund a free rights issue equal to x per cent of their existing equity every year. The fund could likewise acquire an $x/100 + x$ share in the ownership title to real estate and art objects valued over a certain sum, that share to be realized whenever the item changes hands. In this way, the fund could slowly build up. If the dilution were 2 per cent, the fund would acquire half the national wealth in 36 years, three-quarters in 72 years.

The more important part of the idea is the counterpart of the slow build-up: the slow addition to the number of beneficiaries, age group by age group. Let all those who reach the age of 16 next year receive a social dividend, a variable sum depending on the profitability of the fund's equity holdings, but also age-related, perhaps by some compulsory savings device, so that it builds up over three or, if possible, five years from a teenager dividend to a full adult dividend at, say, something like 40 per cent of the average wage, a good deal more for a couple with two children than the 62 per cent of average wage provided by supplementary benefit now. The following year, the 17-year-olds and the 16-year-olds would be covered, and so on until, in about 80 years time, we have special TV programmes to mark the death of the last unendowed man, or more likely woman, with pictures of her drawing the last old-regime pension.

With the endowment the teenager receives the right to study, the right to work and also, of course, the rights to use the National Health Service, to be protected by the police, and so on, which he already had. He also assumes duties of unpaid community service, duties which are compulsory and universal, though widely flexible in form. Only in this way can one achieve what all the schemes for voluntary youth community service cannot achieve, namely, a genuine sharing in community work, on equal terms both of motivation and performance between the bright ones for whom community work is an interruption in preparation for a rewarding work career, and those for whom the alternative would be unemployment.

Some implications

The variability of the dividend depending on national profitability would provide everyone with an additional incentive to take part in the producing economy, over and above the wages they might receive: an enormous free-rider problem, the reader will say. No one will be able to believe that his own contribution makes a measurable impact on his own dividend. True indeed, but that means that everyone *does* have a strong interest in stopping *everybody else* from being a free-rider. Hence we shall see the schools suddenly revitalizing the ethic of duty and responsibility, which will not be at all a bad thing.

The overall reduction of wages which could increase work opportunities would take place gradually as new age-groups come on to the market. What the existing Young Workers' Scheme tries to do, selectively, to bring down youth wages, would happen as a result of the manner of the Scheme's introduction. Within a few years the concentration of unemployment among the young should end. The low-wage cure for youth unemployment would inevitably lead to displacement of some older workers at first, and it is admittedly difficult to foresee the counter-measures necessary to deal with the problem of having dividend-receivers and non-dividend-receivers competing in the same labour markets with different reserve prices. It seems certain that they would involve abandonment of the strict principle of equal pay for equal work in favour of some kind of seniority differential. This is easier to envisage since a larger proportion of the jobs which will remain will be the kind of jobs for which incremental scales are already common: middle-class jobs in which accumulated experience counts. The fact that it is existing older workers who dominate the trade unions should also ensure that the lowered labour-supply price of younger workers does not simply result in unemployment for older workers.

The other nub of the matter is that factor shares in national income would have to shift over time from something like 70 per cent labour: 25 per cent capital (1983 figures, 5 per cent imputed income from personal property excluded) to something closer to a 40:50 ratio. This is clearly problematic, though given the large element of conventional determination in factor shares and the nature of the new political forces which a capital fund/social dividend scheme would set up, not beyond the bounds of possibility.

But could we get by with only 40 per cent of national income distributed according to effort? Can we afford, yet, to have an economy in which choosing to do one's own thing in modest poverty is wholly compatible with citizen dignity, a society in which the material incentive to work is much reduced? That was a major concern for Marshall when he wrote *Citizenship and Social Class* in 1949. At a time when full employment had been established, by means which we thought would work forever, he did not foresee that beyond the minimum income problem there might be a minimum dignity problem. He did wonder, though, whether people would put their backs into their jobs if income guarantees became too strong, whether, in Mandeville's terms, there was anything but their wants which could 'stir workers up to be serviceable'. He sought hope in the thought that increasingly the search for status and for the intrinsic satisfactions of work would replace Mandeville's wants as means of stirring us up. A far higher proportion of the jobs that remain today permits the mobilization of those motives than ever before. If the wages for the remaining unpleasant and unskilled jobs have relatively to rise because of the universal minimum, this would be a useful countervailing force to the tendency for market forces working on talent scarcities to exacerbate income inequalities. And the vast array of fascinating gadgetry and travel and holiday possibilities which our new technologies have brought should provide plenty of genuine new wants of a material kind and, if those fail, we always have our advertising industry to provide spurious ones. There should be no serious lack of work incentives; it seems unlikely that the social dividend would turn us into a nation of layabouts, or harm the drive to make Britain competitive.

What it *would* do, would be to redefine the social significance of jobs and the concept of a right to a job. It would destroy the idea that it is through their jobs, and only through their jobs, that men and women have a right even to a basic livelihood, a really solidly grounded right, a right valid even in the eyes of a Tebbit or a Thatcher. That would have a number of consequences. It would, for example, make it less likely that anyone would strike, as the miners did in 1984, for the principle that the community has an obligation to ensure that anyone who has a job should be able to keep it forever, irrespective of all economic considerations, whatever the subsidy costs to the community. It might also lead to some compression of wage differentials. The pressure to *have* a job would be reduced. There should be a weakening of the idea that income is a reward for fulfilling work *duties* and should therefore be proportionate to the importance of those duties. We might come to think of interesting jobs more as a luxury, a piece of good fortune for their possessors, or rather, since we already do in fact half think so, come to think and talk more explicitly and overtly in those terms. If that happens, then 'Why should I put in extra effort if nobody's going to pay me for it?' would be balanced by 'When you've got an interesting job which gives you prestige, power and a sense of accomplishment that other people are not lucky enough to have, why should you *also* expect more money than they have, too?' And out of the new balance between the two logics should come a pattern of income differentials closer to an Israeli or a Swedish, or even a Japanese one than to the one which is growing steadily wider in Britain today.

12
Home thoughts from America

'Taking Japan Seriously', thought the American publisher, may be fine for the complacent, slow-to-catch-on British public. It might have been appropriate in the United States, too, seven or eight years ago. But after a steady stream of books in recent years telling Americans how to learn from Japan and how to understand their menacing Japanese competitors, there can hardly be any doubt that Americans do take Japan seriously already. That is not necessarily to say, however, that there are many Americans who would draw the same lessons from Japan as are suggested in this book. The US, indeed, as in many ways an extreme exemplar of the genus 'individualistic Western economy' – a good deal more extreme than his own – offers an Englishman an excellent vantage point from which to reflect on the general implications of Japan's demonstration that very efficient economic organizations *can* be built on very unindividualistic lines.

The basic arguments of this book can be summed up in two propositions.

1 A good number of the features which give Japan competitive strength are *emerging trends* in the UK (as in other industrial societies). They are responses to the technological and organizational opportunities and requirements of the late twentieth century, responses which the Japanese have got to before us in part because of their 'late developer' advantage. These include trends towards:

(*a*) Increasing intervention by an increasingly developmentalist state to improve the economy's international competitiveness:

(*b*) Increasing attempts to develop consensual regulation of money-income increases to control inflation;

(*c*) Increasing trends towards lifetime employment of workers with flexible if specialist skills, and a concomitant shift away from 'Company Law' enterprises towards more 'Community model' enterprises;

(d) An accompanying tendency towards a hierarchy of enterprises and a wage spectrum reflecting presumed worker quality and firms' innovativeness/price-making power, and not just occupational differences;

(e) An increasing tendency for employers to bear the cost of occupational training;

(f) An increasing tendency towards meritocracy, towards the hierarchical ranking of schools and colleges according to the presumed ability of their students, and the increasing use of educational records for selecting recruits to work organizations.

2   The other theme of this book has been the economic and social importance of a concern for fairness and compromise, for not allowing market forces alone to determine the allocation either of resources or of rewards. It is an argument for creating mechanisms – conventions, precedents, norms – which allow for a little give and take and make sure that the powerful do not drive their bargains so hard for short-term advantage that they destroy the relations of trust and cooperation which may be necessary for their own and others' long-term benefit. It will have been clear that I argue for the virtues of such mechanisms partly because of a personal preference for the quality of interpersonal relations which such a society sustains, partly because it does also seem to promote greater economic efficiency.

Here the Japanese advantage in being able to develop these compromise mechanisms seems to be not a late-development effect but a cultural one, the result of long-standing preferences for obligated, trustful, as opposed to impersonal and wary relationships. And there is less obvious reason for believing that long-run structural changes are making for the *natural* unplanned, un-preached-for evolution of the individualistic profit-maximizing ethic of Anglo-Saxon economies in such a direction. Nevertheless, taking thought, preaching, deliberate effort, might modify our practice in a Japanese direction, *if* we could liberate ourselves from the imprisoning rigidities of the marketist ideologies which make hungry self-interest not just an instinct but a duty.

How do these arguments look when one's reference society is not Britain but the USA? Are there any signs of a rethinking of marketism in the United States, some appreciation that the invisible hand working through short-term profit-maximizers may not be enough to secure the general benefit, and that short-term profit-maximizing, for most individuals, may not be the best way of maximizing their utility? Let us look first for the postulated trends listed earlier, beginning with industrial policy.

Trends: Industrial policy

What is unmistakably true is that the *debate* about industrial policy – about how far the patterning of investment which shapes the structure of the economy can be left to free-market forces – is vigorous, not to say heated, and that.hardly anyone manages to participate in it without mentioning Japan. A symposium on US competitiveness was recently published by a group of active interventionist economists. Its index has 8 references to Europe as a whole, 9 to the UK, 29 to Germany and 116 to Japan (Scott and Lodge, 1985).

There is an edge of passion and even anxiety in these debates which is missing in Britain. It is already a good many decades since thoughtful Englishmen could convince themselves that industrially and in terms of scientific and technical power, Britain was undisputed world leader. She manifestly lost that position to the United States early in the century. Of course, not all Britons are thoughtful. The forces of patriotic complacency are strong. In some of the more egregiously complacent corners of Oxbridge or the City of Westminster one can find people who still speak as patronizingly of their American counterparts as their grandfathers did in the nineteenth century. But by and large the British have come through the major trauma of ceasing to be number one.

But not so the Americans. When a Harvard professor, Ezra Vogel, wrote a book with the title *Japan as Number One*, he was clearly speaking to deep anxieties, and so, more overtly, was his second book, *Comeback America*. The sense of a threat to America's natural and proper dominance of the world (which, of course, the world is seen to need for the sake of world order as much as America needs it for its own self-interest) is as much a factor in the continuing debates about Japanese trade as the penetration of particular American markets by Japanese imports and the threat to particular producer interests. As Japanese firms do to the American market for dRAMs, and seem subsequently set to do to the market for EPROMs, what they did for motorbikes and VTRs and facsimile machines, many Americans react with cries of 'unfair', a note struck quite forcefully by President Reagan in a speech on trade problems. And the fact that Japanese investors are covering the US budget deficit ('buying up America') to the tune of nearly $50 billion a year may seem to exacerbate rather than mitigate the offence. For exponents of the more extreme forms of patriotism, Japan, as the major threat to US supremacy in the economic sphere, is no less incarnate wickedness than the Soviet Union, the antagonist in the global power sphere.

That makes for a lot of 'noise' generated by hidden agendas in American debates on the meaning of Japan. This is nowhere more the case than in the field of industrial policy. Some of the most common positions are:

1 Admiration for what is seen as Japan's skilled and judicious support of sunrise industries and wise handling of adjustment in sunset industries, and strong advocacy of the need for Americans to do likewise (Vogel, 1985; Reich, 1984; Scott and Lodge, 1985), very much a minority view in an America where the expression of fundamental doubts about the society has come to seem disloyal.

2 Similar attribution to government of a major role in Japan's success, but branding this as an unfair way of conducting international competition, and one which contrasts with Americans' rejection of socialist interventionism, and their honest belief in fair and unsubsidized competition (the 'Japan-bashing' version, as it is called by those who find its self-righteousness offensive or are in some way influenced by the $50 million per annum reputedly spent by the Japan lobby in Washington (Morse, 1983).

3 A denial that Japanese government policy has any but the most marginal importance in giving Japanese firms competitive advantage, a message coming variously from (a) those reacting to what they perceive as Japan-bashing, (b) economists, and others devoted to free-trade ideals, reacting against any argument which is used to justify protectionist measures, and (c) economists unable on theoretical grounds to believe that any governmental reallocation of resources can ever lead to greater economic efficiency than reliance on the market.

By column-inch criteria, views which minimize the importance of industrial policy probably predominate, although a former Chairman of the Council of Economic Policy Advisers seemed to assume otherwise when he put that view forcefully in a 1983 article and entitled it 'Industrial policy: A dissent'. (In that article he characterized as 'sheer nonsense' the idea that without MITI's guidance, Japan's massive industrial investment would have been directed into textiles, shoes, plastic souvenirs and other non-growth areas in which Japan had revealed (static) comparative advantage. 'Given the quality of Japanese business executives, those massive investment funds probably would have wound up roughly where they actually did. And to the extent that there would have been differences, there is no reason to believe that MITI's influence, on balance, improved the choices in any way' (Schultze, 1983).

Nevertheless, in practice, the US is no exception to the general tendency for the increasing pressures of international trade competition to bring a steady increase in 'developmental interventionism' – intervention to enhance the international competitiveness of selected sectors of the economy. The US was a pioneer, for example, in providing, under the 1974 Trade Act, general (rule-bound, not *ad hoc*) compensatory assistance to workers in industries affected by import competition, designed to deflect the demand for tariff or quota protection from declining industries.

At the other end, in the promotion of sunrise industries, government initiative and expenditure has been on a considerable scale. Some has been directed specifically at civilian production: tax advantages for research and development introduced in the Economic Recovery Tax Act of 1981, for instance, and the amendment of the Anti-Trust Laws by the National Cooperative Research Act of 1984, designed to encourage research cartels, by making absolutely clear that combining for the purpose of promoting long-term 'pre-commercial' research was not an actionable Anti-Trust offence. (By April 1986, some 36 of these research clubs had been registered.) The bulk of the vast and – under Reagan – increasing, expenditure of government funds on research and development, however, has been via the defence budget. A recent summary by Rothwell and Zegweld (1985) makes clear that the aim of making American industries strong and capable of competing in the civilian markets of the world has been intermixed fairly overtly with the aim of making the American armed forces strong and capable of outfacing any military rivals in the world, and a good deal has been made of these indirect effects in arguing for appropriations before Congress. 'One important side product of what the Department of Defense does should be to help US industry', said the organizers of the Very High Speed Integrated Circuit Program back in 1978 (Yoshino and Fong, 1985).

Since then, of course, the rhetoric has changed a little with the arrival of a Reagan government wedded in theory to marketist philosophies. But it is not so clear that the trend of policy has changed. The Office of Technology Assessment (OTA), set up by Congress in 1972, is an interesting bell-wether since its choice of research themes reflects the centre of gravity of Congressional opinion. It responded, first, to concern with the environmental effects of technology choices, notably with energy and the nuclear means of producing it. By the end of the Carter administration it was publishing reports calling in general terms for an industrial policy. If the language of its reports became somewhat more guarded with the arrival of Reagan, the proportion of the Office's activities devoted to work with clear implications for particular industrial policy issues has certainly not diminished. The OTA report on the electronics industry (1983) was the first explicitly to make international comparisons of policy devices for the promotion of high technology industries, and makes no bones about its message. International competition is intensifying, particularly in high-technology sectors like electronics. Increasingly industrial policy has become 'a routine activity of all governments':

> In the end it comes down to this: If other countries are developing ambitious and comprehensive programs to support certain of their industries, can the United States assume that *absence* of Government action is the best response? . . . We can continue to leave industrial policy to the random play of events, or we can try to improve the system (OTA, 1983, pp. 500–1).

Trends: Incomes, employment and training

If industrial policy *is* a live issue in the US, incomes policy is not. It has been tried once – by Nixon as a desperate expedient to curb the inflation set off by the Vietnam war – and got such a bad press as a result that it has practically no advocates, quite apart from the very real difficulties of organizing anything except a very temporary rough-justice sort of policy in a country of the scale and regional diversity of the United States.

Trends in employment relations, however, are another thing again. The evidence is accumulating that, whatever the strength of the 'hire and fire' ideology, however true it is that employers *can* lay off redundant workers more readily and with less likelihood of last-ditch union opposition than employers in almost any country in Europe, it is still the case that (to quote a recent survey of 'the importance of lifetime jobs in the US economy'):

> The typical worker today is holding a job which has lasted or will last about eight years. Over a quarter of all workers are holding jobs which will last twenty years or more . . . The jobs held by middle-aged workers with more than ten years tenure are extremely stable. Over the span of a decade only 20 to 30 per cent come to an end (Hall, 1982).

That point is not new, of course, and the classic work identifying the emergence – and the reasons for the emergence – of long-tenure jobs in what they called the upper tier of a two-tier economy was that of Doeringer and Piore (1971) written in and about the United States. It was an essential part of their argument that the growing importance of firm-specific skills and hence of firm-specific training – a product of the increasing sophistication of technology – played a key role in generating these trends. The evidence for these trends remains fragmentary and anecdotal, multiple reports of intensive training and retraining programmes mounted by individual employers particularly in high-technology fields (American statistical services covering manufacturing industry are as bad as those of the post-Thatcher-cuts UK). There has been one sample survey by a private employers' organization, however. It puts the average expenditure per employee at $283 per annum (Carnevale and Goldstein, 1983). There seems little doubt, however, that the share in the financing of vocational training in manufacturing which is borne by the employer, as opposed to the individual being trained, or public budgets, is steadily increasing. In that respect, too, American firms are getting more and more like lifetime-employing Japanese firms even if it remains true that the willingness of individuals to save, withdraw from the labour market, retrain and return to the market to search for a better-paying job still, probably, remains greater in the US than in either Japan or the UK.

US labour economists have recently looked further at aspects of these trends reminiscent of Japan – some, for instance, at the shape and explanation of the relation between seniority and wages (is it only a reflection of the increase in worker productivity with increasing tenure, or is it a 'pure' reward for seniority, or the result of union influence, e.g., Mills, 1985). Others have looked at the nature of interpersonal wage differences and how far they reflect differences of worker quality as employers perceive them (Ruhm, 1986), though there seems as yet to be less work on inter*firm* differentials and how they might also be rooted in differential 'ability to pay' related to differential market power (through technological or other monopoly). It is, of course, the ability to pay high wages which combines with policies preferentially to recruit workers of high quality, to create the elite firms whose emergence is the start of the process called in Chapter 3 the process of 'spectrumization'.

Meritocracy

As for the other part of the process of developing a spectrum society – the tendency to make educational merit a main criterion of 'worker quality' (and to define that merit in ways which reflect as much judgement of underlying aptitude as of the quality of the educational experience to which the qualification held supposedly testifies) – the obvious place to look is within the 40 per cent or more of each age group who complete a college education. There are indeed some clear signs of the emergence of a prestige hierarchy of educational institutions which is correlated with the minimum score they require in the SAT test, a scholastic *aptitude* test, supposedly measuring not short-term crammed-for scholastic achievement but the underlying ability to acquire basic literacy and numeracy skills in the first eighteen years of life. The 'best' universities have higher minimum SAT entry scores and their graduates are more highly prized and more likely to be recruited at good salaries by the best firms (an advantage which they do not lose in the rest of their careers, even though they are less likely than their Japanese counterparts to stay in their first firm for ever). The system approaches more closely to the Japanese one than does the British in one respect: the SAT test is a good deal more objective, and a good deal closer to being a predictor of the kind of qualities employers look for, than the multiple-standard, bafflingly complex A-level examinations which perform (with Oxbridge entrance examinations) the same functions in Britain. In other respects it approaches less closely. The more wide-spread use by top Ivy League universities of subsidiary selection criteria besides academic merit – athletic or musical talent, ethnic minority status, and so on – is one factor. The much greater importance of rationing by the purse in a system with wide variations in fees (prestige has to be paid for), only partially compensated for by a complex system of scholarship assistance at the top universities, also complicates and introduces a lot of 'noise' into its functioning as an ability-grading mechanism. (The universities, in other words, also retain their function as status-confirming, intergenerational status-transmitting mechanisms.) And the size of the country, and persistent regionalism (bright country boys might still not think of setting their sights any 'higher' than the local state university), mean that the national prestige market – a national consensual ranking of universities – is still only weakly established compared with Britain or, *a fortiori*, Japan.

But the direction of the trend seems clear. That the SAT is acquiring increasing authority and increasing significance in the determination of life-chances is suggested by the popular attention it receives. A school in Dallas reputedly offers $1,500 bonuses to teachers who raise their charges' SAT scores; one cramming school pays its teachers three times the hourly wage of high-school teachers (Owen, 1985). The importance of the test is also shown by the strength of feeling behind the attacks on its 'fairness', or rather the fairness of giving SAT results the importance which they are in fact accorded. A racy journalist's attack on the SAT and its creators, the Educational Testing Service, concentrates primarily on the futility, ambiguity, trickiness, unfairness or lack of validity of the tests, using all the standard arguments and many more (Owen, 1985). But it is clear that the fundamental objection is to the whole 'cult of mental measurement', the fact that the test 'plays a significant role in determining who gets ahead in America and who falls, or stays, behind' (p. xxi). A second objection is that, as we shall doubtless hear more and more stridently in criticism of British and Japanese meritocracy, when the social surveys begin to show more unmistakeably a secular decline in social mobility:

> the real beneficiaries of 'aptitude' testing are the offspring of the advantaged, who ascend from privilege to privilege on the strength of their scores and come to view those numbers as a moral justification for the comforts that are the trappings of their class (Owen, 1985: p. 266).

Trends: The 'Community model' enterprise

If job tenures are of increasing length, what evidence is there of a trend towards the other organizational characteristics which seem to go with lifetime employment, of a trend away from a 'Company Law model' towards a 'Community model' type of firm? It is hard to say. Peters and Waterman (1984), in one of the few passages in their inspirational bestseller *In Search of Excellence* which deals with the nuts and bolts of personnel relations, say that the 'best presidents of the best companies, Messrs Watson (IBM) Kroc (McDonalds), Marriott et al., have been pathbreakers in treating people as adults, in inducing practical innovation and contributions from tens of thousands, in providing training and development opportunities for all, in treating all as members of the family.'

The message from the management literature is loud and clear. It is essentially the message preached by the 'human relations' school back in the 1950s, or embodied in McGregor's much quoted but otherwise not much regarded *The Human Side of Enterprise* (1960). Now that message has been reinforced by influential books on Japanese management published at the beginning of the decade – Pascale and Athos's *Art of Japanese Management*, Ouchi's *Theory Z* – and by the publicity given to the apparently successful importations of Japanese management techniques such as Quality Circles or the Ford agreement combining tenure security, enhanced retirement benefits, and union participation in management, with wage restraint. The book quoted above, *In Search of Excellence*, became not just a bestseller but a number one bestseller and its successor, *A Passion for Excellence* (Peters and Austin, 1986) will doubtless achieve the same status when it appears in paperback.

The core of Peters and Austin's message is: make employees feel involved. In the training of new employees, 'the prime education is "You belong", "You can contribute"'. Once that message is genuinely transmitted and absorbed, then the "technique-learning process" can be shortened by 60 to 90 per cent, for there is suddenly the will to learn' (p. 341). They quote with warm approval from the '40 Thoughts' credo of the Dana Corporation:

> Remember our purpose – to earn money for our shareholders and increase the value of their investment. Recognize our people as our most important asset. Help people grow. Promote from within. Remember – people respond to recognition. Share the rewards. Provide stability of income and employment. Decentralize. Provide autonomy . . .

They use the concept of 'ownership'. 'People who are part of the team, who "own" the company and "own" their job, regularly perform a thousand per cent better – often many thousand per cent better – than the rest' (p. 216). All good companies recognize this: 'some go to extremes to ensure not only a sense of ownership but stock ownership as well. Like Dana's McPherson, Publix Super Market's George Jenkins passionately believes that all employees should own shares in the corporation so that they are "working for themselves"' (p. 218).

'Going to extremes', indeed. The distribution of the proceeds of employees' collective efforts is not something which occupies the authors of this management literature a great deal. It does at least get mentioned in another recent book, again of the direct 'lessons from Japan' kind, Abegglen and Stalk's *Kaisha: The Japanese Corporation* (1985). It is written in very conscious dissociation from the 'involvement' literature just quoted. They will have none of the soft stuff about Theory Z, management arts, leadership and company philosophies. As the sub-title on the jacket puts their theme, it is: 'How marketing, money and manpower strategy, not management style, make the Japanese pace-setters'. Theirs is the hard-nosed story. 'Aggressive' is their favourite adjective when expressing approval – on one occasion it is used five times in a single paragraph. However, they do spare a few paragraphs for what they call the characteristics of Japanese firms as social organizations (as distinct from economic organizations). They acknowledge that it 'may be' that the absence of stock options and managerial performance bonus systems in Japanese corporations has something to do with their greater capacity for inter-divisional cooperation in developing new products. They talk about the relatively narrow salary differentials within Japanese firms, and link this to other characteristics of the Community model.

But when they come to giving their prescriptions, and set out the ways in which American executives might think about beating the Japanese at their own game, all the emphasis is on aggressive long-term strategies for establishing a position of market dominance. There is no suggestion that American executives should, if they want really involved employees, make do with salaries which are a more modest multiple of their employees' salaries. There is no talk of executives taking, as they routinely do in Japan in troubled times, salary cuts themselves before they resort to lay-offs. One does not write a popular book for bottom-line-oriented American executives with that sort of message. They do at one stage commend the notion of 'truly contingent compensation, shared equally throughout the organization', but the idea is not spelt out, and generally, 'the specifics of Japanese compensation and career patterns will not lend themselves readily to adoption in the West.'

In fact some US businesses have adopted some of the practices which Abegglen and Stalk are hesitant to recommend: Eastern Airlines is one example of managers taking considerable salary cuts as a means of evoking cooperation from the staff in surmounting a bad crisis. And there are quite a number which have 'gone to extreme' and distributed stock among their employees, though generally only a tiny proportion of their total stock, making no impact on the pattern of control over the company. Legislation has also encouraged employee stock-ownership and there are a number of ESOPs (Employee Share-Owning Partnerships) in existence, some of which are thriving concerns (Bradley and Gelb, 1983). But these are mostly firms rescued from the brink of collapse and no longer of much value or concern to their original stockholders. There is very little predisposition in this literature to reconsider the basic property system of modern American capitalism.

It is a great merit of Abegglen and Stalk's book, however, that unlike other writers they do discuss the differences in ownership patterns between Japan and the US and all the implications of those differences which were the subject of Chapter 6: the importance of shareholding patterns for Japanese firms' ability to create Community model organizations and for their ability to follow long-term investment strategies, emphasizing, for example, research at a fairly basic level. They quote a survey study of corporate objectives. American managers put return on investment first on their list, and maintaining the value of their shares second. Japanese managers give pride of place to increasing market share. Maintaining share values comes ninth and last on their list.

Abegglen and Stalk point out, however, that *in the event* Japanese shareholders have not done badly, a faster rate of capital gains having compensated for the fact that dividends are conventionally held to less than 2 per cent of current values. This enables them to offer selected Japanese prescriptions to American managers. Be bold. Tell your shareholders to expect low dividends for some time while you aggressively go for growth by investing heavily in projects which will win you a dominant market position in the long run.

That Japanese strategy must have very un-Japanese risks in an American world in which shareholders *expect* 10 per cent and not 2 per cent returns, and where takeover predators are always ready to strike if the desertion of faint-hearted shareholders brings share prices tumbling. Authors who make their living as business consultants are bound to be optimistic perhaps, but some do take the point, and argue for measures which the financial community is not likely to find easily acceptable. Bruce Scott (1985) at the Harvard Business School suggests not only the regulation of takeovers but also graduated taxes on share-ownership to penalize the rapid turnover of shares, encourage shareholder stability and make possible the long-term investment which American firms need to make if they are to stay competitive with the Japanese.

The sense of crisis will have to intensify considerably, however, before any message of that sort has much chance of a hearing. The United States is a nation whose devotion to the notion of the sanctity of private property, including the property rights of shareholders, makes the UK seem like a society clouded over by the pale cast of collectivism. It is a society in which the financial buccaneers responsible for the recent rash of predatory takeovers, often dubiously financed by so-called junk bonds, can actually pose as moral crusaders, because they are reasserting the basic rights of shareholders against the managerial usurpers with their six-figure salaries, their stock options, their executive jets, executive suites and all the rest. And who can deny that they have a point when, as suggested earlier, the division of rewards *within* the corporation is as much open to question in the light of the Japanese comparison as the shareholder–employee division of power and income?

The United States has in some ways a more finance-oriented and less production-oriented form of capitalism, more firmly wedded to the Company Law model of the firm, than the UK. If the growing dominance of lawyers and accountants over engineers on the boards of manufacturing companies is not a reflection of a prestige gap of quite the same dimensions as in Britain – engineering in the land of Yankee ingenuity still has rather higher prestige than in the UK – the importance attached to property rights is, if anything, greater. And more self-assertive, also, are the political forces which have a strong interest in reinforcing property rights. The US *is* a more single-mindedly bottom-line-oriented society than the European societies, and *a fortiori* than Japan. The view that self-interest is the only reliable motivational force has more widespread acceptance, and (in this, the most litigious society on earth) those who fail to assert their property rights to the full are in danger of being branded as weaklings. Another number one bestseller, which stayed on the list for many months in 1977, was entitled *Looking Out for Number*

One, billed as 'by Robert J. Ringer, author of *Winning Through Intimidation*'. And these, be it noted, were no Stephen Potter-like musings on the foibles and vanities of mankind, but proper how-to books written, and doubtless read, in deadly earnest. Marvin Harris (1981) attributes the poor quality of American manufactures to the fact that 'it is very hard for people to care about . . . products to be used by strangers' when they are working for large organizations. 'The intimate sentimental and personal bonds which once made us responsible to each other and to our products have withered away and been replaced by money relationships.' And within organizations, the pervasiveness of cash performance incentives in salary systems must surely be greater in the US than anywhere else. Even a university basketball coach may have a paypacket strictly determined by the number of points his team has scored.

So it is something of a paradox that there do seem to be American firms which are a good deal more successful at generating all the outward appearance of Community model enthusiasm even than some of the 'cooler' Japanese firms. Certainly, some of the expressions of corporate enthusiasm gathered in books like those of Peters and his associates, are such as few Englishmen could utter without fear that their listeners would squirm with embarrassment. But is this a genuine sign of identification with the organization, comparable to the Japanese' less demonstrative loyalty to the firm? Or is it a more superficial manifestation, like the gladhand bonhomie which Americans are more likely than the Japanese or British to show to people casually met in trains or aeroplanes? I suspect that it does not alter the fundamental perception of the organization, not as a community, but as an *arena* in which everyone is primarily – and entirely legitimately – 'looking out for number one'. The parallel between marriage and employment is perhaps a relevant one. American mores permit – indeed may require – fulsome expressions of blissful happiness and mutual devotion on marriage. At the same time, America has a very high divorce rate. Japanese marriages are much more low-key. And *last*. Britain occupies an intermediate position in both respects.

But, even if it is only organizations which are manifestly successful in serving their members' self-interest which evoke these expressions of team enthusiasm, the other side of the medal is that the enthusiasm is usually accompanied by genuinely hard work, which is what makes the organization successful. Avowed and unashamed self-interest, accompanied by recognition of others' equal and opposite self-interest, optimism, outspokenness and a recognition that cooperative teamwork is the only route to mutual gain, *can* be a recipe for an efficient and successful organization, especially if its leaders are people of sufficiently powerful personality to sort out the frictions which arise from the clash of self-interests.

Fairness

So much for my first argument about the adaptive trends which might possibly be carrying the US closer to Japan, simply by dint of endogenously operating forces. What about the second part of this book's thesis, the possibility of that modification of self-regarding individualism which, I suppose, can not only lead to greater economic efficiency but may also, as was suggested in Chapter 11, be the only way of retaining social unity in a world where *laissez-faire* markets would produce only increasing disparities of wealth and power, and possibly increasing social divisiveness?

As was suggested above, in its widespread acceptance of the assumption that self-interest is the only really reliable motivator, there is perhaps no society on earth which approximates more closely than the US to the models of the neo-classical economists. (And no Americans closer to the model than American economists, who appear to be highly prone to act on the principles they attribute to others. In experiments to test the propensity to 'free ride' – to get maximum benefits for minimum contributions to collective endeavours – economics students come out as the most dedicated and consistent free-riders. (Marwell and Ames, 1981)

It is not surprising, therefore, given the moral authority of the market as the only legitimate arbiter between clashing self-interests (government being assumed to be largely corrupt, as well as inefficient, as soon as it strays from its proper classical functions such as military defence into economic management) that the overwhelmingly dominant principle of fairness is (in the jargon of Chapter 2) EPEW – Equal Pay for Equal Work, or more widely and more accurately, Equal Income for Equal Contributions as Judged by the Market.

Hence, any attempt to 'take care of the losers' by modifying or delaying the operation of market forces, is generally seen as a lapse from virtue. It happens in practice all the time, of course. The pressures on Congress and the White House to give tariff protection to this industry, to offer a covert subsidy to that, to tailor a government procurement programme thus, or channel a contract there, are strong and not infrequently irresistible. But this is almost everywhere regarded as the seamy side of democracy, the price, in more or less corruptness of practice, which has to be paid for the accountability of government and freedom from arbitrary oppression which democracy guarantees. It is not seen as *legitimate and sensible* – the way for those who gain from technical or trade developments which are not particularly of their own meritorious making to share those gains for a while with those who lose, even at the expense of allocative efficiency. As mentioned earlier, doing this through the tax system and the worker adjustment assistance of the 1974 Trade Act *was* considered legitimate. But only dubiously so, and under the Reagan Administration, the programme has been cut back so that disbursals in 1985 were running at less than 4 per cent of disbursals in the peak year of 1980.

As for the other, much more difficult and long-term 'taking care of the losers' problem – taking care of those who lose out in the lifetime meritocracy competition, and especially those who fall below what are likely to be, in future, increasingly demanding standards of employability – there is little sign that the US will seek innovative compromises in this field, partly because the whole issue is so intricately bound up with, and overshadowed by, the race issue, but partly also because, as the authors of a recent study of American individualism remind us, self-reliance has always occupied a central place in American values, a place well expressed in a famous essay of Emerson's written in 1841 (Bellah *et al.*, 1985, p. 55). His stress was on both aspects of that virtue: personal effort as the only basis for entitlement to reward *and* the need to stand out against 'illegitimate' claims of society: 'Then again, do not tell me, as a good man did today, of my obligation to put all poor men in good situations. Are they *my* poor?'

There have undoubtedly been upsurges of collective solidarity, notably, in the sixties, the measures to expand welfare summarily referred to as Johnson's Great Society programme. It is America, not Europe, which has experimented in quite radical measures like Head Start to equalize educational opportunities, in negative-income-tax forms of minimum income guarantees, in extensive job subsidy programmes. America, too, was a pioneer in special compensation payments for workers in industries forced into decline by import competition.

But the basic tendency to believe that individuals should stand on their own feet – and that redistribution of income through tax and welfare systems is not only destructive of supply-side incentives (tending therefore to lower economic efficiency) but also morally mistaken – was deeply rooted and strongly revived in the 1980s: made explicit, for example, in books like President Reagan's favourite economic polemic, George Gilder's *Wealth and Poverty* (1981). It is revived even by those who are otherwise opponents of Reagan's *laissez-faire*, the advocates of industrial policy and prophets of a drive to restore American competitiveness: Bruce Scott, for instance, who deplores 'our distributional strategy' which, over time, 'has relieved an ever-larger segment of the population of much of the responsibility for its own welfare and has induced an increased degree of dependence which has become an added burden on the productive part of the economy' (Scott, 1985, p. 142).

The rethinking of the Beveridge principles which is so much a part of the contemporary British scene, has gone further in the United States where those principles were never more than tentatively and half-heartedly accepted in the first place. The process of differentiation of an excluded underclass – predominantly, but not exclusively, blacks in inner-city ghettoes – has proceeded much further. The word 'underclass' itself, still pretty much tabooed in Britain, is freely used in discussion of welfare problems – and employment problems and educational problems and crime problems. But efforts to reintegrate the society, and the social concerns which led earlier to such efforts, seem to be weakened to the point of disappearance.

There are a number of specific reasons, quite apart from the general resurgence of Reaganite conservatism, why this should be so. A major one is that the cities are no longer burning. There is no Black Panther movement. On the one hand, positive discrimination has improved the position of those black people who have remained in the school system until the end of high school and beyond. Whereas, twenty years ago, qualification level for qualification level, the average salaries of blacks were consistently lower than the average salaries of whites, today the difference has disappeared, and at some qualification levels has been reversed. At the same time the prospects for those who drop out on the way – a substantial minority of the black population – have worsened. While 'a large segment of the black population (Kilson estimates roughly 60 per cent) is effectively tapping white middle-class resources for upward mobility . . . another large segment is becoming mired in intergenerational poverty . . . [These are], for the most part, the labor market's analogy to the Displaced Person, without education, without skills that the labor market could use' (Murray, 1984, p. 92). Their plight is reflected in several statistical indicators of relative well-being – the overall black–white difference in employment rates, in willingness to seek employment, in the proportion of 14-year-olds with two parents in the household (down over 20 years from 60 per cent to 40 per cent in black communities) and so on. How – if there is a causal relation – this increasing differentiation within the black community has reduced the manifestations of unrest which so much perturbed white American society two decades ago, is not entirely clear, though it is reasonable to assume that the improved position of the middle-class black must have, if not removed the resentful sense of being discriminated against among those equipped to be the articulate spokesmen for black minority groups, surely, at least, have softened it.

Simultaneously the white world has mended its fences, rather literally. The affluent white areas of Washington – a city with one of the highest homicide rates and one of the worst drug problems – are well policed, calm and secure. One sees fewer burglar alarms than in middle-class Brighton and *a fortiori* than in Hampstead or St John's Wood.

The other part of the change is the loss of confidence of the liberal Left in the solutions which they advocated in the 1960s and 1970s. Few have much changed the positions they publicly acknowledge, but their inner faith in the standard solutions has been badly shaken. They find it hard to point to evidence that greater welfare spending, government programmes to lessen the environmental disadvantages of ghetto children, work opportunity programmes and the like, have had much impact on the problems of the 'displaced persons' most in need of help. They have a hard time trying to refute the arguments of the radical Right.

Those arguments are significant variations on the standard 'welfare hand-outs sap people's will to be self-reliant' theme. The teenage girl who drops out of high school to have an illegitimate child and thenceforth live on the single-parent's welfare allowance instead of entering the labour market is an object of particular concern. ('She will learn to multiply before she learns to subtract' say the posters showing – delicately – a *white* pregnant teenage schoolgirl). So is the widespread escape into drug addiction. And so, also, are the various manifestations of positive discrimination.

Murray, for example, one of the most eloquent of those urging a radical rethinking of the situation, emphasizes the way in which the desire to sustain the motivation of poorly performing pupils in schools leads to a flabby flexibility of standards which provides no encouragement for the not-quite-so-poorly-performing pupils (the sort of pupils who might succeed in climbing out of the ghetto by their *own* genuine achievements). It thus reinforces the defeatism of the poorest performers. Apart from the personal tragedies, this has the national consequences of lowering overall standards of school achievement (as evidenced in declining SAT scores), sapping the work ethic, and generally putting the nation at risk in the competitive arena of the international economy (Murray, 1984). There is now an Attorney General who believes that positive discrimination 'to remedy the lingering social effects of past discrimination makes no sense in principle; in practice, it is nothing short of a legal, moral and constitutional tragedy,' and crucial judicial decisions due in the summer of 1986 are expected to make a significant dent in the legal provisions which have hitherto given ethnic minorities compensatory advantages in the job market.* The abandonment of strictly universalistic achievement standards by a society supposedly dedicated to the principles of individual effort and reward for demonstrated (and valued-in-the-market) merit is seen as an aberration which needs immediate correction.

Moods can change, of course. It is possible that some new concatenation of events will revive the emergent collectivism of the 1960s; there is always the cliché to fall back on that 'these things go in cycles'. But not everything does, and the forces currently at work seem to be pushing in the opposite direction. Patriotism is a very strong sentiment in the United States in foreign policy affairs. It does not seem to reinforce the sort of social solidarity which makes the ordinary American feel that he has to be his brother's keeper. And patriotism, now, manifest in concern for America's declining position in world trade and a determination to beat the Japanese, to wrest back world leadership in technological development, argues for an even higher premium to be placed on efficiency and individual effort, and powerful material incentives – rewards linked to real achievement – tested in the market, the only arena where one can trust the rules.

* *In the event the Supreme Court, in both 1986 and 1987, disappointed the Attorney General*

A choice of recipes

Had I written this book primarily about the United States instead of Britain, I think it would have been harder to discern possible ways in which, by taking Japan seriously – by encouraging certain existing trends which, without the example of Japan we might tend to condemn rather than applaud, by using Japan to jolt ourselves into rethinking some of the values in the light of which we judge our institutions – both economic efficiency and social justice might be improved, and social cohesion enhanced. In the dimension, or bundle of dimensions, which I have, following convention, called 'individualism–collectivism' or 'individualism–groupism', the United States and Japan stand at opposite ends, with Britain somewhere in the middle. It is not unknown for British politicians, looking at growth rates and unemployment levels, to urge us in one breath and a single sentence, to take a leaf out of the book of 'the Japanese and the Americans'. But *they are very different books.*

Today, under a Government dedicated to removing the rigidities of the labour market, reducing the role of government, enhancing supply-side incentives and generally making markets work, there is no doubt that it is the American book that people are most inclined to read. And it is true – see what was said a few pages back about American corporations – that, with or without a rhetorical topping of corporation loyalty, individualistic incentives *can* induce real efficiency. But two things should make us pause before we accept the American recipe as the right one for us.

The first is the view of many perceptive economists that the US is in the grip of a long-run process of productivity-growth decline in relation to its competitors. 'Are we on the downward path the British took?' asked Baumol and McLennan in an 'op-ed' article in the *Washington Post* (23 April 1986). Yes, was their answer, and the answer of many other economists with a sense of history too.

The second factor to take account of is the fact that we are not, in the UK, quite individualistically ruthless enough to follow the American recipe anyway.

Together these add up to very good reasons why we should take the alternative, Japanese, recipe – in many ways not unlike the Swedish recipe – very seriously indeed.

References

Abegglen, J. and Stalk, G. (1985): *Kaisha: The Japanese Corporation: The New Competitors in World Business*, New York, Basic Books.

Aoki, M. (1984): *The Cooperative Theory of the Firm*, Oxford, Clarendon Press.

Armstrong, M. and Marchington, M. (1982): 'Shop stewards and employee involvement', *Employee Relations*. 4, iv.

Ball, J. M. and Skoech, N. K. (1981) *Interplant Comparisons of Productivity and Earnings*, (Government Economic Service Working Paper No. 38, Dept of Employment Working Paper No. 3), London, HMSO.

Becker, G. S. (1975): *Human Capital*, University of Chicago Press.

Becker, G. S. (1980): *Altruism in the Family and Selfishness in the Market Place*, Discussion Paper No. 73, Centre for Labour Economics, London School of Economics.

Bellah, R. N. *et al.* (1985): *Habits of the Heart: Individualism and Commitment in American Life*, University of California Press.

Berg, I. (1971): *Education and Jobs: The Great Training Robbery*, Boston, Beacon Press.

Bessant, J. and Grant, M. (1985): *Management and manufacturing innovation in the United Kingdom and West Germany*, Gower Press.

Best, M. H. and Humphries, J. (1983): 'The city and the decline of British industry: Liquidity without commitment', Paper for the Boston Anglo-American conference on the Decline of the British Economy.

Binks, M. and Coyne, J. (1983): *The Birth of Enterprise*, Hobart Paper No. 98, London, Institute of Economic Affairs.

Blackaby, F. (1980): *The Future of Pay Bargaining*, Heinemann Educational Books; republished 1984, Gower Press.

Bowey, A. M. *et al.* (1982): *Effects of Incentive Payment Systems, United Kingdom 1977–80*, Research Paper No. 36, UK Dept of Employment, September.

Bradley, K. and Gelb, A. (1983): *Worker Capitalism*, Heinemann Educational Books.

Bradley, K. and Hill, S. (1983): '"After Japan": The Quality Circle transplant and productive efficiency', *British Journal of Industrial Relations*, Vol. 23, November.

248   *Taking Japan Seriously*

Brown, W. (1983): 'Britain's unions: New pressures and shifting loyalties', *Personnel Management*, October.

Bullock Report (1977): *Report of the Committee of Inquiry on Industrial Democracy*, UK Dept of Trade, June.

Burns, T. and Stalker, G. M. (1961): *The Management of Innovation*, Tavistock Publications.

Cantley, M. and Sahal, D. (1980): *Who Learns What? A Conceptual Description of Capability and Learning in Technological Systems*, International Institute for Applied Systems Analysis, Luxembourg.

Carnevale, A. P. and Goldstein, H. (1983): *Employee Training: Its Changing Role and an Analysis of New Data*, American Society for Training Development.

Carter, C. and Williams, B. (1957): *Industry and Technical Progress*, Oxford University Press.

Clark, R. (1979): *The Japanese Company*, Yale University Press.

Clark, R. (1985): *Aspects of Japanese Commercial Innovation*, London, Technical Change Centre.

Coopers and Lybrand Associates (1985): *A Challenge to Complacency: Changing Attitudes to Training*, A report to MSC and NEDO, London.

Creigh, S. et al. (1982): 'Sharing the incentive', *Employment Gazette*, April.

Daly, A., Hickens, D. M. W. N., and Wagner, K. (1985): 'Productivity, machinery and skills in a sample of British and German manufacturing plants', *National Institute Economic Review*, No. 111, February.

Daniel, W. W. and Millward, N. (1983): *Workplace Industrial Relations in Britain: The DE/PSI/SSRC Survey*, Heinemann Educational Books.

Daniel, W. W. (1976): *Wage Determination in Industry*, London, Political and Economic Planning (now Policy Studies Institute).

Doeringer P. and Piore, M. (1971): *International Labor Markets and Manpower Analysis*, Lexington, Mass., Lexington Books.

Dore, R. P. (1973): *British Factory: Japanese Factory: The Origins of National Diversity in Industrial Relations*, University of California Press.

Dore, R. P. (1982): *An Incomes Policy Built to Last*, London, The Tawney Society.

Dore, R. P. (1983a): *The Social Sources of the Will to Innovate*, Papers in Science, Technology and Public Policy, No. 4, London, Imperial College of Science and Technology.

Dore, R. P. (1983b): 'Goodwill and the spirit of market capitalism', *The British Journal of Sociology*, 34, iv, (Hobhouse Memorial Lecture), December.

Dore, R. P. (1985a): 'Authority and benevolence: The Confucian recipe for industrial success', *Government and Opposition*, 20, ii (McCallum Lecture, Pembroke College, Oxford).

Dore, R. P. (1985b): 'Japan', *Economic and Social Research Council Newsletter* 54, March.

Dore, R. P. (1986): *Flexible Rigidities: Industrial policy and structural adjustment in Japan 1970–1980*, Athlone Press.

Dore, R. P. and Mars, Z. (1984): *Technical Change and Inter-Industry Wage Differentials: Inflation and Incomes Policy*, London, Technical Change Centre, *mimeo*.

Durkheim, E. (1983): *De la Division du Travail Social*, Paris, Felix Alcan, tr. G. Simpson, *The Division of Labour in Society*, Illinois, Glencoe Free Press, 1964.

Economic Planning Agency, Japan (Keizai Kikakuchō) (1982): *Keizai Yōran*.

Elston, C. D. (1981): 'The financing of Japanese industry', *Bank of England Quarterly Bulletin*, December.

Engineering Council (1983): *Appraising the Technical and Commercial Aspects of a Manufacturing Company*, May.

Evans, A. (1980): 'How the "Great Divide" is slowly fading away', *Chief Executive*, February.

Financial Institutions (1980): Committee to review the functioning of financial institutions, *Report*, London, HMSO, Cmd. 7937, June.

Fox, A. (1974): *Beyond Contract: Work, Power and Trust Relations*, Faber.

Freeman, C. (1982): *The Economics of Industrial Innovation* (2nd edn), London, Frances Pinter.

Gilder, G. (1981): *Wealth and Poverty*, New York, Basic Books.

Goldberg, V. P. (1981): 'A Relational Exchange Perspective on the Employment Relationship', Paper for the Social Science Research Council conference, York, *mimeo*.

Greenwald, D. (1973): *McGraw-Hill Dictionary of Political Economy*, McGraw-Hill.

Hall, Robert E. (1982): 'The importance of lifetime jobs in the US Economy', *American Economic Review*, 72, iv, September, pp. 716–25.

Harris, M. (1981): *America Now: The Anthropology of a Changing Culture*, Simon & Schuster.

Hayashi, C. et al. (1981): *Daiyon Nihonjin no Kokuminsei*, Tokyo.

Herzberg (1966) *Work and the nature of man*, Cleveland, World Publishing Co.

Hirsch, F. (1977): *Social Limits to Growth*, Routledge & Kegan Paul.

Hirschman, A. O. (1970): *Exit, Voice and Loyalty: Responses to Decline in Firms, Organizations and States*. Harvard University Press.

Hirschman, A. O. (1982): 'Rival interpretations of market society: civilizing, destructive or feeble', *Journal of Economic Literature*, 20, pp. 1463–84.

HMSO (Her Majesty's Stationery Office) (1983): *Patents, Designs and Trade Marks 1982: 100th Report of the Comptroller-General of Patents Design and Trade marks*, London, 9 May.

Hosomi, T. and Okumura, A. (1982): 'Japanese industrial policy' in J. Pinder, ed. *National Industrial Strategies and the World Economy*, Croom Helm.

House of Lords, Select Committee on the EEC (1984): *Youth training in the EEC, 1983–84*, July.

Industrial Facts and Forecasting (1985): *Adult Training in Britain. A survey carried out by IFF Research Limited for MSC*, June 1985.

Johnson, C. (1982): *MITI and the Japanese miracle*, Stanford University Press.

Johnson, R. and Ouchi, W. (1974): 'Made in America (under Japanese management)', *Harvard Business Review*, September-October.

Kakizawa, K. (1978): *Kanryō-tachi to Nihon-maru (The Bureaucrat and SS Japan)*, Tokyo, Gakuyo.

Knight, A. (1982): *Wilson Revisited: Industrialists and Financiers*, PSI Discussion Paper 5, London, Policy Studies Institute and Anglo-German Foundation.

Kubota (1980): Akira Kubota, 'The political influence of the Japanese Higher Civil Service', *Journal of Asian and African Studies*, XV, 3–4.

Layard, R. (1981): *More Jobs Less Inflation*, Grant McIntyre.

Leibenstein, H. (1966): 'Allocative efficiency versus X-efficiency', *American Economic Review*, June.

Lydall, H. F. (1976): 'Theories of the distribution of earnings' in A. B. Atkinson, ed. *The Personal Distribution of Earnings*, Allen & Unwin.

Macaulay, S. (1963): 'Non-contractual relations in business: A preliminary study', *American Sociological Review*, 28, i, February.

Macfarlane, A. (1978): *The Origins of English Individualism*, Basil Blackwell.

McGregor, D. M. (1960): *The Human Side of Enterprise*, McGraw-Hill.

Manpower Services Commission (MSC) (1986): MSC and Dept of Education and Science *Review of Vocational Qualifications in England and Wales: A report of the Working Group*, April.

Manpower Services Commission – National Economic Development Office (1984): *Competence and Competition*.

Marsden, D. W. (1982): 'Career structures and training in internal labour markets', *Manpower Studies*, 4, Spring.

Marshall, T. H. (1950): *Citizenship and Social Class*, Cambridge University Press.

Maru, Atsuko (1983): 'Kojin Tōshika no Kabushiki Tōshi ni Tsuite', *Shōken Kenkyū* 67, February.

Marwell, G. and Ames, R. (1981): 'Economists free ride. Does anyone else? Experiments in the provision of public goods', *Journal of Public Economics*, 4, xv, pp. 295–310.

Maslow, A. H. (1954): *Motivation and Personality*, Harper and Row.

Meade, J. (1984): 'Full employment, new technologies and the distribution of income', *Journal of Social Policy*, 13, ii, Summer (T. H. Marshall Memorial Lecture, University of Southampton).

Middlemas, K. (1979): *Politics in Industrial Society*, Deutsch.

Mills, D. Q. (1985): 'Seniority v. ability in promotion decisions', *Industrial and Labour Relations Review*, 38, iii, pp. 421–5.

Millward, N. and Stevens, N. (1986): *British Workplace Industrial Relations 1980–1984*, London, Gower.

Moore, jnr., W. Barrington (1978): *Injustice: The Social Bases of Obedience and Revolt*, New York, M. E. Sharpe, p. 438.

Morse, R. (1983): 'The Japanese lobby in Washington', *Foreign Affairs*.

Murray, C. (1984): *Losing Ground: American Social Policy 1950–1980*, New York, Basic Books.

Mutō, N. (1984): 'Kabushiki Sōkai: Fumie Ka Senrei Ka' (The Shareholders' General Meeting: Moral Test or Baptism?), *Uiru*, March.

Nakagawa, Y. and Ota, N. (1981): *The Japanese Economic System: A New Balance Between Intervention and Freedom*, Foreign Press Centre.

Nakatani, I. (1982a): *The Role of Inter-Market Keiretsu Business Groups in Japan*, Research Paper No. 97, Canberra, Australia–Japan Research Centre, Australian National University.

Nakatani, I. (1982b): 'Risuku-shieringu kara mita Nihon keizai' (Risk-sharing in the Japanese economy), *Osaka-daigaku Keizaigaku*, col. 32, Nos. ii–iii.

Nikkei (1984a): *Kaisha Jōhō*, 84, ii, Tokyo, Nihon Keizai Shimbunsha.

Nikkei (1984b): *Hai-Tekku Jiten (High-Tech Dictionary)*, Nihon Keizai Shimbunsha.

Office of Technology Assessment (OTA) (1983): *International competitiveness in electronics*, Washington, D.C.

Ohmae, K. (1985): *Triad Power: The internationalization of Japanese/US business*, New York, Free Press

Okumura, H. (1982a): 'Masatsu o umu Nihonteki Keiei no Heisa-sei' (The closed nature of Japanese corporate management as a source of international friction), *Ekonomisuto*, 6 July.

Okumura, H. (1982b): 'The closed nature of Japanese intercorporate relations', *Japan Echo*, 9, iii.

Okumura, H. (1982c): 'Interfirm relations in an enterprise group: The case of Mitsubishi', *Japanese Economic Studies*, Summer.

Okumura, H. (1983): *Shin Nihon no roku daikigyō-shūdan (A New View of Japan's Six Great Enterprise Groups)*, Tokyo, Diamond.

Okumura, H. (1984): *Hōjin Shihon-Shugi (Corporate Capitalism)*, Tokyo, Ochanomizu Shobo.

Okun, A. (1981): *Prices·and Quantities*, Basil Blackwell.

Organization for Economic Cooperation and Development (1984): *Employment Outlook*, September.

Ouchi, W. (1981): *Theory Z: How American Business Can Meet The Japanese Challenge*, Addison and Wesley.

Owen, D. (1985): *None of the Above*, Houghton-Mifflin.

Palgrave, R. H. I. (1923): *Dictionary of Political Economy*, ed. H. Higgs, Macmillan, 1923–26.

Pascale, R. T. and Athos, A. G. (1981): *The Art of Japanese Management: Applications for American Executives*, Simon and Schuster.

252   *Taking Japan Seriously*

Peters T. and Austin, N. (1986): *A Passion for Excellence*, New York, Warner Books.

Peters, T. J. and Waterman, R. H. (1984): *In Search of Excellence: Lessons from America's Best-Run Companies*, Warner Books.

Phelps Brown, H. (1977): *The Inequality of Pay*, Oxford University Press.

Postlethwaite, N. (1985): 'The bottom half in lower secondary schooling,' in G. D. N. Worswick, ed. *Education and Economic Performance*, Gower Press.

Prais, S. (1985): 'What can we learn from the German system of education and vocational training?' in G. D. N. Worswick, ed. *Education and Economic Performance*, Gower Press.

Reich, R. B. (1984): *The Next American Frontier*, New York, Times Books.

Ross, A. M. (1958): 'Do we have a new industrial feudalism?', *American Economic Review*, 48, December.

Rothwell, R. and Zegveld, W. (1982): *Innovation and the Small and Medium-Sized Firm: Their Role in Employment and in Economic Change*, London, Frances Pinter.

Rothwell, R. and Zegveld, W. (1985): *Reindustrialization and Technology*, New York, M. E. Sharpe.

Ruhm, C. (1986): *Job Tenure and Labour Mobility: Empirical Tests of Three Labour Market Models*, Boston University, Department of Economics Discussion Paper, *mimeo*.

Sakakibara, H. (1977): *Nihon o enshutsu suru shin-kanryo-zo (Portrait of the new bureaucrats who 'produce' Japan)*, Tokyo.

Salter, W. E. G. (1966): (with an addendum by W. G. Reddaway), *Productivity and Technical Change*, Cambridge University Press.

Samuelson, P. A. (1980): *Economics* (11th edn), McGraw-Hill.

Schultze, C. L. (1983): 'Industrial policy: A dissent', *The Brookings Review*, Fall, pp. 3–12.

Scott, B. R. (1985): 'National Strategies: Key to international competition' in Scott and Lodge, pp. 71–143.

Scott, B. R. and Lodge, G. C. (1985): *US Competitiveness in the World Economy*, Harvard Business School Press.

Seni kindaika (1980): Seni Torihiki Kindaika Suishin Kyōgikai (Association for the Promotion of the Modernization of Trading Relations in the Textile Industry), *Nenji Hōkoku (Annual Report)*, 1980.

Smith, A. (1910): *The Wealth of Nations*, J. M. Dent.

Sogo, S. (1981): 'Gaining Respect', in *Speaking of Japan*, Japan Institute for Social and Economic Affairs (Keizai Kōhō Centre), Tokyo, 1, iii.

Solow, R. M. (1980): 'On Theories of Unemployment', *American Economic Review*, 70, i.

Taylor, C. W. (1972): *Climate for Creativity*, Pergamon.

Thurow, L. (1975): *Generating Inequality*, Basic Books.

Torrington, D. (1980): 'Job Evaluation: A Popular Way to Solve Pay Problems', *Works Management*, November.

Trades Union Council (1981): *Statement on Quality Circles*, London, TUC.

Tsen, K. K. (1985): *Marks and Spencer: Anatomy of Britain's most efficiently organized company*, Pergamon.

Tylecote, A. (1981): *The Causes of the Present Inflation*, Macmillan.

UK Central Statistical Office (CSO) (1985): *Social Trends*, London, HMSO.

UK Central Statistical Office (annual): *Economic Trends*, London, HMSO.

UK (1985): *National Accounts*, London, HMSO.

van Empel, M. (1975): *The Granting of European Patents*, Leyden, A. W. Sijthoff.

Vogel, Ezra (1979): *Japan as Number One: Lessons for America*, Harvard University Press.

Vogel, Ezra (1985): *Comeback America*, Simon and Schuster.

Vonnegut, K. (1952): *Player Piano*, Scribners, 1952; Macmillan, 1967.

Watts, A. G. (1983): *Education, Unemployment and the Future of Work*, Milton Keynes, Open University Press.

Weitzman, M. (1984): *The Share Economy*, Harvard University Press.

White, M. (1981): *The Hidden Meaning of Pay Conflict*, Macmillan.

White, M. and Trevor, M. (1983): *Under Japanese Management*, Heinemann, for Policy Studies Institute.

Whitehead, A. N. (1967): *Science and the Modern World*, Macmillan.

Wiener, M. J. (1981): *English Culture and the Decline of the Industrial Spirit*, Cambridge University Press.

Wiener, N. (1950): *The Human Use of Human Beings*, Eyre and Spottiswoode, revised 1954.

Williamson, O. E. (1979): 'Transaction-cost economics: The governance of contractual relations', *Journal of Law and Economics*, 22, ii.

Williamson, O. E. (1981): 'The Modern Corporation: Origins, Evolution, Attributes', *Journal of Economic Literature*, 19, iv, December.

Wolf, M. J. (1984): *The Japanese Conspiracy: A Stunning Analysis of the Internation Trade War*, New English Library.

Wood, A. (1978): *A Theory of Pay*, Cambridge University Press.

Yoshino M. Y. and Fong, G. R. (1985): 'The very high speed integrated circuit program – lessons for industrial policy', in B. R. Scott and G. C. Lodge (1985).

Index

Abegglen, J. 236
ability testing 205
academics 190
ACAS 82
accountability,
    of shop stewards 159
accountants 27, 31, 141, 187
acquisitions 33
adjustment 33
adjustment assistance 241
administrative guidance 6–7, 194, 202
adversarial relations 63, 152, 188
affectivity 182
affluence 152–4, 188, 208
airlines 206
Alliance 151
altruism 183
Alvey project 193, 201
Anti-Trust Laws 230
Aoki, M. 145
apprenticeship 20, 46
architects 42
Armstrong, M. 55
army 8, 96, 136, 159
ASLEF 80
ASTMS 61
auction economy 190
AUEW 151
Austria 68, 93, 127
authority 85–107, 153, 156, 207
authority,
    legitimation of 95–101
automobile industry 72, 176, 180

Ball, J. 59

Ball, John 95
Bank of Japan 110
bankruptcies 199
banks 109–10
    and groups 178
Bar Association 40
Bar exams 104
barber shop effect 82
Baumol, W. 245
Beauman, C. 124
Becker, G. 183
Bellah, R. 241
benevolence 94, 169–70, 175, 181
Berg, Ivar 34
Berle, A. 145, 157
best practice,
    diffusion of 32, 185
Best, M. 110
Beveridge, W. 242
Bevin, E. 159
Binks, M. 131
black economy 172
black minorities 220, 242
Blackaby, E. 60
Blackburn 187
Boards of Directors 110, 158–65, 178, 187
bonuses for managers 119, 135, 236
Bowey, A. 137
BP 96, 141
Bradley, K. 144, 148, 237
Brazil 184
British Aerospace 121
British Leyland 75, 79, 164
British Medical Association 40, 209
British Oxygen 123

British Rail 60
British Steel Corporation 52, 184
Brown, W. 55
Bullock Report 150–4
bumping down 215
bureaucracy 93, 96, 126, 138
bureaucrats and politicians 6
Burns, T. 134
Business & Technical Ed.
  Council 42
business schools 162

Callaghan, J. 78–9
calligraphy 45
Cantley, M. 140
capital 222
capital dilution 222
capital gains 115, 147–8, 237
capitalism 13, 16, 155, 169–92
  forms of 118, 126, 146, 238
career tracks 96
Carnevale, A. 232
cartels 14, 178, 200
Carter, C. 132
CBI 53
certification monopolies 43
China 198, 204, 209
Chloride 119
Citizens Trust 150, 221–5
citizenship 208, 211
City and Guilds Institute 42
civil service 8, 32, 96, 136, 141,
  194, 209
Clark, R. 113, 120
class 62, 98
class cultures 103–6
class recruitment 204–5
class-consciousness 195
closed shop 137
Coastal Command 140
coercion 153
collective bargaining 51, 55, 68–84,
  152, 157, 163
  professionals 79
collectivism 245

communications 220
community model 53–65, 91,
  107–9, 125–65, 206–7, 234–40
community service 223
Companies Act 59, 146
Company Law model 53, 91,
  107–9, 159
comparative advantage 230
comparative method 4–7
competence 20, 141, 159, 165, 207
  managerial 95, 98, 133
competition 205
  business 140
  policy 64, 190
  interpersonal in firms, 136, 140,
  197
competitiveness 220, 228–31, 244
compliance 83–107
compromise 18, 165
computer operators 60
confucianism 94, 98, 170, 204
conglomerates 117, 119, 146, 178
consensus, creation of 194–9
consent 153
Conservative party 68, 151
contract 135
contractualism 91, 135, 139
cooperation 200
cooperatives 137, 148–50, 175
Coopers and Lybrand 22
Corfield, K. 121
corporatism 11, 40, 62, 64, 153
cottage industry 171
Courtaulds 33
Coyne, J. 131
craft skills 41
creativity 47, 133–5
crime 243
crime rates 4
CSE 101
cultural inheritance 145
cultural traditions 91–4, 227
  and consensus 194
  and economic behaviour 179
custom and practice 164

customer markets 186, 190
customer, service to 184–9

Dallas 234
Daniel, W. 55
decision-making 142
declining industries 33, 200, 202, 230, 241
deference 59, 88, 105
  erosion of 156
demarcation disputes 58
democracy 73, 241
Department of Trade and Industry 6, 191
developmental state 5, 40, 193, 226
dignity 189
dignity minimum 211, 219
directors, see Boards of Directors
dividends 114, 118, 147–50, 237
divorce 174, 239
doctors 41
Doeringer, P. 57, 157, 232
Donovan Commission 163
driving test 35, 43, 104
dual economy 48–67
dual labour markets 232
Durkheim, E. 181
dutifulness 182
dystopias 204, 211
earnings,
  differentials 76
  dispersion of 66

East India Company 209
Eastern Airlines 237
Eastern Europe 204
economic growth 5
economics profession 17
Economist 155
economists 229, 240
education 61, 152–5, 173, 204–10, 217, 219, 223, 234, 244
educational opportunity 241
Educational Testing Service 234
EEPTU 151, 157

efficiency 16, 63, 161, 183
  allocative and x- 16, 185, 191
  of stock exchange, 111, 118, 121
  static, dynamic, 122
effort 184, 204, 244
egalitarianism 87, 90–1, 155, 208
electric power workers 51
electrical machinery 72
electronics industry 228–31
elite 196, 211
Emerson, T. 241
employability 213–16
employee share ownership 236
employment 210–21, 231
employment systems, types of 9, 10, 26, 29, 55, 85–92, 157, 176, 183
energy conservation 6, 42
Engineering Council 43, 123
engineers 141, 187
enterprise groups 178–80
enterprise unions 29
entertainment 115
entrepreneurship 125–44
equality 64, 208, 223
equity and efficiency 161
Eton 103
European Community 58, 150
exit and voice 189
expectations 97
expertise 98, 103
exploitation 85, 175

factor shares 220–4
Factory system 171
Factory uniforms 8
fairness 18, 29, 51–2, 74, 161–5, 170, 191, 227, 240–5
false consciousness 88
family enterprises 171
fellow-feeling 54
feudalism 93–5, 151, 207
Fifth Directive 151
fifth generation computer 200
finance, long-term for industry 123

Financial Times 118, 124, 198
financing of enterprises 108–24
Finniston Committee 43
flexibility agreements 58
Ford 164
Fox, A. 54
free enterprise 16
free riders 240
Freeman, C. 129
friendship 170
full employment 63
fund managers 120, 123
future-orientation 180, 194

Galbraith, J. K. 122, 127, 157
GATT 184
GCE 61, 104
GEC 17, 33, 119
Gelb, A. 237
generalist administrators 96
genes 208, 217
Germany 22–3, 127, 160, 217
    banks in, 110
gift giving 177
Gilder, G. 242
Goldberg, V. 174
goodwill 169–92
Greenwald, D. 170
groups, see enterprise groups

handicapped 216
hard work 12
harmonization 56, 57, 137
Harris, M. 239
Harvard Business School 238
hi-tech 26
hierarchy 85–107, 177, 206–7
    new forms 210–3
high technology 228–32
Hill, S. 144
Hirsch, F. 191
Hirschman, A. O. 111, 126, 189
history,
    influence of 91–4
Hitachi 52, 72, 113, 151

homogeneity of Japan 204
Honda 90
Hosomi, T. 112
household assets 114
human capital 60, 153
human capital theory 23–4
Humphries, J. 110
hypocrisy 183

IBM 8, 137, 141
ICI 52, 96, 123, 209
income distribution 86, 150, 163
    206–25
incomes policies 13, 53, 67, 68–84,
    148, 191, 231–3
independent schools 106
individualism 7, 32, 134, 180, 226,
    245
industrial democracy 58, 145–65
industrial participation 103
industrial policy 15, 62, 228–31
industrial property, see patents
Industrial Society 58, 87, 137, 139
industrial structure 62–7, 206
Industrial Structure Council
    180–98
industrial training 231
industrial training boards 27
industry associations 15, 199–203
inequality 48–67, 68
inflation 53, 68–84, 212–13
inflation tax 74, 81–3
information 140, 163, 185
Inmos 121
innovation 125–44, 193, 212
Institute of Directors 59, 158
insurance companies 112
intellectual proletariat 220
interest rates 122
internal labour markets 9, 153
international trade 154
inventors 126, 139, 154
investment 173, 237
    and banks 110–11
investment cartels 10

invisible hand 181, 228
involvement of employees 58, 144, 235
IQ 204, 209
Iran 95
Israel 225
Italy 83
Ivy League 233

Japan,
  British views of 3
  company offices 90
  competition 177
  competitive edge 17
  cooperativeness 12
  Economic Planning Agency 197
  Economic White Paper 197
  education 12
  Enterprise Groups 178
  Fair Trade Act 200
  groupishness 7
  homogeneity 6–7
  investment in UK 3
  Liberal Democratic party 16, 195
  Meiji Restoration 93
  Ministry of Finance 5, 202
  Ministry of Health 200
  Ministry of Labour 41
  Ministry of Transport 200
  party system 94
  politics 89, 93
  Quality of life 4
  right wing 116
  social discipline 86
  Spring offensive 87
  village structure 181
  vocational training 23
  see also MITI, Nissan, politicians etc
Japan-bashing 229
Japan Development Bank 194
Japan Incorporated 193
Japan Spinners Association 174
Japanese firms, in UK 98
Jenkins, Clive 82

job competition 11
job evaluation 57
job grading 57
job leavers 31
job recruitment 206
job rights 225
job security 155, 189, 232
job-sharing 213
John Lewis 148
Johnson, Lyndon 241
Joint consultative committees 55
Jones, Aubrey 74
Joseph, K. 193

keiretsu, see enterprise groups
Keynesian reflation 69
Knight, A. 123
Korea 184, 204

labour markets 9, 57, 183, 223
labour mobility 24, 39, 155, 216
Labour Party 15
labour turnover 56
labour unions, federations 72
Lancashire Evening Telegraph 155
Laszard 216
late-development effect 8, 46, 226
law and society 146
lawyers 41, 81
Layard, R. 81
leadership 89–91, 156
learn-from-Japan movement 226
learning curve 125
learning organizations 33, 45, 46
Leibenstein, H. 17, 184
leisure,
    distribution of 219
    education for 219
levy-grant system 27, 34, 36
Liberal Democratic Party 16, 195
life-expectancy 195
Lifetime employment 4, 29–32, 70, 109, 141, 185, 206, 232
Lloyd's 201
London Business School 120

long-term thinking 108–24, 237
loyalty 39, 137, 170, 184, 189
Lydall, H. 207

Macaulay, S. 187
Macfarlane, A. 180
MacGregor, I. 88
machismo 88
management consultants 143
management ideology 58
managerial optimists 151
Mandeville, F. 224
Manpower Services Commission 20, 47
market imperfections 189
market power 176
market-orientated employment system, see employment systems
marketing 188
marketism 10, 193, 227
markets for intermediates 177
Marks and Spencer 13, 187–8
marriage 174
Marsden, D. 57
Marshall, T. H. 208, 224
Marx, K. 171
Maslow, A. 154, 219
Maxwell, R. 152
McGregor, D. 157, 235
Meade, J. 221
means tests 221
Meiji Restoration 93
mergers 121
merit assessments 29
meritocracy 98–106, 204–25, 233–5, 241
mid-life retraining 22
Middlemas, K. 62
Mill, J. S. 52
Mills, D. 232
miners 51, 80
minimum wages 212
MITI 6, 15, 42, 196, 230
MITI Visions 198
Mitsubishi 180

Mitsui 180
modernization 176
money illusion 78
monopoly 189, 191
Morgan, J. P. 170
Murray, C. 242–3

Nakatani, I. 180
national character 91–3, 180
National Freight Consortium 148
National Health Service 217, 223
Navy 136
NCB 62
NEDC 158
NEDO 6, 15, 21, 198–9, 201
Netherlands 127
new Right 196, 211
newspapers 118, 146, 195
Nishiwaki 171–3
Nissan 113
Nitobe, I. 182
Nobel prizes 132
non-price competition 125
non-tariff barriers 184
North Sea oil 75, 120, 197
Norway 68, 127

obligational contracts, see relational contracting
OECD 31
oil crisis 69
Okumura, A. 112
Okumura, H. 115, 176
Okun, A. 190
oligopoly 10, 71, 126
operational research 140
opportunism 173
organization theory 134
organizational complexity 153, 154
organizations 239
   and individuals, 239
   mechanistic and organic 134
OTA 231
Ouchi, W. 143, 235
Owens, D. 234

ownership and control 145, 153
Oxbridge 61, 103–5, 209, 228
Oxford Economic Forecasting 50

Palgrave, R. 170
Parsons, T. 182
Party System (UK) 94
participation 58, 75, 144
particularism 182, 201, 227
Pascale, R. 143, 235
patent law 139
patent registration 197
patents 127–31, 139, 201
paternalism 107, 137
patriotism 229, 244
pay, see wages
PAYE 81
peasant revolts 94
pension funds 112, 115, 120, 137
Peters, R. 235
Peters, T. 119
Phelps Brown, H. 215
Pilkington 119, 164
pioneer industrialization 9
Piore, M. 57, 157, 232
plant size 56
police 32, 83
politicians 16, 195
  and bureaucrats 6
politics 89
Polytechnics 61
population, aging of 197
positive discrimination 243
post-innovation phase 140
Postlethwaite, N. 217
Prais, S. 217
Prato 173
price-consciousness 188
price-bargaining 175
price-earnings ratios 120
price-tag economy 190
prices 175, 188, 221
Prices & Incomes Board 74
production coordination 172
productivity 77

professions 141, 187, 219
profit motive 187
profit-maximization 238
profit-sharing 147
profit-sharing schemes 137, 147
promotion 140–1, 195, 207
property rights 153, 157, 238
protectionism 193, 238
Prutec 129–31
public service 195–7
pump industry 7

qualifications 21, 40, 61, 96,
  100–10, 205
quality 108
  and consumers, 188
quality assurance 191
quality circles 12, 18, 58, 88,
  102–3, 119, 143–4
quality control 186
quality of life 190

R and D 120, 125–44, 139, 143,
  154, 230
radical Right 10
railways 46–7, 60, 71
rationality 164–5, 185
recession cartels 10
recruitment 141
regulatory state 5, 193
relational contracting 173–91
relative prices 82
Rent Act 147
research and development 108
research clubs 200
research institutes 71
respect 211
rhetoric, uses of 164
rights issues 114
rigidities 189
Ringer, R. J. 239
risk 180, 185
robots 185
Rockefellers 184
Rogers, E. 125

role of women 4
Ronson, C. 152
Ross, A. 52
Rotary Club 158
Rothwell, R. 129, 230
Rowlands, T. 152
Royal Society of Arts 42
Ruhm, C. 233
rule of law 84

Sainsbury 187–8
salaries, see Wages
Salter, A. 62
Samuelson, P. 170
SAT 233
Saudi Arabia 198
savings rate 14
Scargill, A. 88
schools, see education
Schumpeter, J. 129
science 47, 208
science faculties 196
Scott, B.
Scott-Bader Commonwealth 137, 148
SDP 73, 147
security, see risk
self-actualization 219
self-employment 39, 41, 75, 83, 206,
   212
self-interest 169–70, 179, 227, 238,
   240
self-regulation 201
self-righteousness 74
semi-conductors 228–31
seniority 29, 32, 46, 70, 96–7, 136,
   140, 196, 207
shareholders 54, 55, 75, 108–24, 143,
   145, 158, 162, 235, 237
   employees 148
shipbuilding 65, 72, 199, 202
shop stewards 55, 73, 159
short-term thinking 108–24
Singapore 204
single status 56
Skill Olympics 41

skills, general and enterprise
   specific, 22, 57, 232
skill-testing 40–41
Skoech, N. 59
small firms, 86
   and innovation 129–31
small government, 14
Smith, Adam 169, 181
social cost-benefit 34
social dividend 150, 221–5
social engineering 106, 145
social label 218
social mobility 234
social security 30
socialism 157
Solow, R. 174
Sony 116
spectrumization 48–67, 233
Spencer, H. 181
spot-contracting 174
Sri Lanka 87
stagflation 189
Stalk, G. 236–7
state, views of 5
statistical services 6
status 156, 161, 163, 205, 225
STC 121
steel industry 72, 177, 180, 184
Stock Exchange, 111–24, 149, 201
   reputation of 116
   stamp duties 123
   turnover 116
Stockton, Lord 211
strikes 71, 72, 155, 164
subcontracting 13, 65, 169–92
submissiveness 87
suggestion schemes 139
sunrise industries 230
supermarkets 202
supply-side incentives 241
Sweden 68, 165, 225, 245
   Meidener Plan 149
synchropay 75–81

takeovers 114, 116, 117–18, 146, 237

talent, flow of 101, 105, 117–18, 209
Taverne, D. 99
taxation 5, 14, 230
taxation-allergy 172
taxi drivers 69–70
teachers 83, 219
Tebbit, N. 225
technocracy 195
technology 22, 57, 59, 125–44, 153, 154, 208
   and complexity 98, 208
   and employment 210–21
   and prices 64
   gains of, 62–7
   transfer 46, 132, 185
temporary workers 29
Tesco 187–8
textile firms 63
textile industry 60, 171, 180, 185–7, 202
Thatcher, M. 211, 225
Thatcherism, 196
Thorn EMI 121
Thurow, L. 10, 48
Tokugawa period 93–5
de Tocqueville, A. 156
Tokyo University 99, 204–5
Torrington, D. 57
Toshiba 52
Toyota 176
Trade & Industry, Department of 47
trade liberalization 184
trade unions, see unions
trading relations 173–92
training industry 33
training scheme (ETLIS) 34
training tax 33
transaction costs 173
transfer of institutions 19
transparency of government 199–203
transport 220
Treasury 73, 78
Treasury model 50
Trevor, M. 98
Trollope, A. 88

trust 54, 95, 98, 107, 163, 170, 179, 182, 185, 188
   & institutionalized suspicion 160
TSSA 61
TUC 62, 68, 77, 141, 151–2
turnover, see labour mobility
TV 71, 93
two-income families 216
Tylecote, A. 52

U-boats 140
UGC 105–6
underclass 242
unemployment 25, 210–21
   psychological effects 221
unfair dismissal 37
Unilever 209
unions 29, 59, 153, 157, 158, 198
   adversarial stance 85
   enterprise basis 62, 73
   nature of power 53
   officials 73, 80
   power of 74
unit trusts 115
United States 22, 87, 142, 155, 179, 182, 226–45
universities 61, 96, 98–106, 110, 195, 233
university degrees 141

venture capital 133
ventures 138
VHSI 231
village structure 181
visions, MITI 180
vocational training 21–34
   market paradigm of 23
   expenditures 23
   see also training tax 34
Vogel, E. 228
Vonnegut, Kurt 211, 221

wages 30, 49, 136, 160, 163, 172, 190, 221
   annual round 53

differentials 56
going rates 50, 53
principles underlying 29, 137
profit sharing 53, 56
youth wages 223
wage competition 11
Wage Councils 68
wage differentials 48–67, 86
wage relativities, inter-industry 66, 82
wage share 221
wealth tax 222
weaving 171
Weber, Max 62, 93
Weighell, Sid 80
Weitzman, M. 147
welfare benefits 212, 241–3
welfare minimum 211
welfare services 221–5
Welfare State 153, 154
West Germany 150
Westinghouse 87
Which 188
White, M. 55, 98
white-collar unions 56, 61

Whitehead, A. 126
Whittle, Frank 134
wholesale trade 179
Wiener, N. 105, 210
Williams, B. 132
Williamson, O. 172–4
Wilson Committee 112, 120
window-guidance 110
Wood, A. 52
work 219
   comfort at 51
   ethic 137, 220, 221, 239, 244
   hours 172, 213
   incentives 136–9, 157, 239
   meaning of 219

X-efficiency 17, 184

Yellow Peril 85
Young Workers' Scheme 223
Youth Training Scheme 218

zaibatsu 113
Zegweld, W. 129, 230